AF545268

ROLLEI TLR — THE HISTORY

The complete book on the origins of Twin-Lens photography

EDITED BY IAN PARKER

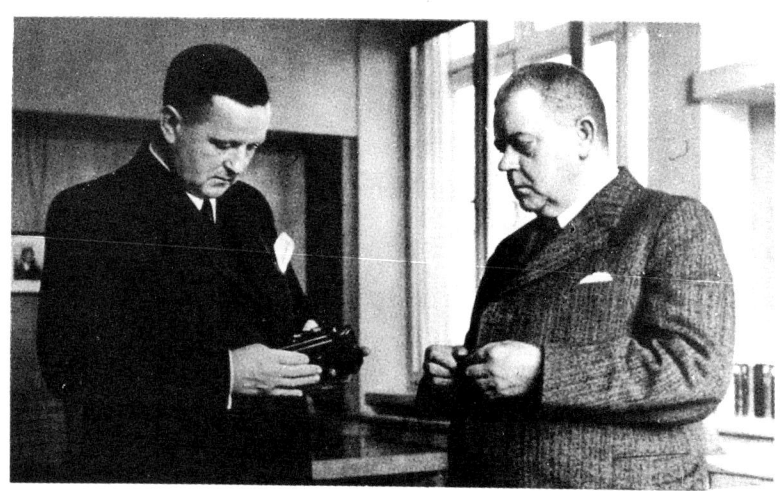

The Founders: Paul Franke on the left Reinold Heidecke on right.

ROLLEI TLR
THE HISTORY
The complete book on the origins of Twin-Lens photography

EDITED BY

IAN PARKER

Published July 1992
World copyright by Club Rollei
Hotel de France, St. Saviour's Road,
Jersey, Channel Islands JE4 8WZ

British Library Cataloguing-in-Publication Data.
A catalogue record for this book is available from the British Library.

ISBN 1-874657-00-9

Distributor:
Newpro (UK) Ltd.
Old Sawmills Road
Faringdon, Oxon. SN7 7DS
Tel: 0367 242411
Fax: 0367 241124

Printed by Hartnolls Ltd.,
Cornwall PL31 1EG

CONTENTS

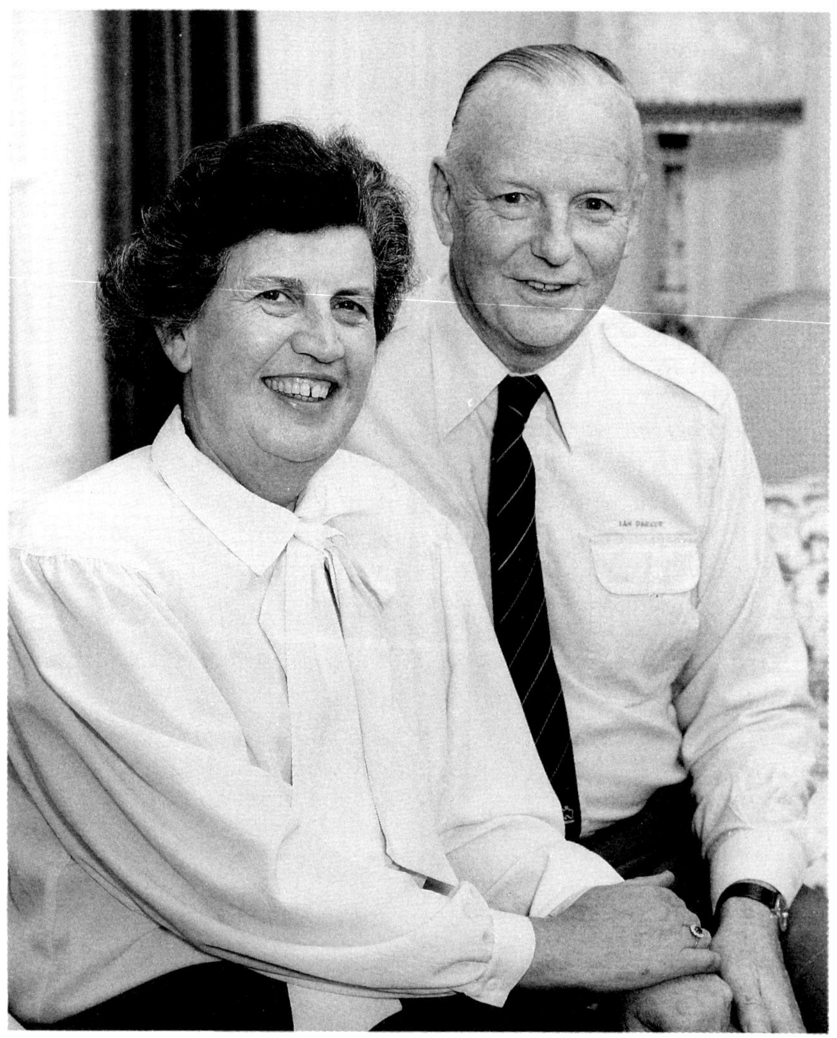

Hazel and Ian Parker.
Photo: Hardie Hass and Nigel Hodgson.

AUTHOR'S PREFACE

This book really started in 1950, was put away to gather dust, and resurrected during the last five years when additional material from Wolfgang Saß and Dietmar Kanzer of Rollei Fototechnic enabled the final chapters to be completed.

Many Club Rollei members have assisted with material and obtaining old Rollei prospectus. In the U.K. Terry Sheehy and Peter York of the British Museum in London; Carl Jurgon in the U.S.A. and the University of Adelaide, South Australia, have all been very helpful. The British Military archives have supplied information on the occupation of Rollei's factory at the end of hostilities in 1945/6 together with copies of Franke & Heidecke trading accounts and information on the production run up to 1946, including an inventory of equipment within the factory when occupied by the British 21st Army.

Mention must also include British Island Airways, now Air U.K. pilot David Smart, whose regular visits to Jersey encouraged the writer to part with money as he discovered many Rollei cameras not already in his museum. David, a keen Rollei collector and enthusiast, founded the Rollei Collectors Club and now resides in Samos, Greece.

This book is dedicated to the management and staff of Rollei Fototechnic, "long may they manufacture cameras to give pleasure to their many friends, collectors and serious photographers".

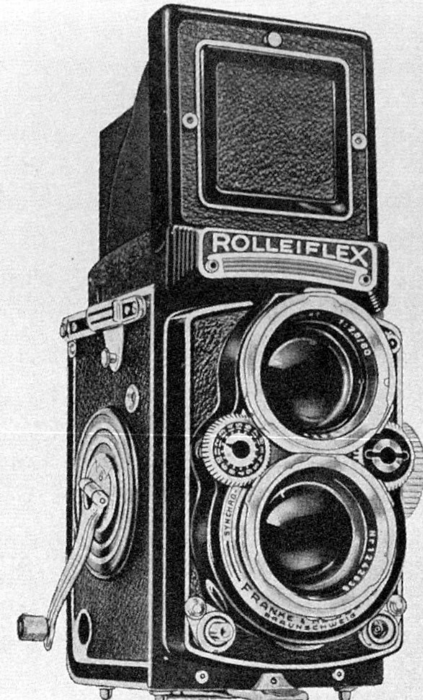

IMITATIONS

Come and go!

It requires more than a commercial philosophy based strictly on copying, to reproduce the quality built into Rollei cameras. It requires *original thinking, original design concepts, highly skilled craftsmanship, plus* manufacturing standards of the highest order. That's why no copy of a Rollei has ever approached Rollei in *quality*, in *features*, in *picture results* . . . why no Rollei owner has ever found himself with an orphan!

Burleigh Brooks, Inc.

10 W. 46th St., New York 36, N. Y.

PONDER & BEST, INC.

814 N. Cole Ave., Hollywood 38, Calif.

1955 USA advertisement using a prototype 2.8D.

CHAPTER 1

THE HISTORY OF ROLLEI

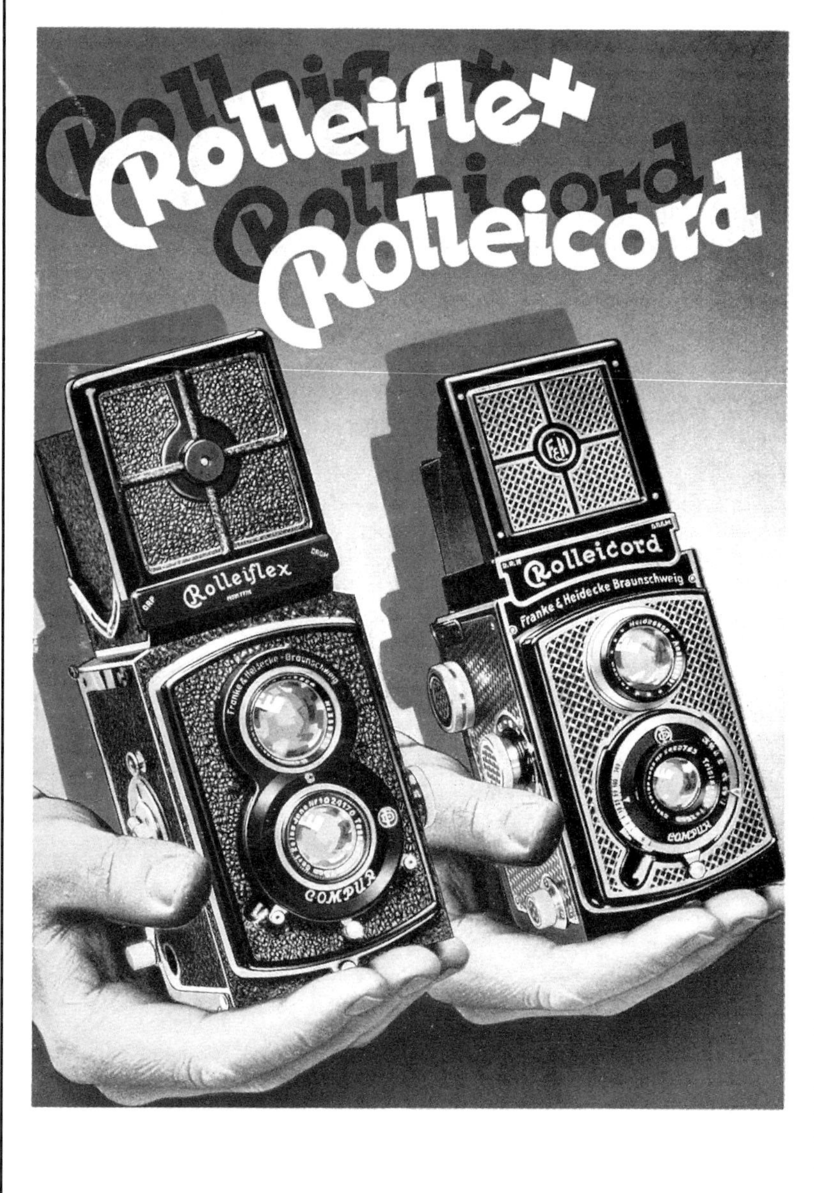
Rolleiflex
Rolleicord
Rolleiflex
Rolleicord
Franke & Heidecke Braunschweig
COMPUR
COMPUR

THE HISTORY OF ROLLEI

Far beyond the next century, when historical camera enthusiasts consider which cameras to collect, a few names will stand out. Kodak for their earlier cameras, cheap, simple and easily available today at a budget price , especially those taking 120 film which is readily available, and therefore the collector can actually take photos as his great-grandfather did in the 1920s or earlier.

Another name is Leica, the innovators of the 35mm miniature camera. The appeal of the Leica is that many of its accessories and lenses are pleasing to feel and touch; the superb workmanship, intricate yet complex and very functional, is a joy to handle. From the 1930s through to the 1990s it was every photographer's dream to hold and own one of these small cameras, that oozed quality, as did the images produced by so many well known photographers, from the Magnum Agency to the likes of Bernard Shaw, who used his Leica to illustrate a number of his books.

The Leica Rangefinder, whether screw or bayonet M type, will live on and on. Many copied the Leica; it is said over 300, including Nikon and Canon, but today they have both entered the electronic age with their miracle wonders which like the early plate cameras will not have the same following as those cameras that can still be used today, easy to repair and films readily available.

This book is about the Rolleiflex T.L.R. More 50- and 60-year-old Rolleiflex cameras are still being used today than any other camera of that vintage. More often than not, the professional wedding photographer even now is using a 1960s or later Rollei. Also it is surprising the number of pre-war Rolleiflexes or Cords that are in everyday use today .

The Rollei story will take you through those early days, the original conception, to the ultimate of the 1990s, the 2.8GX.

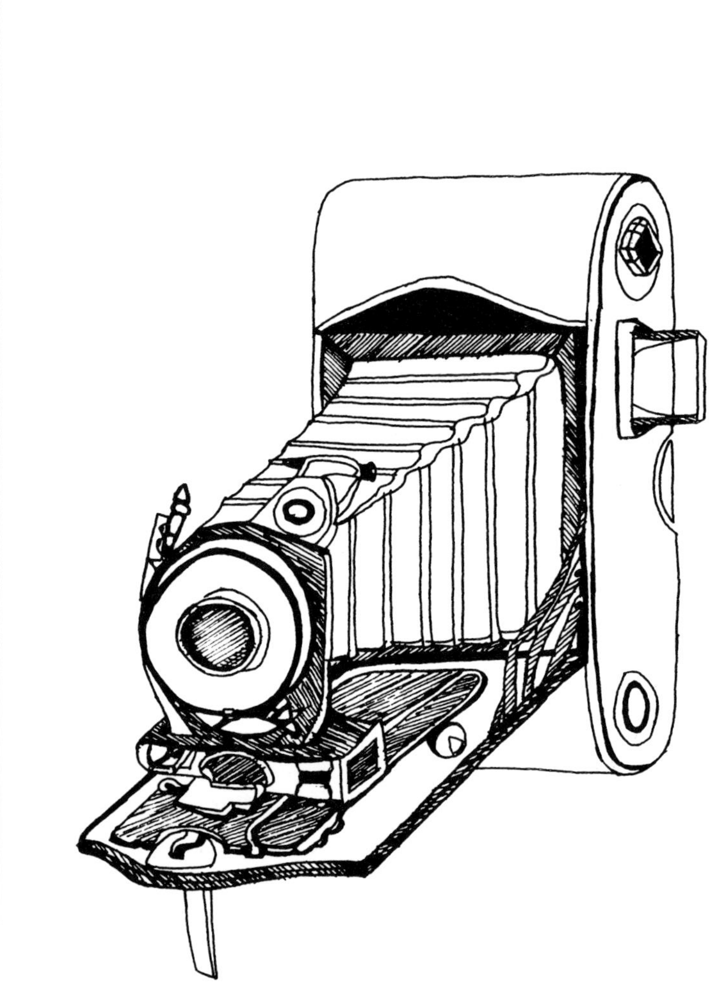

U.S. Army Signal Corps folding T.N.C. 1919 Kodak 3A camera fitted with Zeiss f6.3 Tessar and special coupled rangefinder. Their first camera with a Tessar lens was the 1906/14 Kodak No.4A.

CHAPTER 2

THE INCEPTION

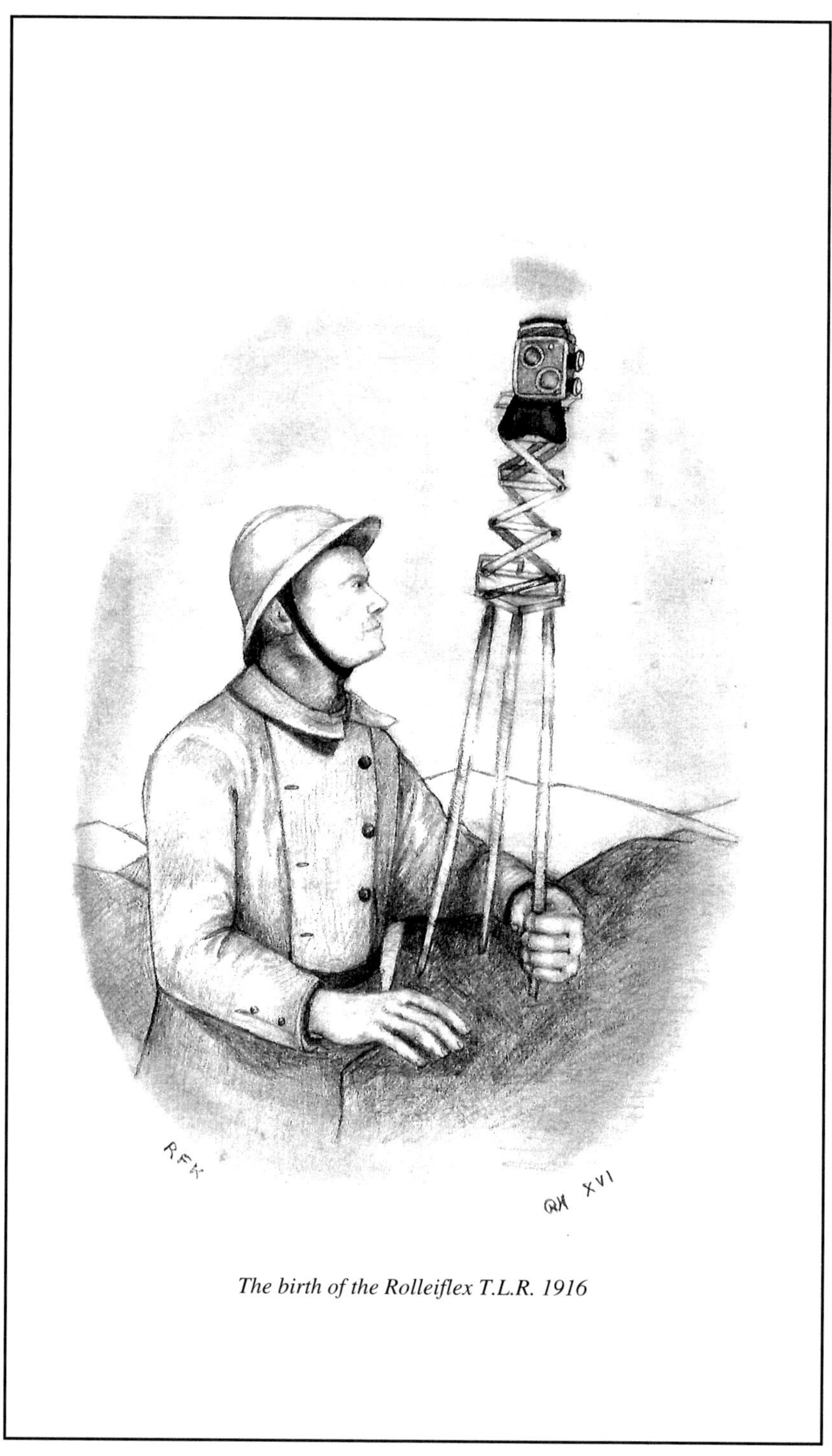

The birth of the Rolleiflex T.L.R. 1916

THE INCEPTION

Rollei had its beginnings in January 1909 when Paul Franke, coming from quite a wealthy family with a boyhood interest in telescopes, joined Voigtländer & Sons as an unpaid apprentice in the export accounts department. At the young age of 18 Franke was very outgoing, and liked to stray into the design department in an endeavour to handle the latest binoculars and telescopes, which were Voigtländer's main business prior to their starting on the manufacture of popular cameras in 1905.

Reinhold Heidecke had also rejoined Voigtländer in 1905 at the age of 25 to start in the new camera design department. Their meeting laid the foundation stone for Rollei, and who would have guessed that some 60 years later the respected name of Voigtländer would be acquired by Rollei. Franke stayed at Voigtländer for just two years, then joined the optical firm of Gerhard, who specialised in telescopes and binoculars, as a junior in their export accounts department. After four years, aged 24, he became the Commercial Director.

During the 1914 -18 war years, Franke never saw active service, perhaps because his job involved the selling of optical equipment throughout the world and brought in valuable foreign currency to the German economy. The firm of Gerhard suffered when on 6th April 1917 America came into the war and they lost this valuable export market, so Franke lost his job. On leaving Gerhard, Franke opened a photography dealership in Kurfürstendamm in Berlin which he named Franke & Co.

The shop started by selling microscopes, telescopes and binoculars, which were very popular for those who went hunting. Besides their uniform, military officers also had to buy binoculars, or if in the Navy they might also require theodolites, so the business very quickly flourished.

At that time, obtaining scientific instruments to sell was extremely difficult. Franke later recalled that one of his best-selling lines was a butterfly collector's outfit; complete with a 21-drawer cabinet, only 40cm high, which would hold over 200 butterflies or moths, a simple brass microscope, a box to hold your live butterflies, and a book giving pictures of the more common species. With many officers living under canvas, the lights within the tent attracted moths so they were easily caught and their collection helped to pass those weary days on the battlefield. With many requests from officers requiring easily portable cameras, Franke decided to visit Voigtländer, to see if he could obtain supplies of photographic cameras to sell in his shop, and once again he met up with Reinhold Heidecke. Heidecke remembered when they both worked together, and was interested to hear all about Franke's scientific instrument store in Berlin. In turn, Franke learnt about Heidecke's promotion from the design section to Production Manager of Voigtländer's camera section and about his ideas for a new camera, which was still only a dream. Voigtländer agreed to supply Franke's store in Berlin. On returning home that night Heidecke spoke to his wife of Franke's visit and she wondered whether Franke would be prepared to invest money in the manufacture of her husband's new camera.

Heidecke, the inventor, had always wanted to be a professor of ophthalmology, but without the opportunity of attending university this was impo sible. He sometimes resented that his parents had not been wealthy enough to allow him to stay at school. Heidecke would avidly read up technical papers, study patent applications, and in particular he wanted to know about the latest developments taking place throughout the world; possibly in the same way as we all try to absorb the latest news contained in our favourite photo-magazine today, even though most of the information supplied by advertising agents may not be strictly correct, as their job is to create interest followed by actual sales.

In 1916 Heidecke heard that Carl Zeiss had received an order for 100 f6.3 Tessar lenses from America, to be supplied to the American Army Signal Corps. At that time there was no simple roll-film camera available in Germany, and many German soldiers wished they had the opportunity of buying a simple reliable camera so that they could take photographs of the many places that they had visited. World War I gave many people an opportunity to travel, which they had never experienced before. Unlike today, when flying in an aeroplane is commonplace, in 1914 passenger planes did not yet exist.

Heidecke obtained a Kodak folding No.3 camera made in 1914, and started to design his own in the basement of his house. Returning home one night he found that a rat had eaten through the bellows! Clearly this was not a camera to take into the trenches, which contained more rats than soldiers.

Another problem with the Kodak camera was that to use the viewfinder meant that your head would be above the parapet of the trench, a sure way to commit suicide. Why not have a camera based on an army folding periscope, he thought? So the twin lens idea, using roll-film, was conceived.

Between 1916 and 1918 Heidecke made a prototype but, due to ill-health, the war, and Voigtländer not being interested in any new designs as they were selling all the cameras they could make, he almost forgot his T.L.R. With the war nearly over, who would buy a camera built principally for use in the trenches?

Heidecke was always presenting ideas to Voigtländer, and in fact, before one modification was able to come into production he was suggesting an improvement. So he was not always popular with his superiors, which is often a common occurrence today when trying to get inventors to design something which is commercially viable. In early 1919, with many returning soldiers bemoaning the lack of a travelling camera, Heidecke "polished up" his prototype and again spoke to Voigtländer about a roll-film camera. Again they were not interested in any new designs that would require finance and new tools as they could sell their entire production, including those products made in their military section, which had by then switched to civil work.

In 1919, after World War I had finished, stereo cameras were, as we would say today, "the flavour of the month". So many people were wanting to visit the old battlefields to take stereo photographs that it was perhaps understandable that Voigtländer would concentrate on improving their existing range of products.

Reinhold then decided he would start manufacturing his own twin lens reflex camera, and visited the bank to find out if he could borrow money to start the new business. The Bank Accounts Manager to whom Heidecke spoke, later wrote and told him that they were receiving many applications for loans from returning soldiers, that designers could be bought for almost two a Deutschmark, that anyone starting a business without commercial and financial experience would have very little chance of success and that his dreams would come to nothing. This advice was to prove valuable as Heidecke had the brains, but he was later to find out that Paul Franke's financial expertise and juggling would save the firm on more than one occasion.

Reinhold Heidecke was easily upset. He was one of the two sons of Bergmanns and Elizabeth Johanna Heidecke and was born in Aschersleben, Harz, on the 2nd of January 1881. His parents were very religious, belonging to the Protestant Church. It could well be that this strict religious upbringing turned Reinhold into a rebel; he had a number of jobs on leaving school and never settled for long.

His first job at Voigtländer was in the tool and wooden pattern department. He started after the traditional New Year holiday in January 1900, but very shortly this difficult to control 19-year-old was moved to another section. After four years he left, only to return in September 1905.

Reinhold was "living in sin", which was unheard of at that time, and this further separated him from his parents. He married Wilhelmine Biethan on the morning of Saturday 7th April 1906. Erich Vollenweider, one of Reinhold's colleagues at Voigtländer, recalled the embarrassment when everyone realised that Wilhelmine was pregnant. She was unable to join in the normal post-matrimonial pleasantries and her father was constantly reiterating the shame she had brought to the family.

Reinhold was as determined as ever, and passed off the wedding with the comment "I have acted like a gentleman and done the right thing". On Saturday the 16th June, exactly 10 weeks after they were married, their first son was born and they named him Reinhold Ernst Friedrich, the last two names being the same as his grandfather's which pleased Reinhold's parents. They had a daughter, Lotte Anna Johanna, born on the 14th January 1908. Reinhold's mother's last name was Johanna. Sadly, Wilhelmine's parents never forgave their daughter and they often complained about Reinhold's arrogant manner. In 1906 morals were very strictly observed and it certainly was not easy for Wilhelmine. Nevertheless, Erich Vollenweider recalled that she was a very good mother, a hard worker and was able to tame her volatile husband. In fact she eventually suggested that Reinhold should approach Paul Franke with a view to starting a joint business.

We all know that Reinhold Heidecke took his wife's advice and wrote to Franke in Berlin, and that Paul Franke, together with his friends, provided the original capital to start the business. More about that later, let us look at the origins that Heidecke always referred to when designing his camera. We know that as a young lad he always wanted to become a designer, and, not having a university education, he would write to manufacturers requesting information on their products and whilst he was at Voigtländer most firms were happy to send him their brochures.

Peter W.F. Voigtländer was born in 1812 and joined the optical manufacturing business which was established by his family in 1756 in Vienna. In 1841 he started to manufacture what some consider could well be the first camera ever designed, the famous Voigtländer Petzval, together with a portrait or landscape lens. In 1849 he opened a new branch in Braunschweig where he manufactured both his camera, and optical instruments. Voigtländer at that time was one of the most respected manufacturers. It was in 1905 that it was decided to start up a new camera division to produce a range of plate cameras. Young Heidecke started work on a rigid-bodied stereo camera known as the Stereflekyoskop, which was based on the pattern of Richard's Verascope (Jules Richards of Paris, France). The later Stereflektoskop was advertised as the smallest stereoscopic reflex camera manufactured, and it offered an almost negative-sized finder located, as in the Verascope and Stereflekyoskope, between the camera's "taking" lenses, and it was on this design Heidecke's original Heidoscop was based.

1. In the design department was a press release from Eastman Dry Plate & Film Company dated 1st January 1885 which was used as a book mark in the patent book giving a list of Eastman's inventions, stating as follows:-

2. Eastman invented the first film, a coated strip of paper, the coat or pellicle of which was stripped after exposure and developing, making a transparent photographic negative.

3. Eastman was the first to begin experiments with nitro-cellulose as a possible base for film.

4. Reichenbach obtained the first patent on transparent, flexible, nitro-cellulose film, which he made by discovering the importance of camphor, fuel oil and amyl acetate.

5. Eastman invented the machinery and processes for making film.

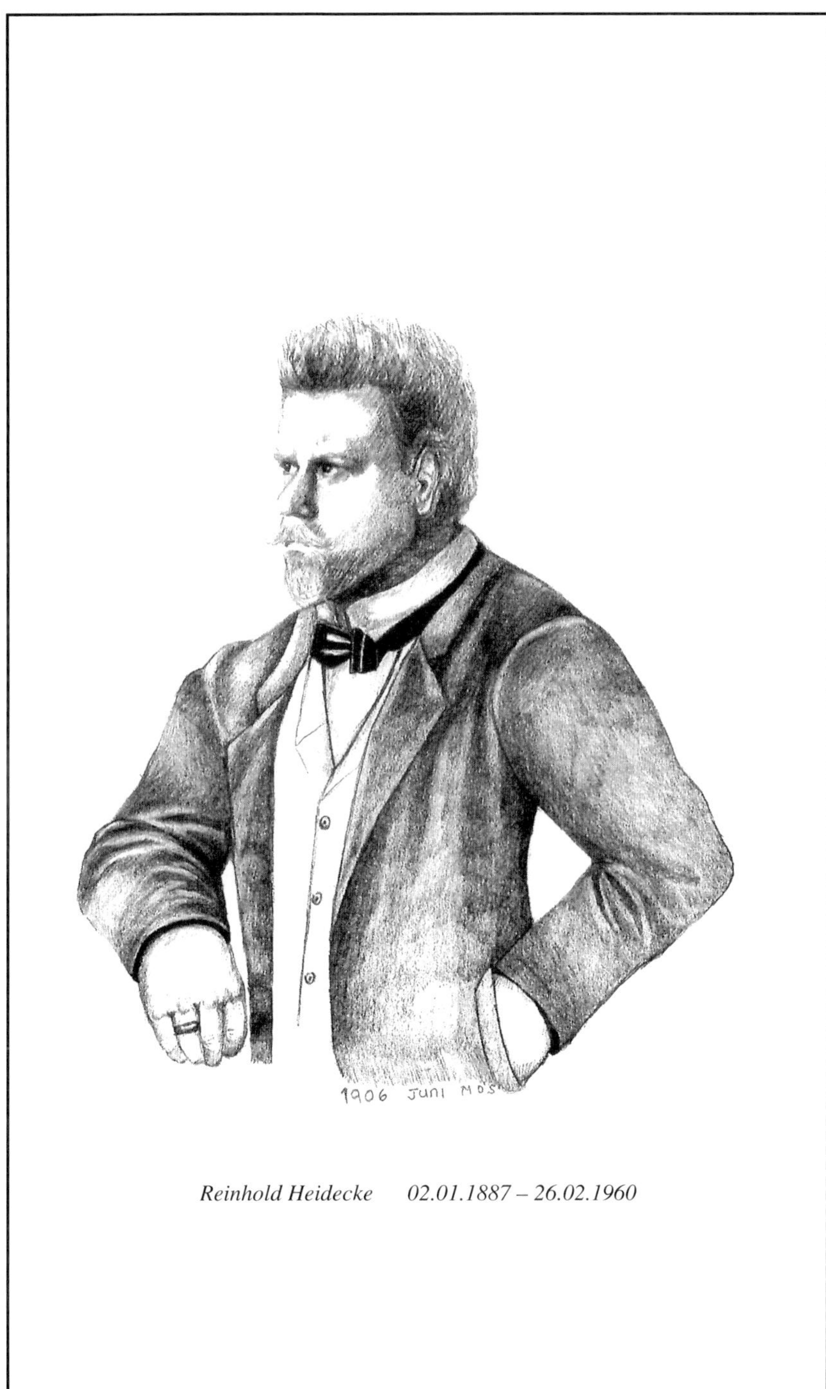

Reinhold Heidecke 02.01.1887 – 26.02.1960

6. The Eastman Company was the first to manufacture and sell both kinds of film. This company created the market for film by developing the Kodak camera which was the first great consumer of the film.
7. This company made the first film for Edison's Kinetoscope, the first motion picture camera.
8. Eastman was the first to eliminate electricity from film, which had caused marking in cold weather.
9. Eastman was the first to produce, manufacture, and market film in continuous strips on reels.

Heidecke thought at that time "Why are we using glass plates when obviously roll-film is available?" He wrote to Eastman and obtained samples of film but it was pointed out that Voigtländer were making plate cameras and not film cameras. This probably spurred Heidecke into designing a roll-film camera to compete with Voigtländer, who quite bluntly told him to mind his own business and get on with the job he had been given.

Heidecke could not understand why Eastman company (who became known as Kodak in 1889) bought Tessar lenses in 1910 when there were so many good lenses available in America. However, those people he met who had used the Kodak camera with the Tessar lenses, spoke very highly of the magnificent high contrast pictures which the camera took, and which could be enlarged and used for exhibition purposes. It is interesting to note that one of Cecil Beaton's first cameras was a Kodak autographic folding camera with a Carl Zeiss Tessar lens.

The autographic feature was invented and patented in 1913 by Henry Gaisman and the patent rights were subsequently bought by Kodak. This feature allowed the photographer to write information on the film at the time of exposure. Gaisman's invention carried a tissue, similar to a typewriter carbon paper, between the backing paper and the film which could be made transparent by using the metal stylus, and the light filtering through the backing paper would expose the sensitive film, giving a permanent record on the film when it was developed. So, the likes of Cecil Beaton and journalists could write the names of the people they were photographing on the actual film. Although Heidecke was interested in this development, Kodak had spent a very considerable fortune on buying the patent rights, so he was unable to incorporate it in any of his cameras. Later on when the U.S. Army Signal Corps purchased the 3A autographic Kodak with Tessar lenses, he decided that the camera he would finally make would have a Tessar lens.

The Tessar lens was also popular with Field Marshall Rommel, who besides owning a Rolleiflex had a Contax and a Leica, all fitted with Tessar lenses. Today, the "T" for Tessar T.L.R. is a firm favourite and can be seen in use by many professional photographers, and is often seen at weddings.

In 1935 Rollei cameras with Tessar lenses were so popular that Zeiss had to stop the production of their 35mm super Nettel cameras, with Tessar

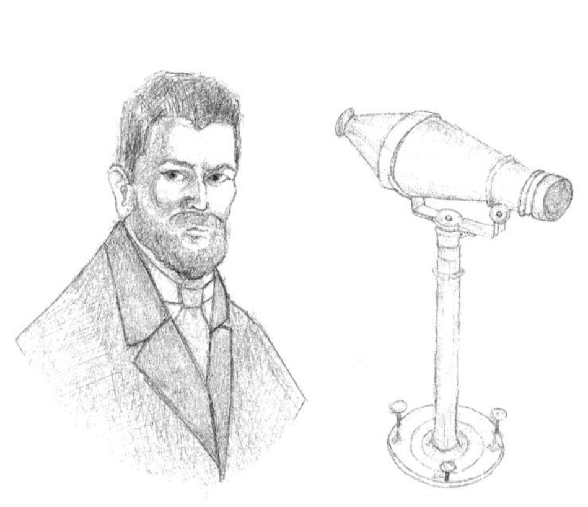

Peter Voigtländer with his 1841 Petzval

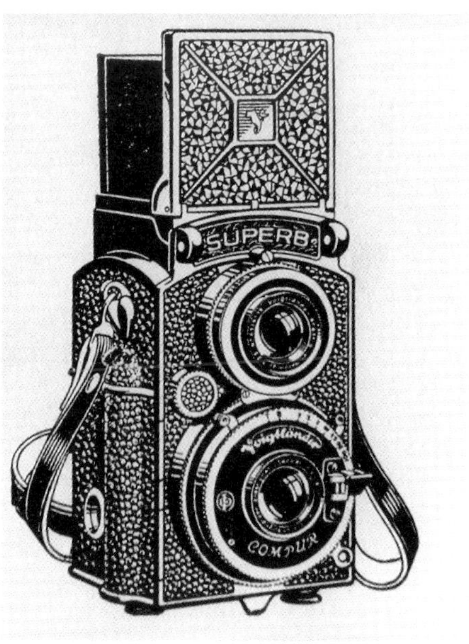

The Superb: Voigtländer's reply to Franke & Heidecke's T.L.R.

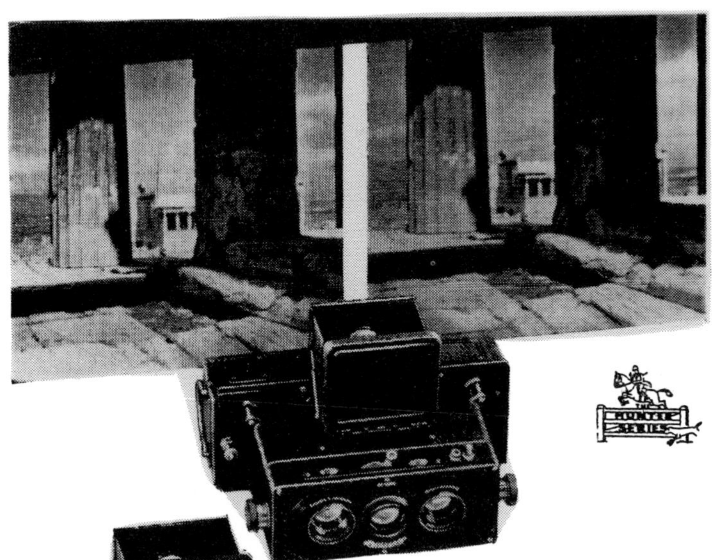

HEIDOSCOPE

The precision Stereo Camera for serious work

The housing is made of light metal, cast in a single piece. This ensures the handiness and precision necessary for stereo cameras with high speed lenses, and keeps the weight down to the lowest possible limit. The shutter is rigidly built into the housing, the two-part shutter is permanently identical. The famous qualities of the Zeiss Tessars guarantee sharpness and plastic brilliance in the pictures at any focal distance. The Heidoscope changing-box is recognized as the most perfect instrument of its kind.

PRICES :

6 × 13 cm. **£55 0 0**
4.5 × 10.7 cm. **£49 5 0**

ROLLEIDOSCOPE

For stereo work with Roll Films

The special high speed finder objective throws a clear and bright image on to the focussing screen, so that the exposure can be estimated with confidence.
The Rolleidoscope is as easily and simply operated as the Heidoscope.

PRICES :

6 × 13 cm. **£47 5 0**
4.5 × 10.7 cm. **£39 10 0**

FULL DESCRIPTIVE CATALOGUE OF THE ABOVE TWO CAMERAS POST FREE ON REQUEST.

1932 advertisement by R.F. Hunter, the English importer.

lenses, so that they could supply the large orders they were receiving from Franke & Heidecke.

The Tessar lens, a Zeiss product, produced sharp images. It was designed in 1902 by Dr. Paul Rudolph and its original idea came from the Cook Triplet designed by H. Dennis Taylor. Although designed after the Zeiss Planar, with fewer air-to-glass interfaces, an inferior lens was preferred to the Planar because the lens coating technology was not available. The Tessar, with the resources of the Carl Zeiss empire, was the best-known and advertised lens for over 40 years. The Tessar was made under licence at the end of World War II in Japan by Nikon and used in their own cameras. Leitz copied the design and it was known as the Elmar.

This lens differed from the Triplet in that the third element was manufactured from telescopic flint. But as on the Triplet, the first and fourth elements were made from dense barium crown and the second element on both lenses was made from light flint. This design, with a small modification in the casing to overcome patents, was made by Leitz as the Elmar. Herr Oskar Barnack started working for Carl Zeiss in 1902 and in 1909 suggested a 35mm camera based on motion film with a fixed speed of 1/40th using a Tessar f3.5 lens. Carl Zeiss was not impressed, and Oskar Barnack left Zeiss and joined Leitz in 1911. He built the first model in 1913 using a f3.5 anastigmat lens of 50mm. It was not until 1925 that the Leica first went on sale with a Tessar copy lens, the Elmar.

The reason why Voigtländer were not keen to manufacture a roll-film camera in 1907 was that the earliest roll-film was prone to curling and it was not until 1903 that Kodak improved their film by adding an anti-curl backing layer of gelatin, and this was not known to Voigtländer.

Heidecke considered writing to Franke about investing money in the photographic manufacturing business but was worried in case it would not be a success. Nevertheless, he worked out what would be required to start manufacturing on a modest scale but in November 1918, with Christmas fast approaching and World War I coming to an end, he did nothing. In February 1919, however, Paul Franke once again visited Voigtländer and on the insistence of Heidecke's wife he was invited to stay the night at their house and Heidecke told Franke of what he would like to do.

Luckily, Paul Franke was extremely worried about living in Berlin and the fact that 3000 Freikorps had to be called in from outside Berlin as a result of the Communist uprising in January of that year. Also, two of the Communist leaders, it was claimed, were murdered while in police custody. This, coupled with the difficulties of getting cameras to sell, interested Franke more than Heidecke suspected. Franke was impressed with the information Heidecke had told him about the Tessar lens and the availability of non-curl film.

Franke was already thinking of moving his business and home out of Berlin, here he thought was an opportunity to be carefully considered.

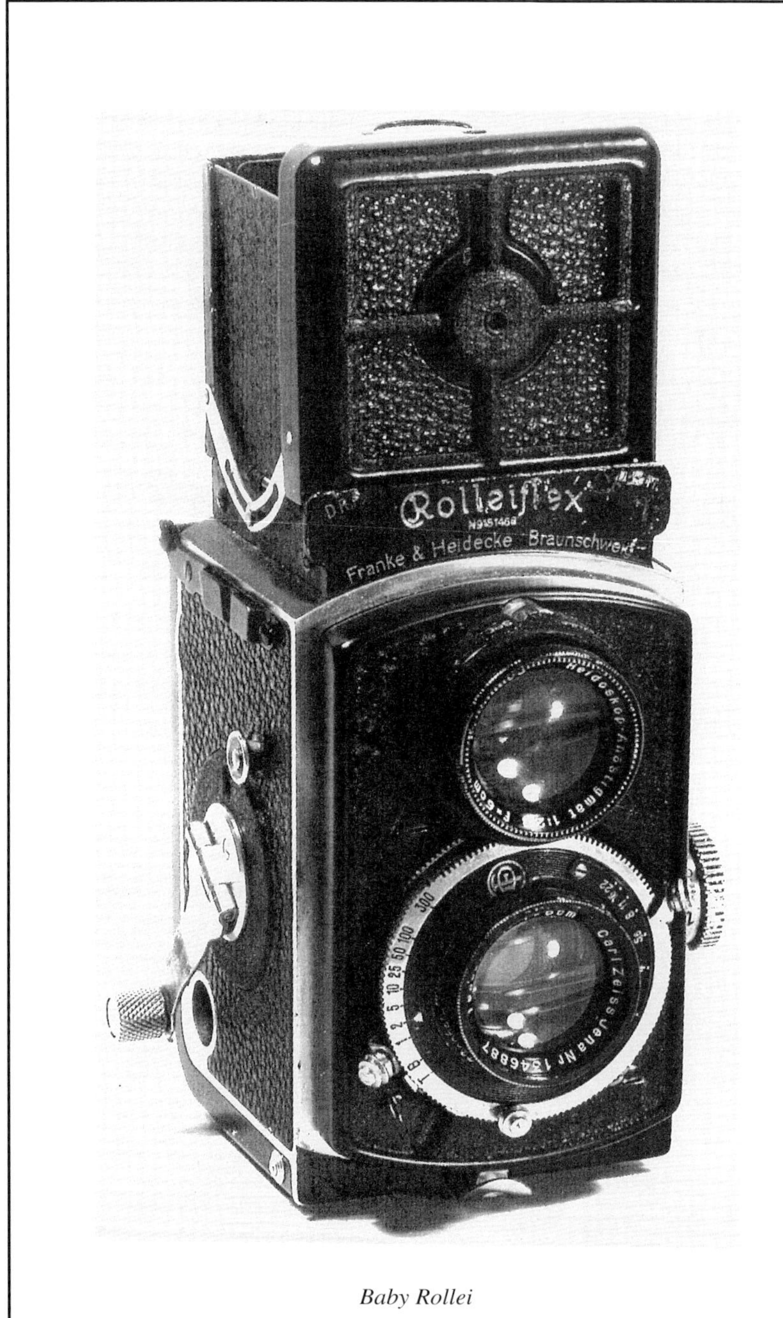

Baby Rollei

CHAPTER 3

THE BIRTH OF ROLLEI

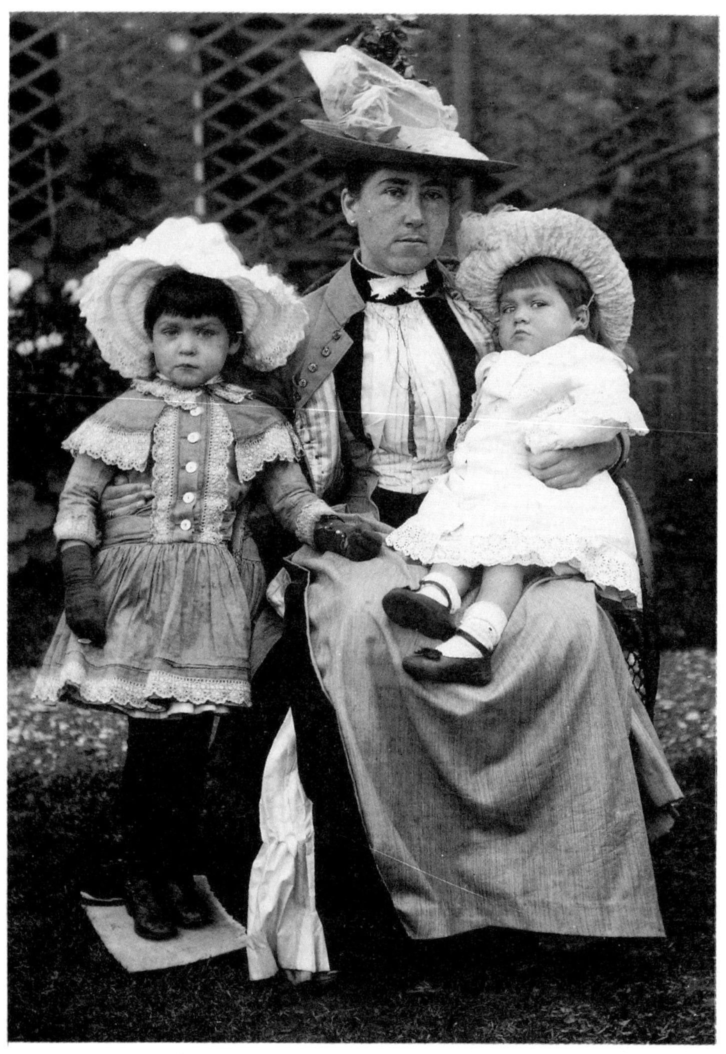

Paul Franke, left, aged 1 year with his mother and Hannah

PHOTO J.P.M. & H.R. *MÜHLHAUSEN 1889*

THE BIRTH OF ROLLEI

Paul Franke was born on 30th November, 1888, in Mühlhausen/Thüringen, the son of quite wealthy parents, and on leaving school at the age of 15 he started work as an apprentice in a large pharmaceutical shop in Dusseldorf which had a photographic department. He remained there for three years, before joining Voigtländer in 1909. After his visit and stay with Heidecke in February 1919 Franke carefully considered a new life in Braunschweig, the city he adored; he would be prepared to put 75,000 Marks into the new business and he began to enquire where he could raise further finance. He was most insistent that they should first manufacture a stereo camera, as he knew that he could sell all they could make in his photographic store in Berlin.

Heidecke readily agreed to these arrangements as he could see the sense in producing a camera which he knew how to design and to manufacture; he was after all Voigtländer's Factory Manager on the photographic section. By November 1919 they decided to start a small business and looked around for premises, eventually renting rooms in the basement of a Braunschweig apartment house at Nos. 31 & 32 Viewegstraße, many other rooms of which were used as a dancing school. They then went ahead with getting their partnership registered in the name of Franke & Heidecke, to commence on the 1st January 1920. The application was sent in at the end of November. Meanwhile, Voigtländer was not aware that they were about to lose one of their designers. On the 10th December 1919 the Certificate of Registration was signed and sealed.

We have some interesting recollections about their first premises in Viewegstraße from a former pupil of the music and dancing academy, Frau Helga Kunstmann, who visited England to see her au-pair daughter in 1954. She recalled the academy had taught ballet, pianoforte and violin, and that the older children were taught the military formal dancing of the period. The academy was located on the corner of Viewegstraße and could easily have been mistaken for a bank. It was a very imposing building with a large lofty basement, two floors with studios and living accommodation on the top floor. Unlike a bank, there was no front door. She recalled that as children they had regarded the building as a high class prison. The entrance was hidden at the back of the building. Inside, where the front door should have been, stood the baby grand piano. When each class was dismissed, the teachers would get up from their piano stools, stretch, turn around and admire the view from the corner window, thus missing those delinquent students who extended their tongues, obviously not realising that their teachers could sometimes see their reflection in the glass.

Frau Kunstmann remembered well the time when a photographic manufacturing company moved into the basement of the building, which she

Wohnung: 6

Geschäftsstelle: ...... 32.

Gewerbeanmeldeschein.

Es wird hierdurch bescheinigt, daß Herr ...... Heidecke

geb. 1) 2.1.81 ...... Franke, Paul

2.) 30.11.88. Mühlhausen i/Th. Absicht, hierselbst das Gewerbe:

......

Fa. Franke & Heidecke

vom 1 Januar 1920 ab zu betreiben, angemeldet hat und daß der Ausführung dieses Vorhabens kein gesetzliches Hindernis entgegensteht.

Wenn der Gewerbebetrieb **dauernd** eingestellt wird, muß derselbe bei Vermeidung der Weiterzahlung der Gewerbesteuer **sofort** unter Rückgabe dieser Bescheinigung **ab**gemeldet werden.

Braunschweig, den 10 Dezbr. 1919.

Der Rat der Stadt Braunschweig

Wagner.

Certificate of Trading Franke & Heidecke 10th December 1919.

thought belonged to the City of Braunschweig. The tenant who ran the dancing school had died and it was being run by the remaining teachers until it was decided what would happen. Some of the students had already left the school and so there were a number of studios available for hire. At this time, besides ballet for young children and classical dancing, a lot of emphasis would have been on ballroom and military dances. With the ending of the war, interest in this type of dancing had declined considerably. Frau Kunstmann recalled that when the manufacturing started in the basement, the gas lights used to shake and sometimes go out. It was the teacher's job to light the gas lamps before class started. This was done by pulling a chain which rubbed a small wheel against a flint, thus causing a spark in a similar way to a cigarette lighter, which then ignited the gas lamp. If this failed then they would light the lamp with a taper.

Within a year, the noise from the basement was greater than that of the children dancing, and on the top floor music lessons were impossible, so the remaining parts of the school closed down and the photographic company took over the whole building.

When looking at the photograph of the building it is evident that, at one time, it must have been a very prosperous dancing academy, and was the type of building one would have associated with a bank rather than a school, and it was here that Franke and Heidecke were able to start their business.

Surprisingly, with so much of Braunschweig destroyed by bombing in World War II, the original building is still standing and today looks exactly as it was way back in the 1920s. Most of the surrounding property has been replaced due to bombing or development of large office or apartment blocks. Today the property is owned by a cousin of Franke & Heidecke, and has been converted into very attractive and spacious apartments, some of which are occupied by Rollei pensioners at a reduced rental.

The main alterations from the outside are new windows, some without bars; the chimney is on the other side, and several ornaments are missing. New electric street lights replaced the few gas lamp standards. The building is now divided up into flats, and the basement, on looking through the window, appears to be used by a bicycle repairer and stores. The marks of the original machine pulleys can still be seen. Obviously the building has been constructed and built in the same manner as the original cameras and will survive many more years.

Franke and Heidecke's choice of location for their first factory in 1920 was very fortunate; only two years later they were able to acquire the entire building, with the help of a mortgage from the Frankfurter Hypotheken Bank. However, the city fathers did not take kindly to the idea of a noisy industrial manufacturing unit within a residential area, and even in those days neighbours were quick to complain. So agreement was reached only six months later for the "factory" to be relocated to a site just outside the city, beyond the railway on Salzdahlumer Straße, covering 60,000 square metres (approx. 15 acres).

In 1919 the official exchange was 43 Marks to the £1 or the equivalent of 68 loaves of bread at 63 pfennigs each. By January 1923 the price of a loaf of bread had risen to 250 Marks, then in September it was 1,500,000 and in November, when the currency finally collapsed, 201,000,000 Marks (quite a few wheel-barrow loads) were required to buy just one loaf.

Contracts for the Salzdahlumer Straße site were completed on 10th January 1923, fortunately before the Mark collapsed, so in fact Paul Franke acquired this site for virtually nothing. It was not until 1930 that the new factory was ready.

Paul Franke was often referred to as the "financial juggler". As most of the partnership's sales were overseas they received payment in foreign currency. David Robertson recalled that he was asked to collect money due to Franke & Heidecke from Wallace Heaton in 1923 and bank the money in the U.K. until requested to transfer it to the Frankfurter Bank in Germany. Hard currency was a very valuable commodity at the time of the collapse of the German Reichsmark. Words cannot describe the anguish that the ordinary person must have gone through. Maybe this information has nothing to do with Rollei cameras, but it does show how the firm, from being tenants in a small basement, were able to acquire a large parcel of real estate and build what today would still be considered a modern factory.

Heidecke wanted a factory better and larger than Voigtländer. He was constantly looking at ways to improve his camera designs and above all to ensure his family of workers had the best tools for the job. The Rollei name became known throughout the world for quality par excellence.

Franke, with the confidence that he was selling the world's best engineered photographic products, was able to obtain large orders throughout the world. With the collapse of the Mark, the timing when payment was received at their firm's bank account was very important, hence his reputation as a financial juggler.

Supplies bought one day on credit could be paid for the next month at a substantial discount. In the early twenties those German firms exporting made enormous profits and expanded, while businesses supplying the local markets and receiving payment for their services in Reichsmarks soon went bankrupt.

The trouble started on 24th August 1922, when rumour had it that French troops were marching into the Ruhr, following Germany's inability to pay a two million instalment of its war reparations. The Mark, which had already been weak during 1921, just dropped 50% of its value within 10 days. The table explains the Mark's movement and the reader will readily understand why exports were so valuable.

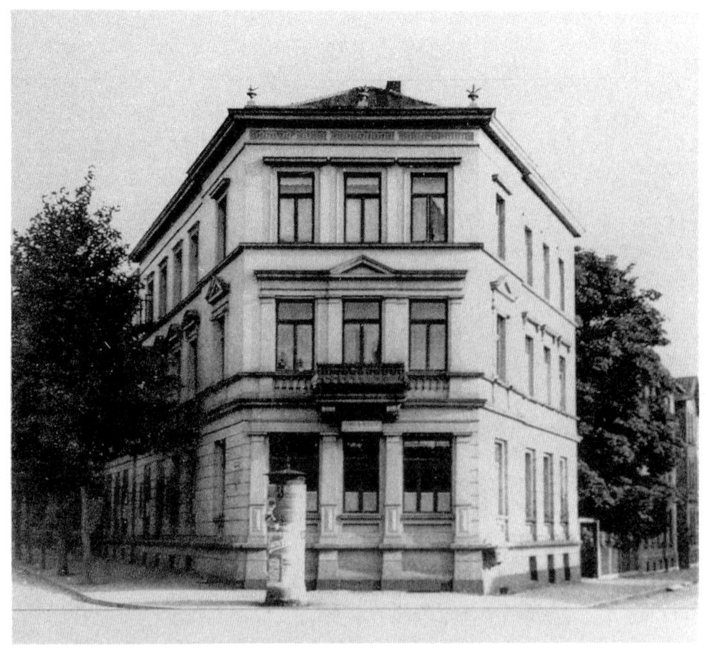

Original Franke & Heidecke works, No.32 Viewegstraße, Braunschweig. Picture c.1925

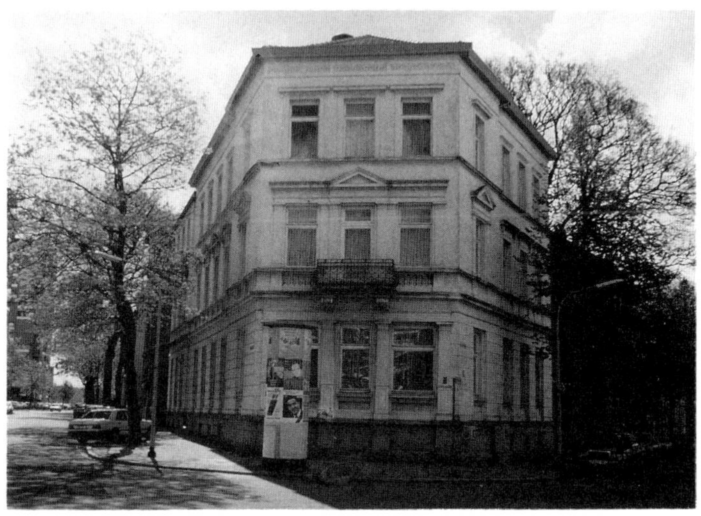

Only the window frames seem to have changed. Picture April 1991.

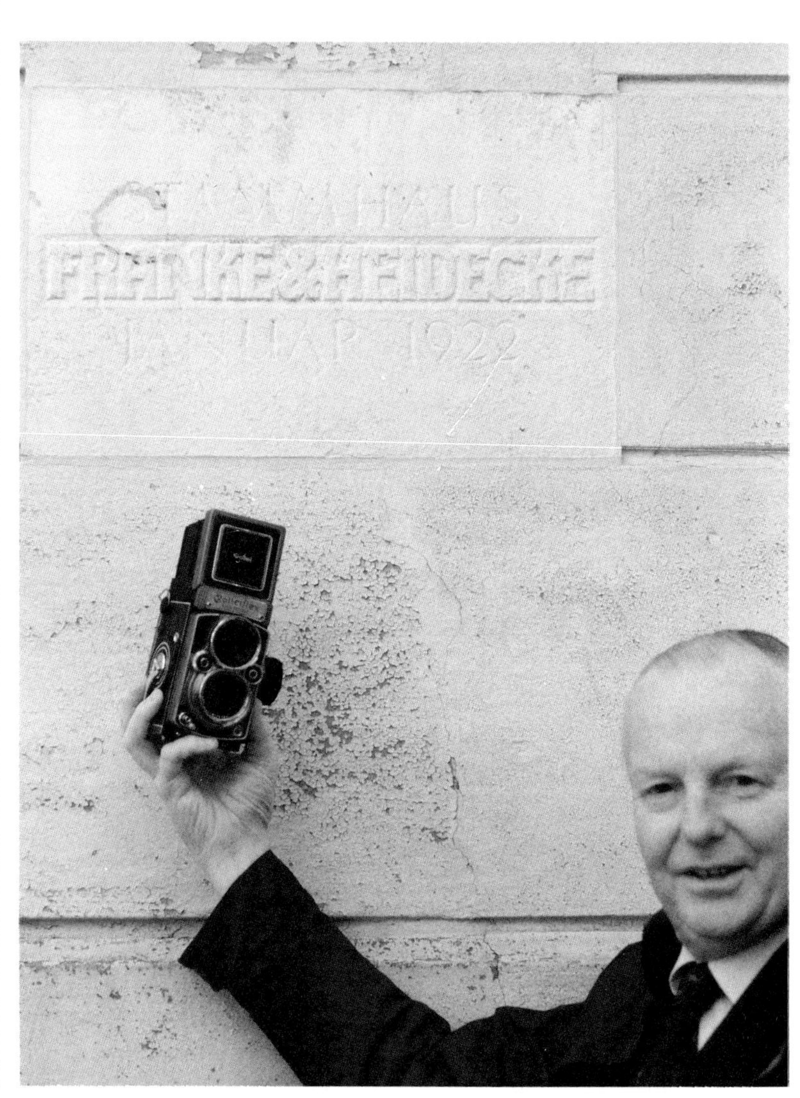

Ian Parker holding a 1991 2.8GX Edition beside the nameplate "Franke & Heidecke January 1922" on the wall of the original small factory at No.32 Viewegstraße, Braunschweig

Photo by Hazel Parker

RELATIONSHIP OF THE MARK TO THE £1

Year	Month	Rate
1918	November	= 4.8
1919	May	= 4.8
1919	July	= 4.8
1921	January	= 85.0
1921	August	= 340.0
1921	September	= 500.0
1921	December	= 750.0
1922	March	= 3,750.0
1922	May	= 4,000.0
1922	August	= 8,000.0
1922	November	= 20,000.0
1922	December	= 80,000.00
1923	January	= 112,000.0
1923	February	= 220,000.0
1923	June	= 600,000.0
1923	August	= 15,000,000.0
1923	September	= 200,000,000.0
1923	October	= 183,000,000.0
1923	November	New Currency

1,000 Million Mark = 1DM

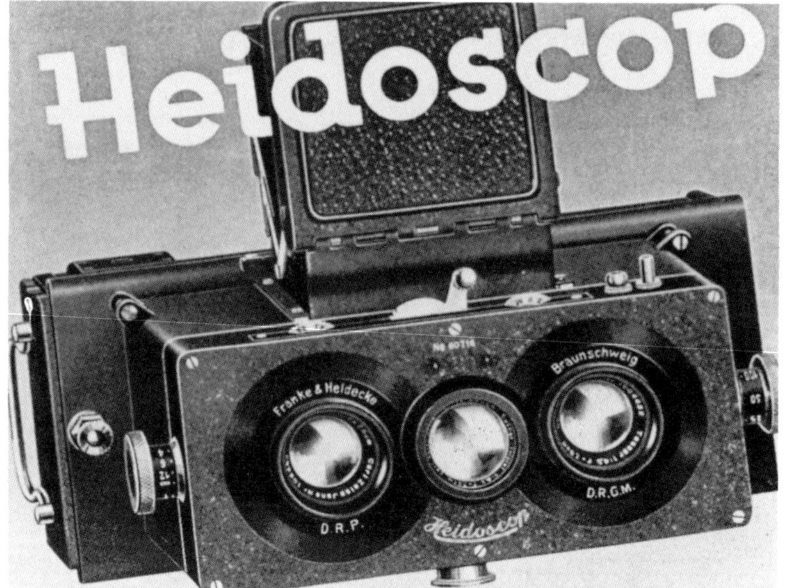

The precision stereo camera for serious work!

The housing is made of light metal, cast in one single piece. This ensures the handiness and precision necessary for stereo cameras with High-speed lenses, and keeps the weight down to the smallest possible limit. The shutter is rigidly built into the housing, the two-part-shutter is permanently identical. The famous qualities of the Zeiss Tessars guarantee sharpness and plastic brilliance in the pictures at any focal distance. The Heidoscop changing-box is recognized as the most perfect instrument of its kind.

Heidoscopy is the best stereoscopy!

FRANKE & HEIDECKE · BRAUNSCHWEIG

To be obtained from any high-class photo-dealer

CHAPTER 4

THE START OF BUSINESS

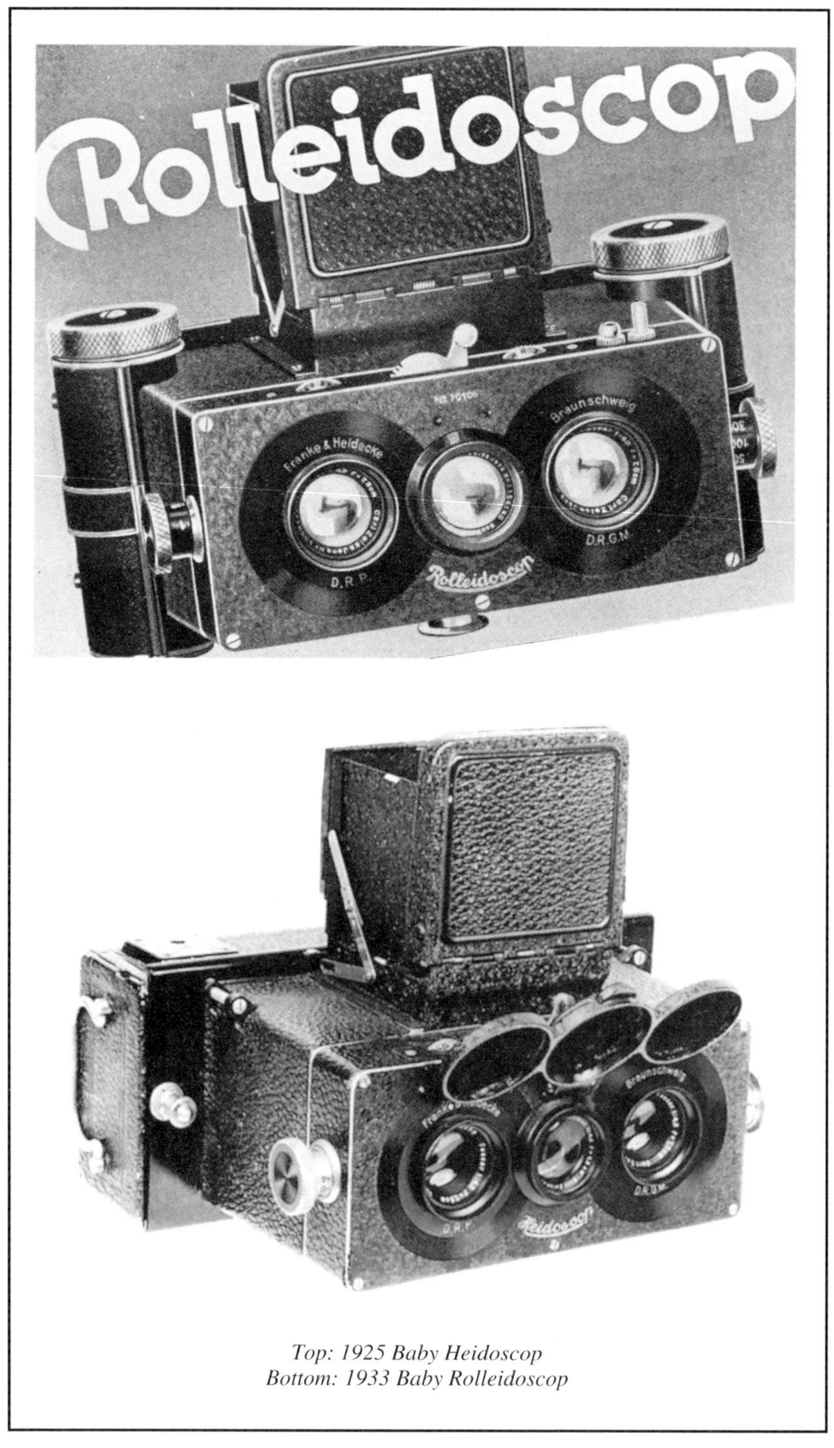

Top: 1925 Baby Heidoscop
Bottom: 1933 Baby Rolleidoscop

THE START OF BUSINESS

Although the tenancy of the Viewegstraße property commenced on the 1st of January 1920, it was not until the 20th that anyone actually moved into the premises. Paul Franke was busy with his New Year Sale, and customers exchanging unwanted Christmas presents, so it was not until February that he could move into a small office which was going to be the counting house (the old name for an accounts office).

Franke at first organised a male accounts clerk who would write the letters, obtain prices for bought-in parts, as well as the thousand jobs which befell the office junior. Franke would visit Braunschweig on a Tuesday and Wednesday, which were the quietest days in his photographic store, travelling by train from Berlin. Little did he realise that within a year the situation would be reversed and he would be living in Braunschweig and visiting Berlin on Friday and Saturday, which were the two busiest days in his store.

Meanwhile Heidecke was waiting impatiently until the 20th January, which was to be his last day with Voigtländer. To start with Heidecke used one of the basement rooms as his drawing office, but mostly he would construct a camera by hand, doing all the cutting, milling and lathe work himself. His early drawings were for bought-in components, so that at first he could obtain competitive prices, and then he finally completed all the drawings for the toolmakers.

Heidecke's first camera to go on sale was a stereo Heidoscop with two Carl Zeiss Jena Tessar f4.5 55mm taking lenses and a Carl Zeiss Jenar Sucher- Triplet f3.2 finder lens. It is said that 26 prototypes were made and discarded. After some two years of frustration, production commenced and the first camera was completed.

The first Heidoscop was the baby for paired exposures on 45 x 107mm glass plates. The body style resembled that of the 1898 Jules Richard Le Verascope. Incidentally, this camera remained in production until World War II with virtually no modifications and is considered the simplest and most reliable stereo camera manufactured. To start with Franke obtained various stereo cameras for Heidecke to select the best features of each, thus not giving the impression that they were copying the Voigtländer Stereflek-toskop. As soon as Voigtländer had seen the Heidoscop they quickly started to patent all their designs.

Another camera looked at was the C.P. Goerz Stereo Tenax. At one time they considered the Goerz lens which was cheaper than the Zeiss Tessar. The first pre-production models were fitted with f4.5 60mm Hoerz Dogmar lenses. The I.C.A. Polyscop with Carl Zeiss lens was also looked at, but in the end Heidecke preferred the reflex viewing lens principle, whereby the photographer was able to see the image rather than looking through a small viewfinder which gave a false picture for those wearing glasses.

The original stereo production cameras were offered in 1921-24 with: (a) Zeiss Tessar lenses and a Zeiss Jena Sucher-Triplet finder lens. (b) Steinheil-Unofokal lenses and a Steinheil finder lens. (c) Heidoscop anastigmat taking and finder lens.

When Paul Franke and Reinhold Heidecke first started to manufacture the Stereo in 1920 they decided on the Baby 45 x 107. Obviously credit and cash were major considerations in those first months before they were able to deliver their first cameras and, what was more important was actually getting paid for those cameras delivered. Carl Zeiss required prompt payment; they had seen many small companies come and go, and leaving a trail of debt.

To start with Franke and Heidecke did not know whether their business would be a success or after a couple of years join the many that went bankrupt. Never did they expect "their" camera to be accepted throughout the world and be so successful.

As a prudent provision, their cameras were offered with three different lenses. If Zeiss stopped deliveries they could offer Steinheil and in turn they had the Heidoscop, a name they could put on any lens.

The only stereo cameras with a Heidoscop lens was the original pre-production model, fitted with a Carl Zeiss taking lens and Steinheil finder lens. The reason that all cameras were fitted with Carl Zeiss lenses was mainly that Carl Zeiss optics, scientific instruments and microscopes were well known and advertised worldwide. Thus Franke & Heidecke were able to benefit; it gave them an entry into many overseas markets.

Advertisements appeared rather prematurely in 1921 announcing the new production of a stereo camera by Franke & Heidecke with a viewing screen the same size as the negative. Then advertisements appeared in *Die Photographische Industrie* in January 1922, again featuring the screen the same size as the negative produced. In fact this style of viewing screen with folding hood can be found on all Rollei T.L.R. cameras, including the 2.8GX, as well as the new electronic 6008 cameras.

The Rollei Stereos were only a means to get started and make some money. In fact, as Heidecke once said, they were a stop-gap until his twin lens reflex camera was able to be sold. The initial success of the baby stereo was far better than they expected, so much so that by the end of 1922 the payroll numbered 12 and 158 cameras were completed.

During 1923 Heidecke made a number of modifications. The shutter setting controls were repositioned from the front of the camera above the viewing/finder lens to the top of the camera on the front. The viewing hood was slightly changed and the shutter release was moved slightly towards the left. Also in 1923 a camera was made to take 117 roll-film and hence the

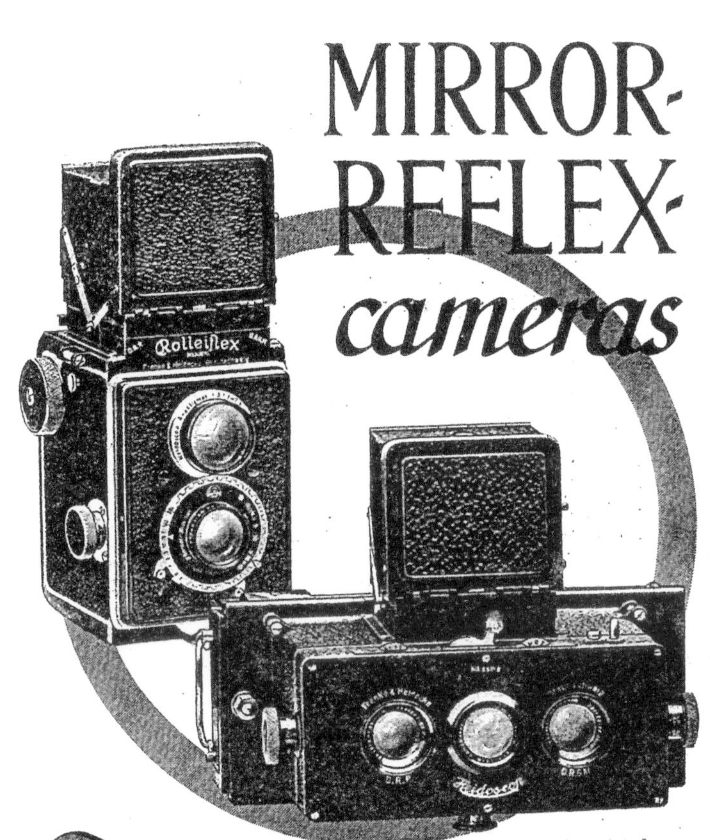

Franke & Heidecke

BRAUNSCHWEIG

1925 AMERICAN PROSPECTUS

Heidoscop 6 x 13	*$200*
Heidoscop 4.5 x 10.7	*$175*
Rolleidoscop 6 x 13	*$160*
Rolleidoscop 4.4 x 10.7	*$125*
Rolleiflex 4.5	*$75*
Rolleiflex 3.8	*$85*

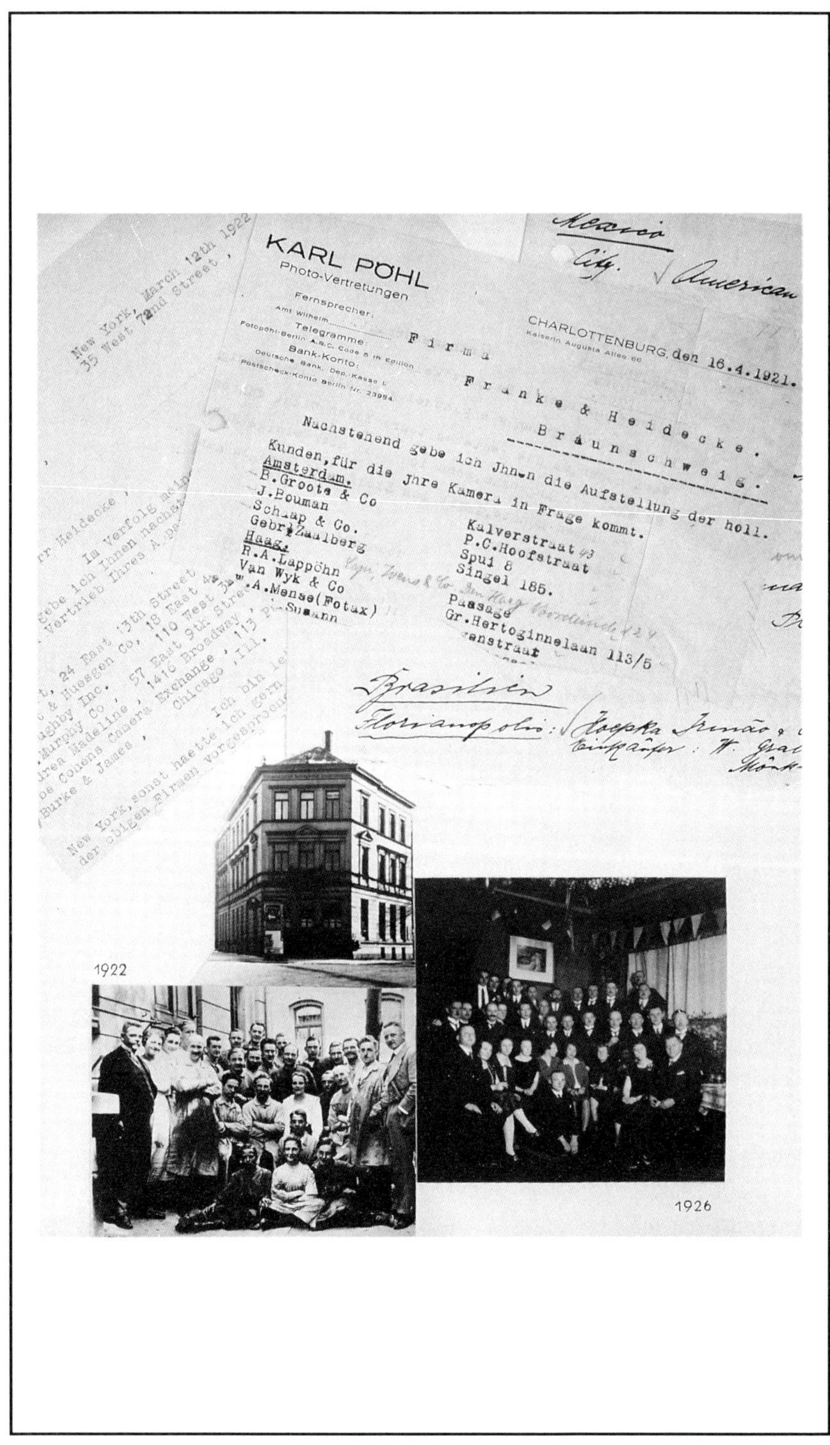
KARL PÖHL
Photo-Vertretungen
CHARLOTTENBURG, den 16.4.1921.
Firma
Franke & Heidecke.
Braunschweig.
Nachstehend gebe ich Jhnen die Aufstellung der holl.
Kunden, für die Jhre Kamera in Frage kommt.
Amsterdam.
B.Groote & Co Kalverstraat
J.Bouman P.C.Hoofstraat
Schaap & Co. Spui 8
Gebr. Zaalberg Singel 185.
Haag.
R.A.Lappöhn Passage
Van Wyk & Co Gr.Hertoginnelaan 113/5
New York, March 12th 1922
35 West 72nd Street,
1922
1926

name of Rollei was born. Heidecke called this camera the Rollfilm Heideck-eoscop. He liked his name to be associated with his cameras, so that Voigtländer would realise the mistake they had made in not allowing Heidecke to have a free hand while working in their design department.

The roll-film stereo camera went on sale in 1926, after problems with the 117 film were solved, and became known as the Rolleidoscop. However, a year earlier a larger Heidoscop, size 60 x 113mm, went on sale with an f4.5 75mm taking lens. By now, annual production exceeded 6000 camera and by the following year had reached the staggering number of 12,090 cameras.

The Heidecke stereo cameras, whether roll-film or plate, can still be seen in use today. Most of the roll-film cameras originally manufactured for 117 film have been converted to 120. The baby Rolleidoscop used 127 film. Later, on seeing the Heidoscop, Voigtländer changed the shutter to a stereo-Compur in 1923.

Production of the Rolleidoscop ceased in 1941, Richard's Verascope in 1940 and the Voigtländer Sterflexoskop in 1936. The Jersey Photographic Museum in the Channel Islands has many stereo cameras from various manufacturers, and a large number of the Heidoscop test plates, plus some of the stereo plates taken in 1921.

In June 1922, confident that their stereo camera was going to be a success, Franke & Heidecke bought the freehold of 31 Viewegstraße, with a staff of twelve in the basement. Paul Franke's son Horst, recounted some of his father's memories, like the story about the footsteps in the drive shaft belting. The machines were driven by a shaft that was suspended from the basement ceiling. This was turned by a large D.C. electric motor bolted onto the floor. There was a small pulley on the motor drive and a very large pulley, about a metre in diameter, on the shaft. From this shaft there were other smaller pulleys which drove through belts the various machines for grinding, drilling etc. Evidently a spare leather belt, some 15cm by 5 1/2 metres was ordered. This belt was quite heavy, with the leather about 8mm thick. As they were all working in the basement moving machinery they did not hear the delivery man and he, not finding the entrance, rolled the belt into the back garden, put it beside the gate and left, intending to take it down to the already locked basement the following day.

Imagine their surprise to find someone had cut out four pieces of leather in the shape of soles for a pair of boots! Two were for a child's shoes and the others quite large. This was the time of Communist unrest with many poor and unemployed.

Another advantage in purchasing the freehold was that it enabled electric lights to be installed. The gas lamps were retained, as often the electric motor would trip the fuse on starting unless all the machine's gears were in a neutral position. At that time the electric supply was on direct current, so they still retained the staple non-flickering gas lights.

Neue Preise

FRANKE & HEIDECKE · BRAUNSCHWEIG

Fabrik photographischer Präzisions-Apparate G. m. b. H.

Format 4 x 4 Code	RM	Rolleiflex-Apparate und Zubehör	Format 6 x 6 RM	Code
—	—	Rolleiflex 6 x 6 mit Tessar 3,8	188.—	Rolleifot
—	—	Rolleiflex 6 x 6 mit Tessar 4,5	178.—	Rolleimin
Rolleirex	200.—	Rolleiflex 4 x 4 mit Tessar 2,8	—	—
Rolleilux	185.—	Rolleiflex 4 x 4 mit Tessar 3,5	—	—
Rextano	12.—	Rolleiflextasche	15.—	Fottano
Rextabe	12.—	Rolleiflex-Bereitschaftstasche	15.—	Fottabe
Rexfihe	5.50	Gelbfilter hell	5.50	Fotfihe
Rexfimi	5.50	Gelbfilter mittel	5.50	Fotfimi
Rexfisky	7.20	UV Hochgebirgsfilter	7.20	Fotfisky
Rexgreen	7.20	Rolleiflex-Grünfilter	7.20	Fotgreen
Rexproun	16.20	Proxarlinsen, Satz 1 (1 m bis 50 cm) .	16.20	Fotproun
Rexprodo	16.20	Proxarlinsen, Satz 2 (50 cm bis 33 cm)	16.20	Fotprodo
Rexsobe	3.60	Sonnenblende (im Lederbeutel) . . .	3.60	Fotsobe
Rexhood	2.50	Aufsteckschacht aus Leder	2.50	Fothood
Rexadapt	10.50	Plattenadapter-Rückwand	10.50	Fotadapt
Rexslide	6.60	Neusilberkassette	6.60	Fotslide
Rexcas	2.85	Behälter für 2 Kassetten	2.85	Fotcas
—	—	Filmandruck-Kassette	6.—	Fotpress
—	—	Mattscheiben-Kassette	6.—	Fotfoc
Rexhead	10.—	Panoramakopf	10.—	Fothead
Rexster	12.75	Stereoschieber	12.75	Fotster
Rexiris	10.—	Aufsteckbare Irisblende	10.—	Fotiris
Rexmir	15.—	Winkelspiegel mit Etui	15.—	Fotmir
—	—	Kinefilmeinrichtung, komplett	27.50	Fotcine
—	—	Ersatz-Agfa-Rolleiflex-Kassette . . .	2.—	Fotcess
—	—	Ersatzmaske für Mattscheibe	—.15	Fotmas

Format 45 x 107 Code	RM	Stereo-Apparate und Zubehör	Format 6 x 13 RM	Code
Heidospeti	427.50	Heidoscop einschl. Wechselmagazin . . .	445.50	Heidosgran
Rollospeti	342 —	Rolleidoscop	414.—	Rollosgran
Heipetano	25.—	Heidoscop-Ledertasche	30.—	Heigratano
Rolpetano	20.—	Rolleidoscop-Ledertasche	22.—	Rolgratano
Ruplan		Wechselmagazin für 25 Flachfilmeinlagen		Rupal
Ruivo	91.80	Reserve-Wechselmagazin	94.50	Rujada
Rukken	10.35	Rindledertasche hierzu	11.70	Rukking
—	—	Rollfilmkassette 6 x 13	67.50	Rollka
—	—	Rindledertasche hierzu	11.70	Rullest

So where did the money come from to start the business? Max Gruel who lived in Charlottenburg, Berlin, loaned the original 75,000 Marks, equivalent to £12,625, and Paul Franke obtained loans for another 75,000 Marks from the Franke Brothers, 50,000 Marks from a friend in London, giving a total of around £30,000. This was sufficient to buy second hand ex-war surplus machinery and materials, and so the business started. Paul Franke's photographic store had to subsidise the second year's payroll and it was not until they were obtaining repeat orders for cameras that their bankers, the Frankfurt Hypotheken, agreed to allow a loan at 3%!

With inflation out of control, Franke would not allow Heidecke to proceed with the twin lens reflex and, as at Voigtländer, their existing range of cameras were selling so well that sales exceeded production. This position, like the war, Franke reasoned, could not last forever and so Heidecke was content designing a new modern factory to build up to 20,000 twin lens cameras a year.

The Rolleiflex T.L.R. finally went on sale in 1929, designed, built and tested in the original factory. The previous six years had seen many problems in Germany, but fortunately Braunschweig, a very attractive cathedral city, had seemed to escape the Communist uprising and it was business as usual.

1929 was the year of the T.L.R., the world business slump and the crash of the New York stock exchange. Franke, the financial juggler, quickly switched sales to the home market that had now settled down. Fortunately, Heidecke's camera was an immediate success, with orders for 800 received in the first month, far greater than either Franke or Heidecke could have ever expected. The Rolleiflex was not a cheap camera, but it was in the high price quality products range that is not usually affected by the rise and fall of stock markets. The price in 1929 was £16.37 (198 RM) for the f4.5 version, equivalent to half a year's wages for a junior clerk or about £3000 today. The f3.8 version sold for 225 RM, £18.75. Photography was certainly not a cheap hobby even then!

Voigtländer & Sohn
Aktiengesellschaft
Optische Werke
Errichtet in Wien 1756

Telegramm-Anschrift: „Voldet"
A. B. C. Code, 5. Ausgabe
Fernsprech-Anschlüsse:
Werk Braunschweig: Nr. 1133 und 4319
Werk Gliesmarode: Nr. 1078
Girokonto:
Braunschweigische Bank u. Kreditanstalt A.-G.
Postscheckkonto: Hannover Nr. 941

Geschäftsstunden: 8 bis 4 Uhr

Braunschweig, den 28. Januar 1920.

Betrifft: Abtlg.
Angabe dieses Zeichens bei Beantwortung erbeten

Z e u g n i s !

Die Tätigkeit des Herrn Reinhold Heidecke bei der Firma Voigtländer & Sohn ergibt sich aus nachfolgender Zusammenstellung.

Sein Eintritt erfolgte im Januar 1900 als Mechanikergehilfe. Bis zu seiner im Februar 1904 erfolgten Einberufung zur Kaiserl. Marine arbeitete er an Prismen- und Zielfernrohren, fotograf. Objektiven und Sektorenverschlüssen.

Nach beendeter Dienstzeit im September 1905 trat er wieder bei der Firma Voigtländer & Sohn ein. Nachdem er einige Wochen als Kontrolleur für Kameras und Objektive tätig war, wurde er Vorarbeiter in der damals neu gegründeten Mikro-Abteilung. Hier wirkte er ein Jahr und wurde im Oktober 1906 unter besonderer Anerkennung seiner Leistungen vom seinerzeitigen technischen Direktor, Herrn Dr. Harting, zum Meister der Fotoabteilung ernannt. Zur Fotoabteilung gehörten seinerzeit ausser Objektiv- und Kamerabau auch die gesamte Dreherei.

Die seit 1904 aufgenommene Kamerafabrikation hatte damals den handwerksmässigen Betrieb noch nicht überschritten und die in Arbeit befindlichen Kameras entsprachen hinsichtlich Konstruktion und

solider

Form. Nr. 218. VII. 19. 20000.

Reinhold Heidecke's reference from the firm of Voigtländer & Son, dated 28 January 1920.

CHAPTER 5

FIRST TWIN LENS REFLEX

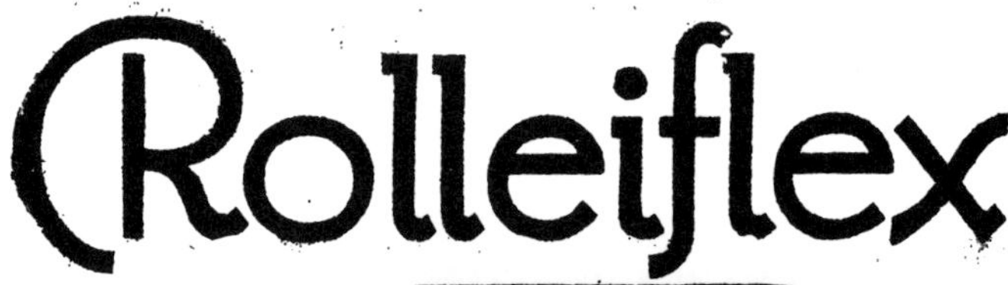

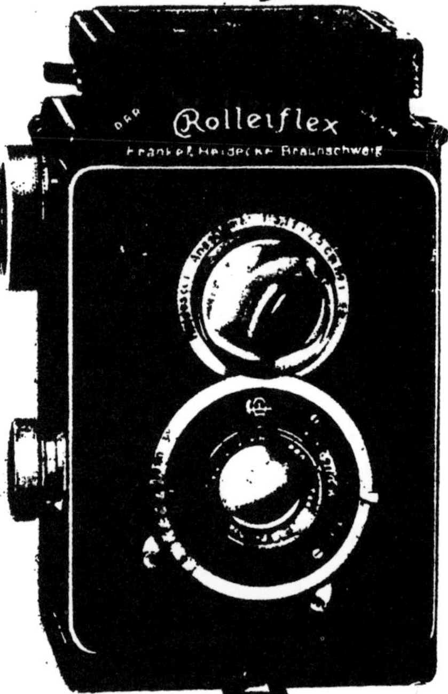

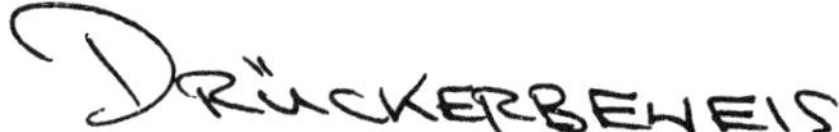

VI.XII. XXVIII

November 1928 printer's proof for the first advertisement and cover of the new Rollei T.L.R. instruction booklet

FIRST TWIN LENS REFLEX

The T.L.R. Rolleiflex was really born in 1916 and, as the reader will readily understand, it was not considered prudent to start manufacturing what might have been a disaster with the limited capital available. Roll-film was a problem as the common 117 film was mainly used for conversions on glass plate back cameras. The film was still inclined to curl and was only designed to take six exposures, with a spool of 0.905 inches, whereas the larger 120 size (for 12 exposures) was 0.990 inches. It was not until 1932 when the camera back was enlarged, adding 2oz. to the camera's weight, that it was possible to obtain 12 exposures. An optional conversion back was available to convert older cameras to take the larger 120 spool, but this was soon dropped as it was discovered that if the film was wound to loosely around the take-up spool, it would stop winding on after the 10th exposure.

Such was the demand for a 12-exposure capability for the original Rolleiflex that Kodak in 1932 introduced another new film size, the 620 (6 x 2 = 12) with a flange measuring only 0.875 inches; as this was smaller than the 117 it was not difficult to alter the winding key to accept the 620 film. Most of the pre 1934 cameras were converted. A number of 120 cameras were made with dual sets on the winding shaft to take 117 or 120 film.

Through 1926, Heidecke made several prototypes, but without success because of the curling problem on the larger 6 x 6 format. He next made a scaled-down version using the 127 film size, known by Heidecke as 12 exposures 1927. This prototype, finally made in 1927, could use 127 film or plate back. The camera worked well, was easily constructed and results were excellent with little sign of flare when the camera was pointed towards the sun. With many cameras of the day focusing was done by adjusting the knob or lever provided, but many users could not judge distances or simply forgot to make the required adjustment. Heidecke's answer, as on the stereo cameras, was to use the screen to focus and compose your picture. The 4 x 4 viewing screen required for 127 film was considered too small and the larger 6 x 6 screen was born the following year when the curling problem was finally solved.

1928 is a historic year for photography, with the introduction of the world's first roll-film twin lens reflex camera. It was hoped to have the camera on dealers' shelves by Christmas, but the world had to wait until January 1929 before supplies left the factory. Production started on 10th August and the first camera No.1 was shown to the press in December 1928.

With just over 20 on the payroll, the excitement within the old dance school was building up. Fredrick Scherreiks, the works manager, recalled how the factory was specially decorated for Christmas by his wife, Frau Nebrkorn,

Frau Vollenweider and Herr and Frau Franke. Meanwhile, all the other employees were cleaning and painting to ensure the factory looked very smart for the invited press to see the new wonder camera. Even the employees' wives and girlfriends were all working that Saturday, the 8th December, and were invited by Paul Franke to a dinner and dance that evening. By around 4.00pm they left the works looking more like a department store with so many Christmas decorations. Reinhold Heidecke was worried in case the decorations caught fire and forbade the use of gas lights and they had to fill up some containers with sand, which they obtained from a pile conveniently left at the top of the road, ready for snow, plus some buckets of water.

Scherreiks recalled that Heidecke was the practical serious person who was always interested in how to improve each and every component they were making. Some of his ideas were very simple but unlike most engineering managers he knew how to do every job within the works. He loved writing letters to fellow scientists, but would give an immediate cold shoulder to anyone he thought would not further his knowledge. That afternoon they left the works cleaner than Scherreiks had ever seen it and, as there were no glasses, they all had a metal mug of wine before they departed to their homes to get ready for the evening dinner. Hannah, his wife, was instructed by Paul Franke to buy some glasses and plates so they could offer the press some refreshments on the following Monday, and someone suggested she should buy a tablecloth to camouflage the old table. Paul Franke, however, thought this was too extravagant and said he would bring one from home. He knew only too well that a new tablecloth would soon be cut up for rags or used as a bandage for someone, cut by the unfinished sheet metal panels. Such was life in the works. In those early days, Scherreiks reflected, they were one large happy family, fortunate in the knowledge that they were part of a team, assured of their earnings, unlike many of their friends working elsewhere who never knew how long their jobs would last.

For Scherreiks those were happy days. He recalls that the move to the new factory was quite an achievement for a small team. Sadly and very quickly, however, he found out that some of the new employees were only interested in their pay packet, rebelled at authority and had no commitment to Rollei's customers. Nor could these new employees understand that a well made product, with no faults, ensured a contented buyer, who would be proud of their purchase and so act as an unpaid salesman, thus promoting further sales which would safeguard the jobs of all at Rollei. The workers, however, thought otherwise. The 1930s were the times of Fascists, Hitler and general political unrest. The workers could only see that they were working the same number of hours as Franke and Heidecke but benefiting less. Eventually, however, the original work team won the new employees over to their way of thinking and those not interested in their job soon left.

Scherreiks remembered that the dinner was a great success. Paul Franke thanked the fifty or so present for all their hard work and presumed, looking at

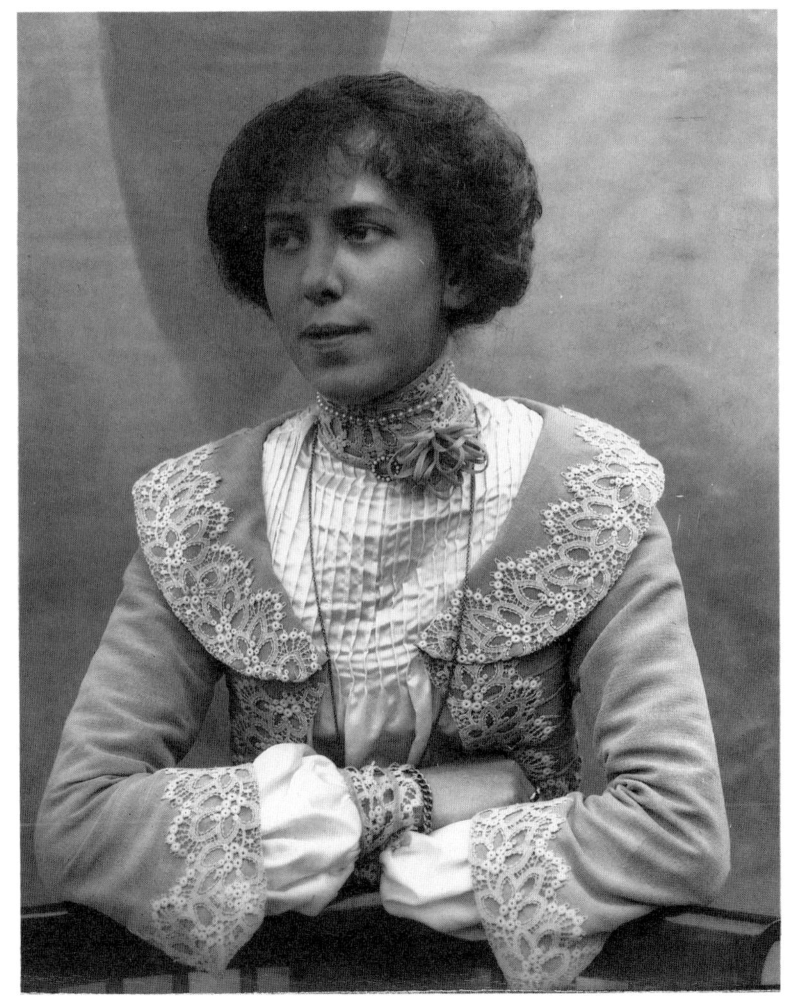

Frau Vollenweider. Photo: Paul Franke, taken with the first Rolleiflex prototype T.L.R. November 1927.

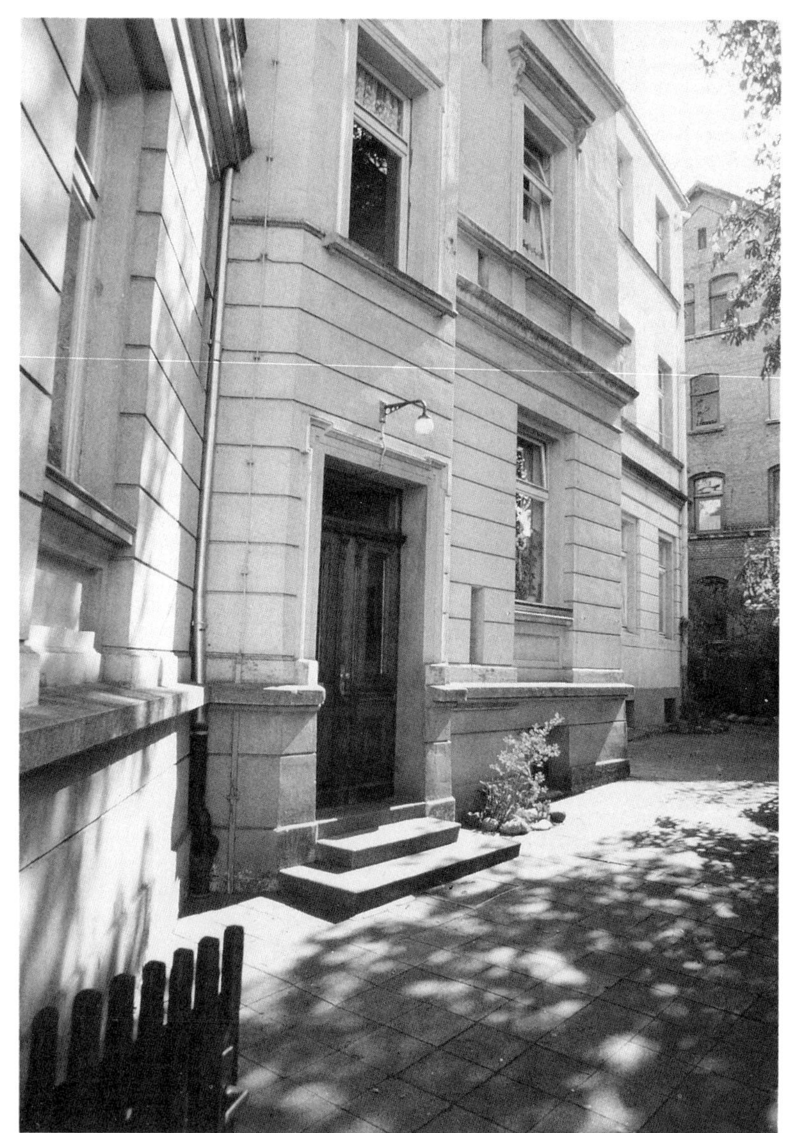

The entrance to the basement 31/32 Viewegstraße

his wife, that someone would thank him for all the work he had done that day. This was the best laugh of the evening as Paul Franke, immaculately dressed with shoes well shined, white spats, blue suit, waistcoat, gold watch, his usual white coat, but on this occasion with no flower in his buttonhole, had walked around the works giving unwanted advice on either cleaning the machines or putting up the Christmas decorations. Paul Franke was a born showman, a circus ringmaster who cracked the whip for others to do the work.

On Monday 10th December at 11.00am. about a dozen newsmen arrived, mostly from the local press, and shortly afterwards Scherreiks remembers about four from the local photographic press arriving, who seemed more interested in obtaining advertising for the new product. Within two months many newspapers, technical magazines and books were reporting on the original T.L.R. Looking back he considered the star turn of this historical announcement to the world would have been the press release package Paul Franke had prepared. Young sales representatives were able to hand to their editors all the information they required to present a good story. One photo magazine gave a test report, the contributor having neither seen or handled a camera! When everyone was seated, Paul Franke thanked them all for coming and introduced the designer and those employees who would escort the honoured guests around the works. Little did they realise that the boxes of completed cameras, already sold and waiting to be packed up were empty. So keen were they to give a good account of themselves.

Paul Franke spoke about the firm and how they were selling all over the world and Heidecke spoke about the design of the camera, of how he had suggested the idea to Voigtländer and of their lack of interest. It was then that they realised they had not fully patented the camera, so the next day they hurriedly applied for provisional patents in all the countries which they hoped would become customers.

Question time was also very interesting, when one reporter asked whether part of the building was used for the manufacture of paint. With the cold weather and no heat in the works over Sunday, the paint on the machinery had not dried and was smelling. Worse still, dust etc. flying about was happily embedded into the paint and did not look so wonderful. It was so cold when the employees arrived on Monday morning that the water and sand in the fire buckets had frozen.

Someone asked to see some photographs taken with the new camera, but they had none. Paul Franke said that there were photos in the press packs which would be handed out when they left, but Scherreiks knew there were none which they could quickly put in, as the staff had taken all the test photos and had not thought to keep any copies for publicity. This must have been an embarrassing situation and Scherreiks recalled the German saying: "The cobbler's children always have no shoes".

As soon as the journalists had departed Franke and Heidecke walked down the road to Friedrichplatz und Autorstraße, near to the Viewegstraße works, which was the home of the Heidecke family, to tell his wife Wilhelmine about all the day's events. Now aged 22, Reinhold Junior was not very interested in the manufacture of the cameras. He did show some interest in later years, but, unlike Paul Franke's son, Horst, he did not follow in his father's footsteps.

Christmas came and went. 1929 promised to see the production of the new camera absorbing all the space at the old dance school , and by the end of January boxes and boxes with either f4.5 or f3.8 Tessar-lensed Rolleiflexes went on sale. France granted the first provisional patent No. 604896 on the 17th January 1929, shortly to be followed by Germany with patent No. 526509. World patents were applied for and by the end of the year back orders numbered over 8000, thus allowing their bankers to agree a loan to build a new factory, which was now essential to retain the goodwill of their new customers.

Meanwhile, throughout the year, problems arose with sub-contractors who could neither deliver as expected nor cope with frequent modifications and improvements to the Rollei T.L.R. By the time the new factory was ready in 1931, the original works had started to build the new T.L.R. alongside the stereo camera.

PROGRESS OF THE ROLLFILM T.L.R

1927	1	Prototype camera
1928	10	Prototype cameras
1928	12	Production cameras
1929/30	3881	Production cameras
1930/31	1634	Production cameras
		Total production of old works: 4260
1932	23,720	1st year in new factory

On moving to the new factory in 1931 all the plant was bought new and within four years the payroll numbered 496, at a time when there was a world wide depression. The firm were fortunate in that, as they were providing employment, everyone was keen to help. Overseas exports assured, with many unfilled orders, the confidence of the two partners caught the imagination of the banks who backed them all the way.

To fully understand the twin lens reflex perhaps an explanation of the make-up of the camera is necessary. All Rolleiflex and Rolleicords have a basic aluminium diecast body that is drilled and turned with great precision. A metal housing fits within this aluminium body holding the two lenses, which are moved forwards or backwards by the focusing knob which works through four worm gears, driven by a concentric gear behind the taking lens. The gears were cut out of hardened bronze with oilite bearings to ensure a long life. The

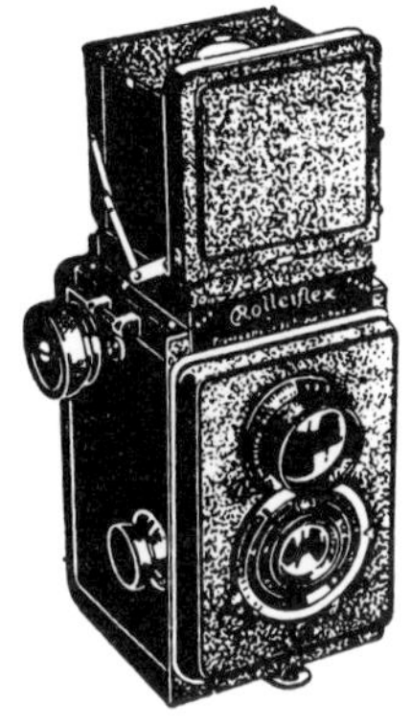

Rolleiflex

Anleitung zur Handhabung

FRANKE & HEIDECKE

G. m. b. H. • BRAUNSCHWEIG

First instruction booklet for the 1929 Rolleiflex

Lichtschacht

Öffnen: Durch Niederdrücken des Hebels *h* öffnet sich der Lichtschacht „blitzartig schnell". Das Mattscheibenbild liegt frei.

Scharfeinstellung mit der Lupe: Lupenklappe *L* mit dem rechten Mittelfinger über den Lichtschacht klappen bis sie festhakt (Abb. 1). Auge dicht an die Lupe bringen, Einstellknopf *D* drehen und Mattscheibe beobachten. Durch leichten Daumendruck gegen die rechte Seitenwand springt die Lupenklappe wieder zurück.

Beobachtung in Augenhöhe: Mit dem linken Mittelfinger den unter der Deckelklappe liegenden Spiegel am Knopf *k* fassen und niederdrücken bis er einschnappt; Lupenklappe dann nach oben schwenken. — Rückbewegung durch leichten Daumendruck erst gegen die rechte, dann gegen die linke Seitenwand.

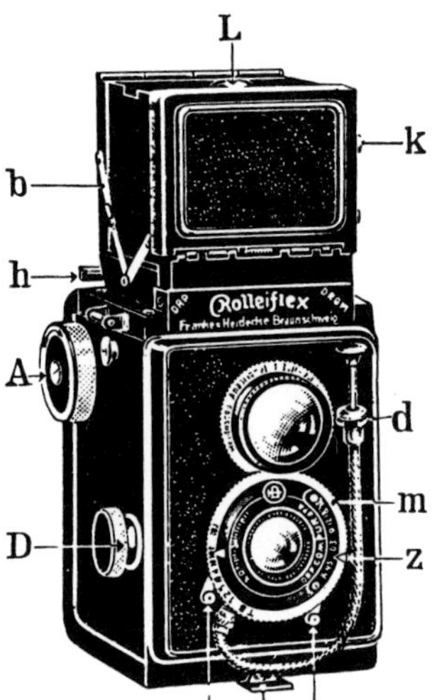

Abb. 1

Schließen: Es erfolgt durch Umlegen der 4 Seitenwände mit rechtem und linkem Daumen abwechselnd in der Reihenfolge: Rechte Seitenwand, linke Seitenwand, Einknicken des Scharniers *b*, Rückwand, Deckel.

Rückwand der Kamera

Öffnen: Riegel *R* mit dem rechten Daumen nach unten ziehen, unter Gegendruck mit

First instruction booklet for the 1929 Rolleiflex — Page 1

der rechten Handfläche auf die Rückwand *W*; diese hochklappen (Abb. 2).

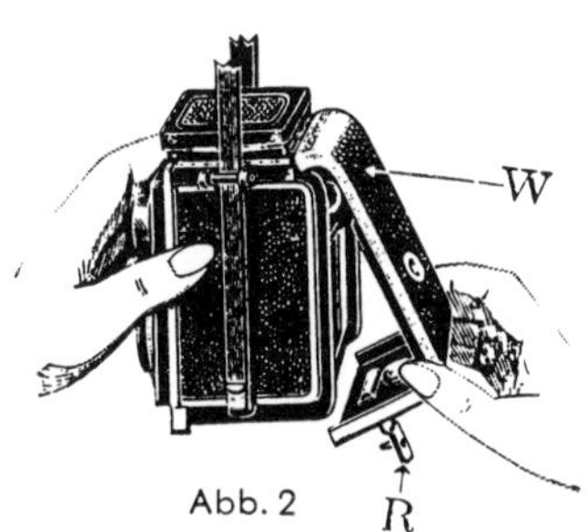

Abb. 2

Schließen: Rückwand *W* mit Daumen und Handfläche fest gegen den Kamerakörper drücken (Abb. 2) und den Riegel wieder einklinken. Die Rückwand ist scharnierartig angelenkt. Um aber die Rolleiflex auch für den Plattenadapter verwenden zu können, kann die Rückwand durch einen leichten Druck gegen die linke, federnde Öse abgenommen werden. Die Rückwand ist *vorher* hochzuklappen.

Filmwechsel

Vorbereitung: Belichtete Rolle zunächst vollständig aufwickeln. Rückwand hochklappen, Aufzugknopf *A* drehend herausziehen, Filmspule dabei links andrücken. Sie springt sofort heraus und wird zugeklebt. Möglichst wieder lichtsicher verpacken! Nicht in greller Sonne auswechseln!

Die leere Abwickelspule wird durch schnellen Druck auf den Hebel *H* selbständig herausgeschleudert. Sie dient jetzt als Aufwickelspule. Zu diesem Zweck: Aufzugknopf *A* drehend herausziehen, Spule links auf den Zapfen setzen, einschwenken. Aufzugknopf drehend in den Schlitz der Rolle drücken.

Laden mit Rollfilm B 1 (6×6): Die neue Spule *S* wird einfach unter die federnde Klappe *k* geschoben (Abb. 3), das zugespitzte Ende nach oben über das Bildfenster hinweggezogen und in den breiten Schlitz der Aufwickelspule gesteckt. Aufzugknopf einige Male umdrehen und achten, daß das Filmband parallel zu den Führungsleisten läuft.

First instruction booklet for the 1929 Rolleiflex — Page 2

Verschluß

Die Einstellung der Geschwindigkeiten erfolgt bei dem neuen Compur lediglich mit Hilfe des großen Metallringes *m* (Abb. 1); im übrigen wird der Verschluß in bekannter Weise bedient. Steht also eine der Ziffern neben dem blanken Pfeil, so muß der Verschluß vor dem Auslösen noch gespannt werden (Hebel *a* anziehen bis zum Einschnappen). Wird dagegen auf *B* oder *T* gestellt, so arbeitet der Auslösehebel unmittelbar. *B* öffnet und schließt die Sektoren mit jedem Anziehen des Auslösehebels; bei *T* wird das Objektiv erst durch nochmaliges Anziehen geschlossen. — Die Auslösung des Verschlusses erfolgt entweder durch Anziehen des Hebels *s* oder mit Hilfe des Drahtauslösers (Abb. 1, bei *d*). Im letzteren Falle wird mit dem linken Daumen ausgelöst.

Bei der Einstellung auf 1/300 Sekunde wird eine zweite Feder eingeschaltet. Deswegen ist eine mittlere Geschwindigkeit zwischen 1/100 und 1/300 nicht möglich, während sonst die Geschwindigkeiten von 1/1 bis 1/100 fortlaufend ansteigen. Ferner ist zur Einstellung auf 1/300 ein gewisser Widerstand zu überwinden, und außerdem darf der Verschluß erst nach erfolgter Einstellung des Ringes gespannt werden.

Aufnahme

Aufzugknopf drehen bis im Bildfenster Nr. 1 erscheint. Nach erfolgter Exposition sofort weiterdrehen bis zur nächsten Ziffer und so fort.

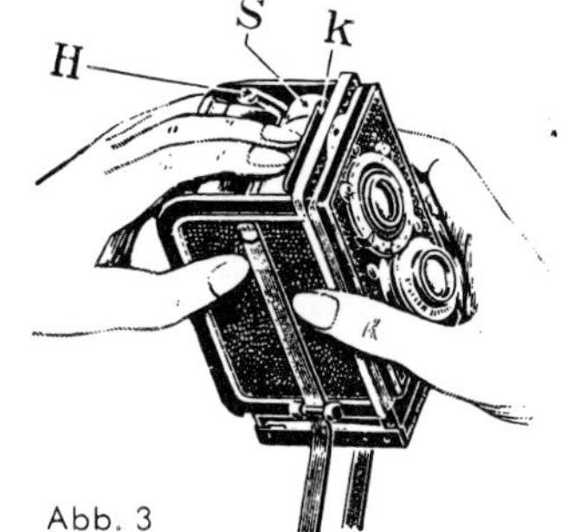

Abb. 3

First instruction booklet for the 1929 Rolleiflex — Page 3

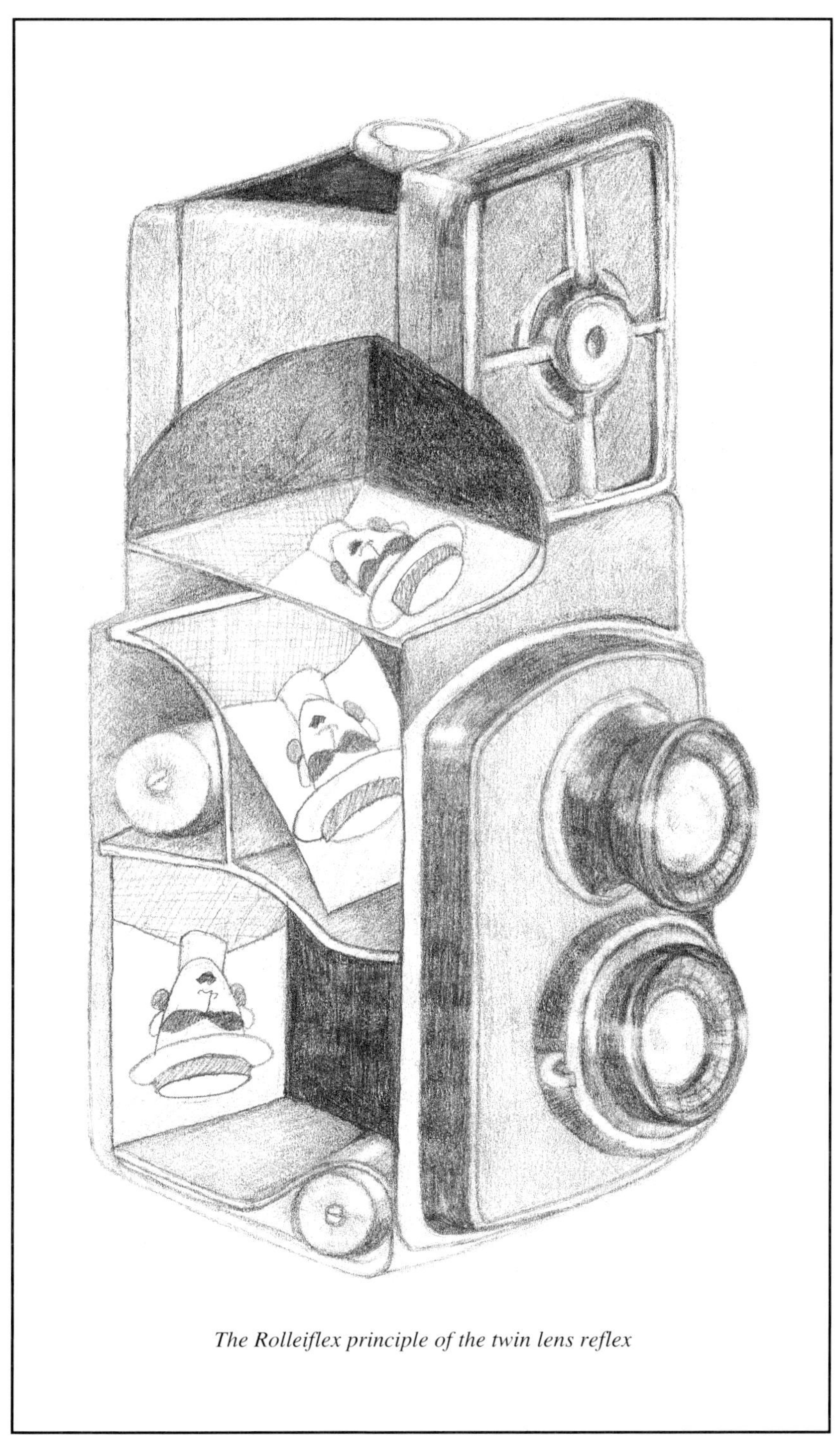

The Rolleiflex principle of the twin lens reflex

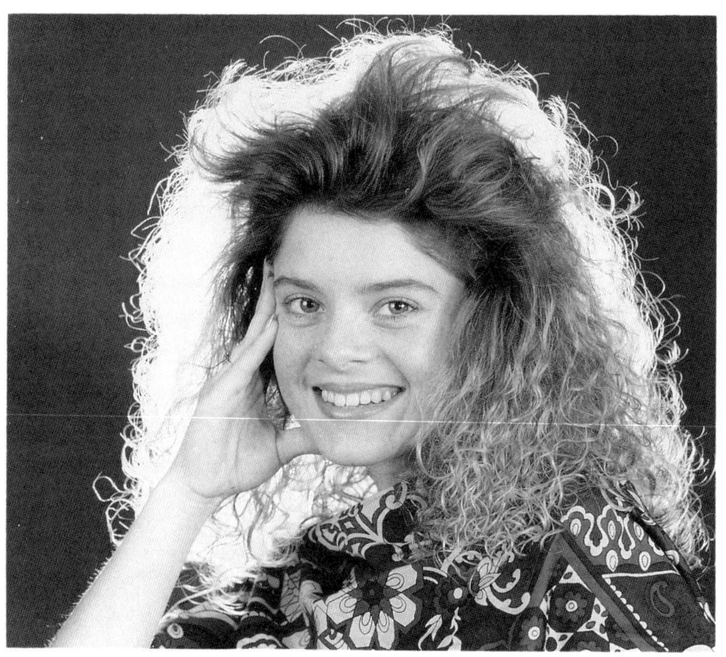

Note the quality of this portrait taken on a Jersey Photographic Museum 1933 Rolleiflex with modern studio lighting

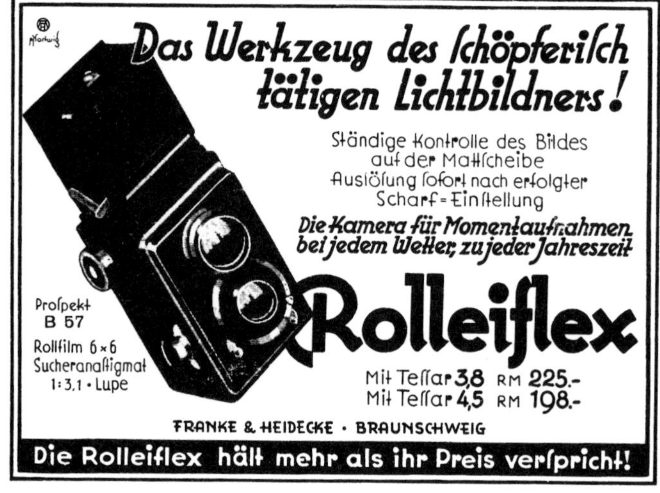

wind-on knobs were made from brass. The aluminium hood was stamped out and shaped, as were the metal back strap lugs and the inside metal work for the chamber, as shown on the drawings. The design was brilliant for its simplicity, easy to repair and with components all over-engineered this accounts for why so many cameras over 60 years old are still in use today.

The weakest part was the aluminium hood, stamped out in soft aluminium and easily shaped in manufacture, but this soon changed shape if misused. The soft aluminium pressed back panel was also easily damaged in use and the steel back, as used in the first Rolleicord, was not much better. Zeiss supplied the Tessar lens and results fully lived up to expectations. Zeiss quality control was known the world over as being better than any other lens manufacturer's and advertisements quoted "the guiding factor in all Zeiss products is perfection with quality control of paramount importance at all stages of construction". Heidecke chose Zeiss to provide a special rim-set Compur shutter made at Zeiss Deckel Works. Remembering the bellows on the Kodak camera, Heidecke had designed his camera with a metal bellows. It became widely accepted that without a cloth shutter or leather bellows the new Franke & Heidecke camera, known as the Rolleiflex, was the ideal traveller's companion. The camera would not attract insects, nor unwanted animals, and contained no parts that would rot, even in the tropics or jungle. The Rolleiflex was an outdoor camera which contentedly purred on and on through rain, snow or hail, provided that the lens was covered, and a lens hood soon cured this problem with the result that sales and marketing required no real products effort, unlike today when inferior products well-presented and advertised sell to the seemingly gullible public.

Altogether, around 28,000 original Rolleiflexes were sold between 1929 and 1932. To identify a camera is not easy and most collectors are confused about the numbers engraved on the body and lens on the original T.L.R. Paul Franke reasoned that if camera numbers corresponded to invoice numbers, it would be easier to find out about a camera – when it was made, to whom it was sold – just by looking at the number on the nameplate and then the invoice number. In the case of the early Rolleicords, the number was inside the camera. This explains one reason for having two different numbers on one camera. On going through copy invoices you would find items for push-on filters, cases, spares, even films and of course stereo cameras. Paul Franke was the business manager and travelling salesman. His tricks of the trade would include showing a potential buyer a new camera with the serial number of 60,000 when only 15,000 had been made, thus giving the impression that the camera was selling well.

Today, as 60 years ago, Rollei camera numbers cannot be relied upon. Suffice it to say that from the start of the first stereos in 1921 to Dec 1938 300,000 cameras of all models were sold. So many wild guesses have appeared regarding numbers of cameras actually constructed that a table giving this information can be found in the *Rollei T.L.R.* Manual published by Club Rollei in 1992.

There were two models of the original Rolleiflexes, both with a wind- on knob. The change to lever film wind-on was in 1932 after the move to the new factory, and the famous Rollei lever wind-on was made in-house. The original film wind-on knobs were bought-in components as the old works was not equipped to undertake this work; similarly the diecast aluminium bodies were also supplied by a sub-contractor.

f3.8 or f4.5 lenses were available on both models simultaneously, otherwise they were identical. The original cameras were not synchronised for flash. The external film counter to be found on some early cameras on the left side of the camera body was not manufactured by Rollei, who had neither the employees nor the equipment to carry out this work. Walter Talbot of Berlin advertised modifications to improve your Rolleiflex, which besides converting the camera from 117 film to 620 could also provide an external film counter for 12 exposures.

Inside pressure plates were black and later were replaced by in-house polished metal plates. The very first cameras 1925/1929 had no provision for cable release. This improvement, with a cable release socket, is found on the left lower side by the taking lens. Any early 1928/1929 Rolleiflexes in excellent condition must surely appreciate in value. A mint example must be worth a small king's ransom.

In 1932 Rollei once again surprised the photographic world with the Mark II version of the T.L.R., claiming that the new standard Rolleiflex with lever wind was the best camera of its kind throughout the world. Heidecke, with a chip on his shoulder, was determined to prove to the world that he was not as we might say today "a punk rocker", or in those days a non-conformist, both of whom were looked down upon by their conservative elders. Later, when he was successful, few of his colleagues would have suspected that the now portly Dr. Reinhold Heidecke was, in his formative years, a rebel.

The new standard Rolleiflex was the world's best T.L.R. medium format camera. There were no competitors! The design was new, designed to take either 117 or 120 film with windows, either at the side of the base for aligning the film for 120, or in the centre on the back for the 117 film. After 1934 there was no centre window on the back thus today providing a quick identification of whether you have the original camera. 6-exposure film was numbered on the backing paper in the centre. The hole in the pressure plate could cause scratches and it was not possible to place the window at the centre of the base as the tripod bush had priority. 120 film was numbered at the sides and centre, so later cameras only required one window which could be located next to the tripod bush and this in turn reduced one operation, the stamping of the hole in the pressure plate.

Many features were taken from the baby Rolleiflex which was the first product of the new factory. The reason why the baby was relegated revolved around the poor image displayed on the focussing screen, so a larger 6 x 6 format with a much improved display was selected.

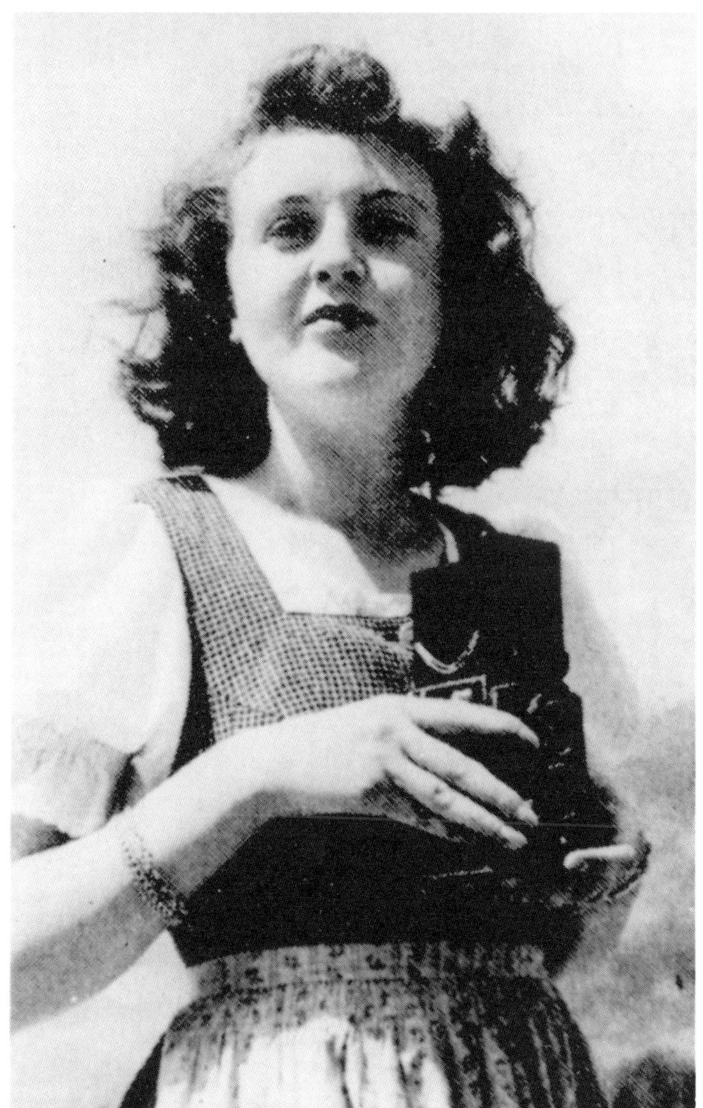

Hitler's mistress Eva Braun with a 1933 standard Rolleiflex

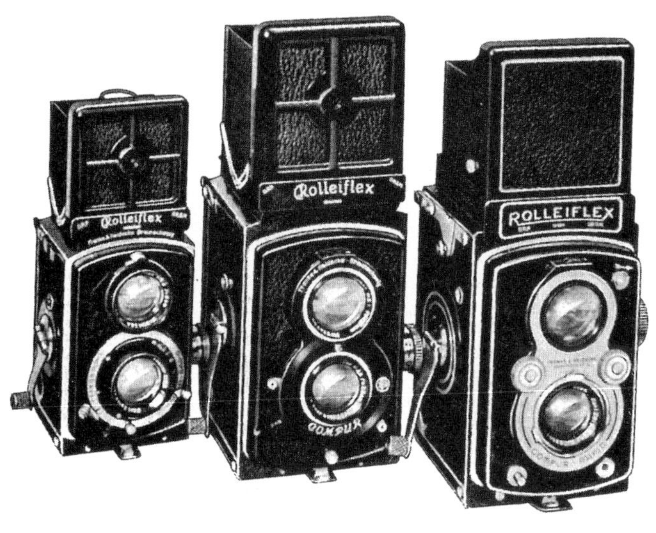

VIER x VIER
Die Handlichste von allen

STANDARD 6x6
Die Standard-Kamera mit großem Bildformat

AUTOMAT 6x6
Die Königin, die Kamera ohne Fehlermöglichkeit

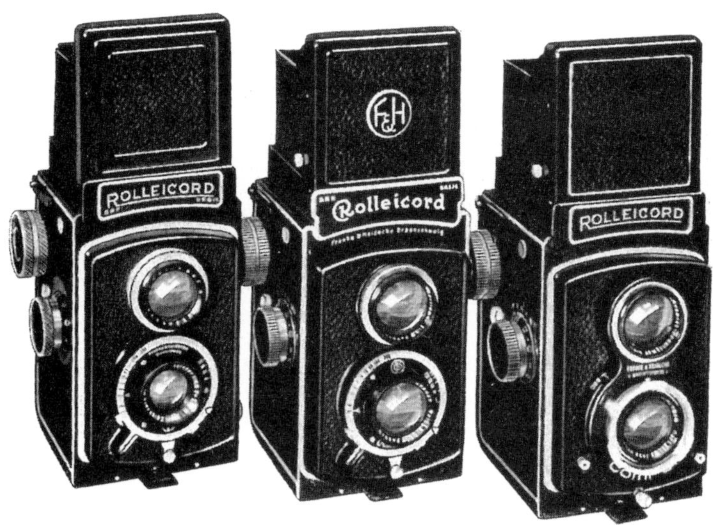

ROLLEICORD Ia
Die Präzisionskamera für den schmalen Geldbeutel

ROLLEICORD II 4,5 ROLLEICORD II 3,5
Die Präzisionskameras für den mittleren Geldbeutel

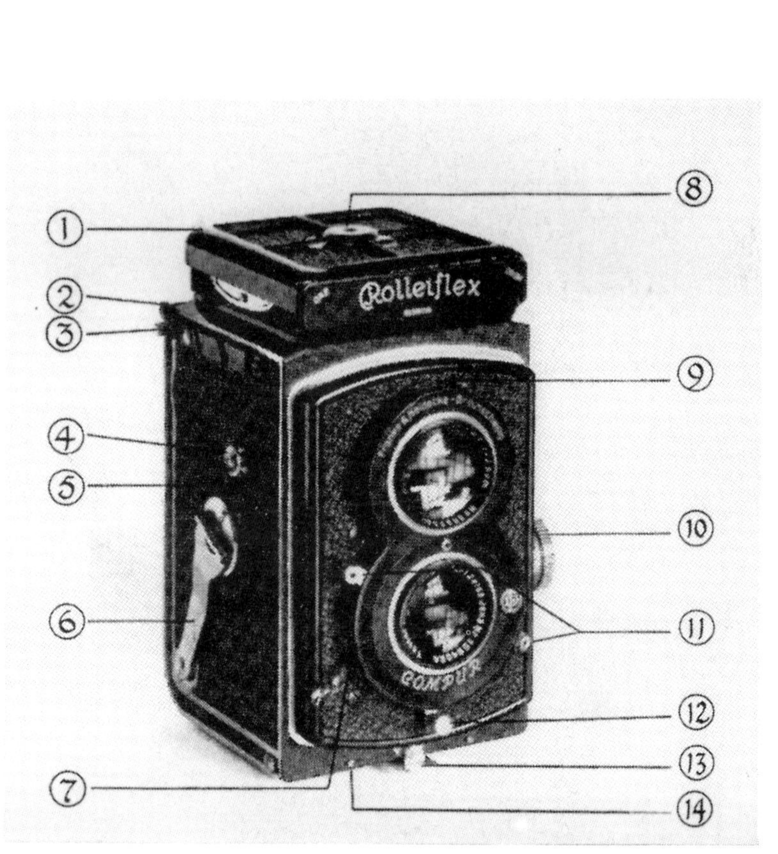

1933 Lever Wind Rolleiflex:

1. *Focusing hood, closed*
2. *Back hinge*
3. *Back hinge release lever*
4. *Film numbering trip*
5. *Film number peephole*
6. *Film transport lever*
7. *Cable release socket*
8. *Dioptre finder, closed*
9. *Shutter speed and lens aperture window*
10. *Focusing knob*
11. *Speed and aperture setting levers*
12. *Double action shutter set and release button*
13. *Base clip*
14. *Locating studs*

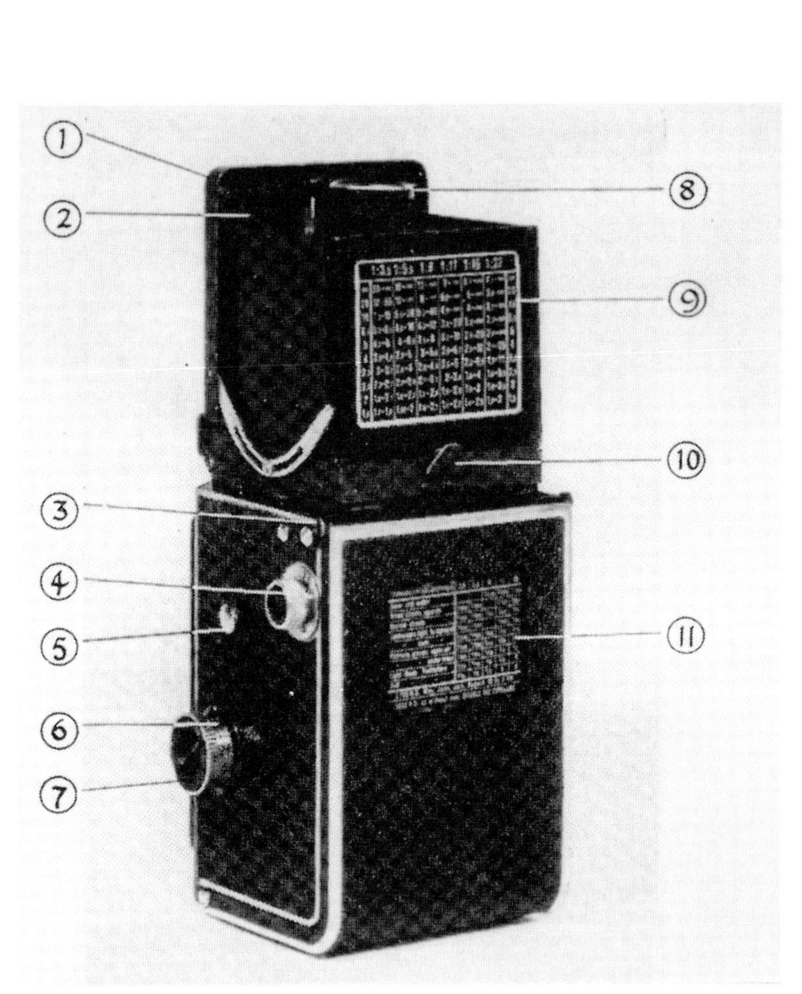

1933 Lever Wind Rolleiflex:

1. Focusing hood
2. Collapsing frame
3. Back hinge
4. Take-up spool retaining knob
5. Neck strap anchor
6. Focusing scale
7. Focusing knob
8. Screen magnifier
9. Depth of field scale
10. Double purpose hood catch
11. Exposure chart

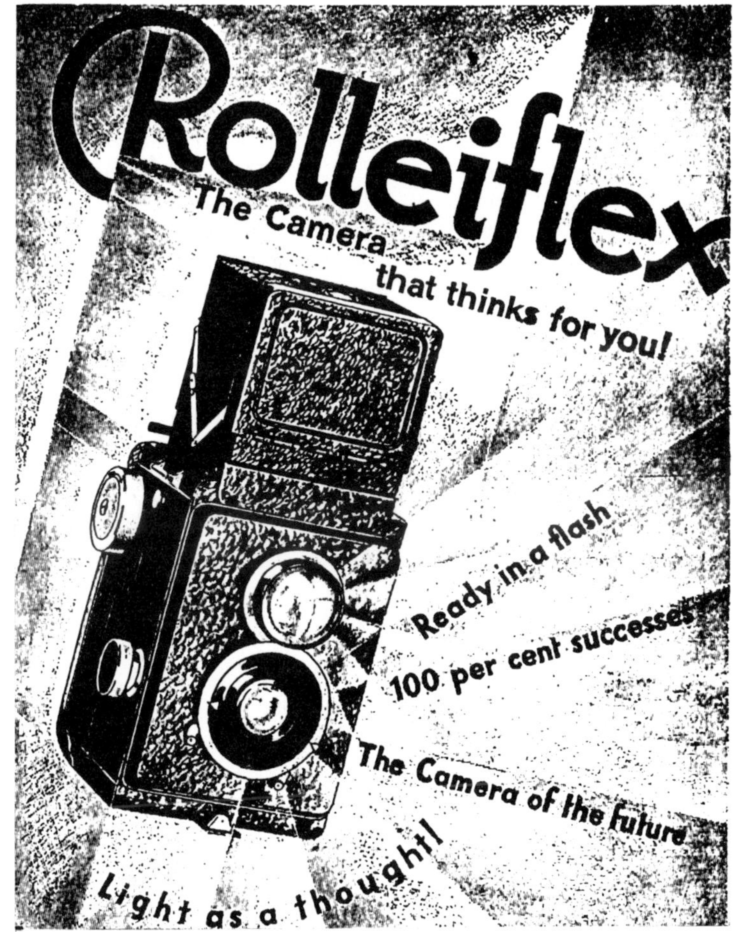

1929 British advertisement by Wallace Heaton Ltd.
Britain's No. 1 photographic dealer

Four years later Heidecke was able to obtain an f2.8 60mm lens which he named the f2.8 Heidoscop anastigmat 60mm. The additional brightness was such that Wilhelmine, his wife, encouraged him to build a lady's camera. This gave Heidecke an opportunity to redesign the current model and incorporate all the improvements that had been suggested. Furthermore, he was able to design the camera's components in such a way that they could make them within their own factory.

The baby used 127 size film, giving 12 4 x 4 cm negatives, and was the first Rolleiflex to use the famous crank advance lever. On placing the film into the camera you attached it to the take-up spool, cranked a turn or two, closed the back, and cranked on to No. 1, as seen in the little window on the base of the camera, pressed the small button above the crank and No. 1 appeared in the small aperture with a definite click. From then you shot and cranked until you heard a continual clicking as you were winding on the end of the film. This clicking enabled sports or machine-gun photographers to know that they had come to the end of the film. Apertures marked in white were readable when the camera was at waist level. The shutter speed was another matter. The times, in red with a black background, were not so easy to read. However, with the speed and aperture controls easily adjusted, the shutter tensioned and released directly below the taking lens, the camera was simple to use and fitted nicely in the hand. Although controls were few, the film cranked on without the need to line up the numbers in the little window. One control in those early days which was hidden within the camera could catch out the unwary modern photographer. Forget to wind on the film and you could have many multi exposures. I am sure we have all done this many times.

All these improvements on the baby were incorporated into big brother a year later, in 1932. One new design sometimes forgotten was the redesigned hood for the baby which included the cruciform sports finder, much appreciated by many, and oddly enough discontinued on the 1990 Rollei 6008. The sports finder on Rollei cameras has changed over the years but basically it is the same, whereby you can look through a square incorporated in the hood. The Rollei, painted black , became the first truly professional camera. From 1932, with manufacturing space able to absorb more and more workers and production soaring, T.L.R. cameras became readily available. It became the dream of most photographers to own a Rollei.

By 1937, when the Automat appeared, annual production exceeded 35,000 camera units with over 600 employees. Sales boomed as the press turned in their 4 x 5 plate Speed Graphics for the roll-film T.L.R. Rollei still had no serious competitors.

The Rolleicord sold 19,987 in 1938 alone, such was the popularity of the "Cord!". Paul Franke's son Horst was asked in 1949, while in the U.K., whether Rollei would repeat the art deco design on another camera. He replied "The Rolleicord first appeared in early 1932 in a deco design of the period" – end of story. Horst Franke did not like the art deco design and his father, whilst later speaking to Alec Pearlman, author of The Rollei Manual, said that Heidecke was not getting his own way and purposely designed the deco finish in a defiant temper. Once again, as with his disappointment with the Baby Rolleiflex, Heidecke learnt the hard way when the new Rolleicord failed to win substantial orders. Even though there was a back panel showing depth of field scales or an exposure guide, the black leather Cord was very popular and outsold the art deco model by three to one until production was halted. The art deco model sold well in the U.S.A. and the U.K. Those of you who are designers or work closely with them may well understand the frustrations they suffer. Perhaps a little time spent carrying out their own research by watching who buys what on a crowded Saturday afternoon's shopping trip would pay dividends. Heidecke's wife thought a baby Rolleiflex T.L.R. would appeal to the ladies, travellers and mountaineers, as had the baby Heidoscop stereo camera. Why this improved version of its larger brother did not sell in large number may never be clearly understood. At the time it was thought that many amateurs of the day were content to accept contact prints for the family album.

The art deco Rolleicord disappointed Heidecke who determined to find out why this camera, which he thought would sell well and bring him another accolade, had failed and what had gone wrong, and this he did. Let us compare the two versions of the Rolleicord. Design work started in 1932, a year after production had started on the baby 4 x 4. It was decided that there should be a budget-priced T.L.R. camera available to counter rumours that several would-be competitors were planning to market a cheaper copy. Heidecke had already designed the 1932 Rolleiflex that was in production and on sale. His first thoughts were to make cosmetic changes to the Flex, but the two cameras on the dealer's shelf would look the same. He thought an art deco panel of engraved and painted brass would be the quick answer. Later the panels were brass-plated. One cannot argue that the nickel finish caught the eye. The hood was better designed than that of the later Flex. Bought-in focussing knobs, as on the very original 1928 Flex, were used together with a cheaper lens, but with the same shutter. Shutter speed and aperture controls were simple to construct, and on looking at the early Rolleicords, seemed more professional than the Flex if you did not understand the difference. Both versions were identical, except for the colour and lens.

In December 1934 the art deco cost 88 RM, the black cost 105 RM the Rolleiflex 192 RM and the baby 200 RM. Which would you buy, not knowing anything about cameras or their performance? Certainly not the baby if you wanted your money's worth. The black Rolleicord was, at 105 RM, the star but at almost half the price of the Rolleiflex. When the first Rolleicord went on sale at 88 RM it was too cheap and looked like a toy. The image on the screen was not very clear and a f4.5 Zeiss Triotar lens, bless it, could be found on many cameras selling for 40/50 RM. After two years the camera had a sister. Paul Franke was confident that a black amateur Rollei costing 100 RM would be a winner, so the MK2 version of the Rolleicord, costing 5 RM more

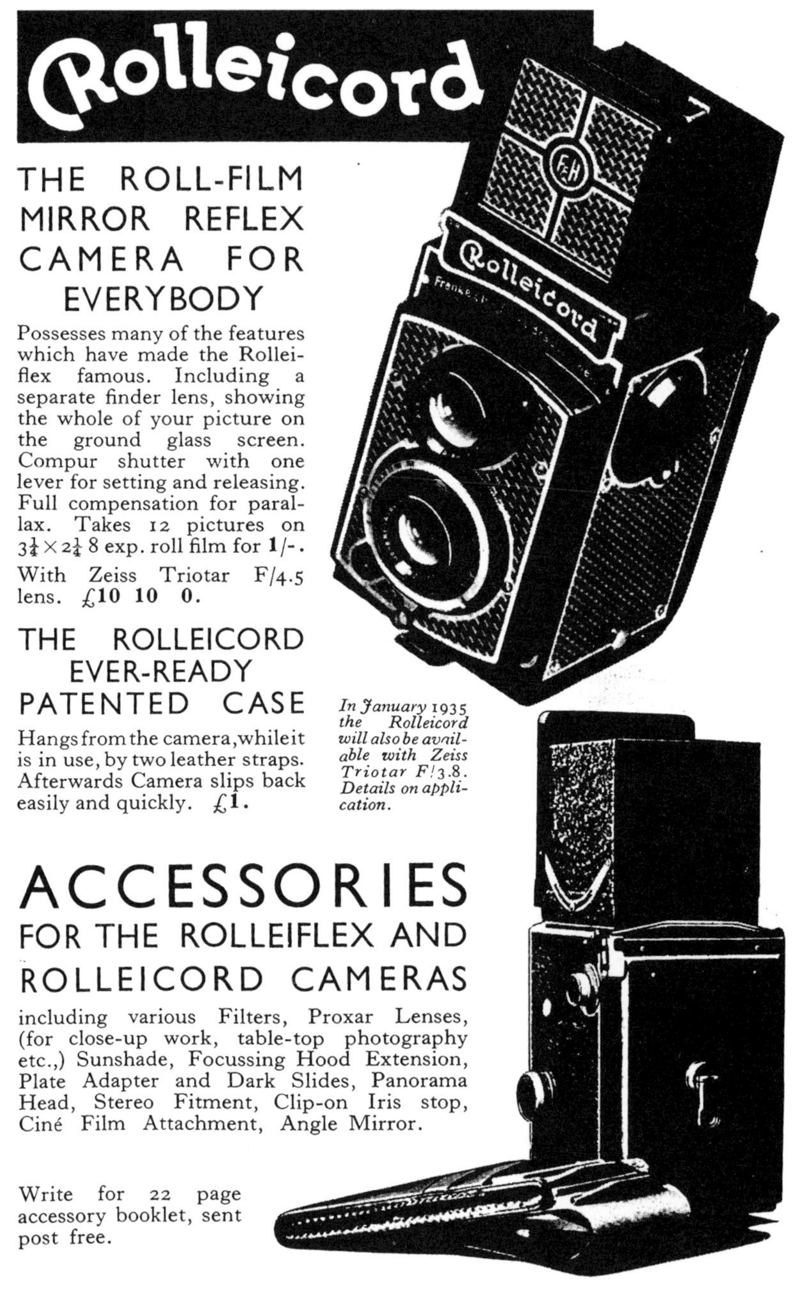

1933 advertisement by R.F. Hunter, the English importer.

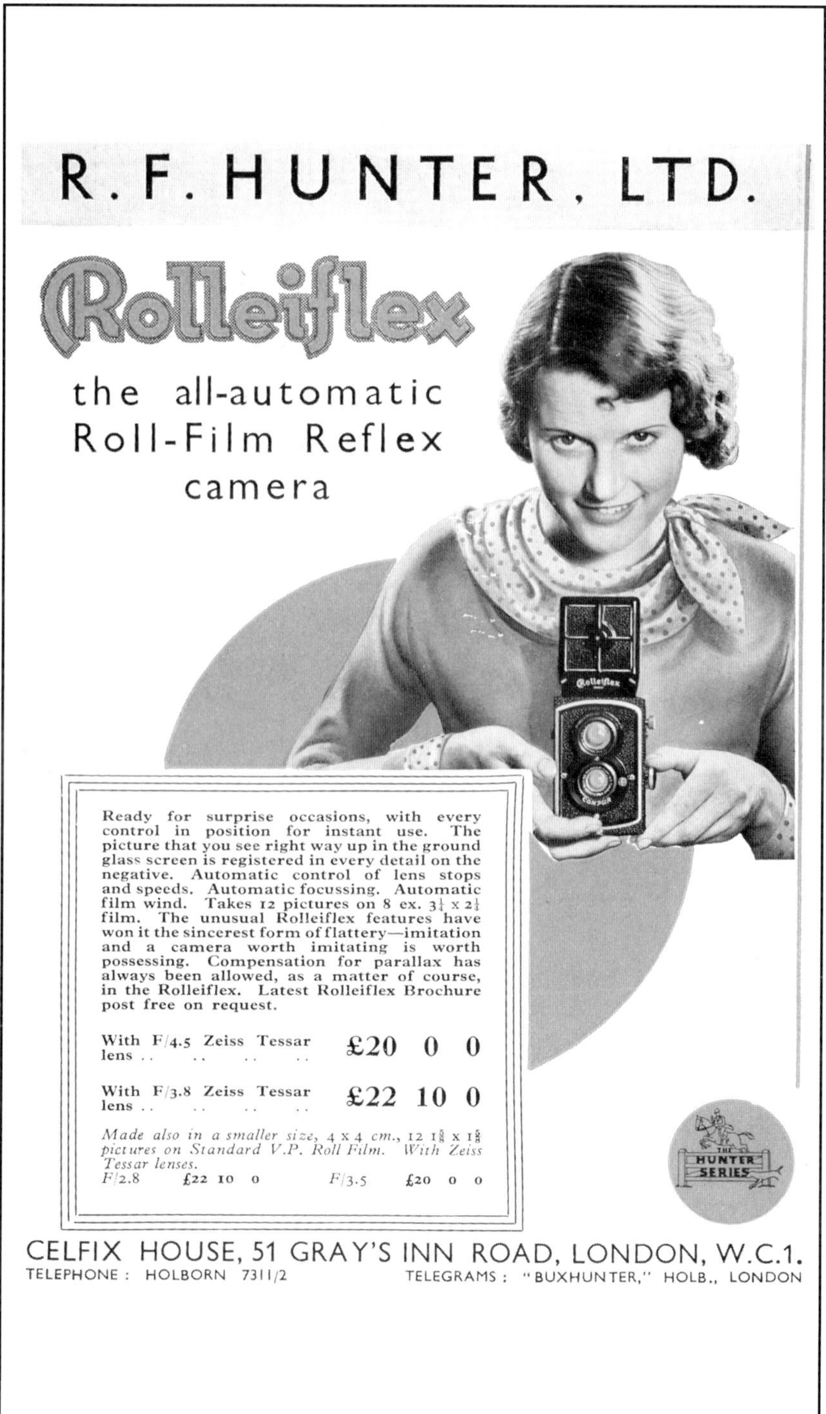
R. F. HUNTER, LTD.
Rolleiflex
the all-automatic
Roll-Film Reflex
camera
Ready for surprise occasions, with every control in position for instant use. The picture that you see right way up in the ground glass screen is registered in every detail on the negative. Automatic control of lens stops and speeds. Automatic focussing. Automatic film wind. Takes 12 pictures on 8 ex. 3¼ x 2¼ film. The unusual Rolleiflex features have won it the sincerest form of flattery—imitation and a camera worth imitating is worth possessing. Compensation for parallax has always been allowed, as a matter of course, in the Rolleiflex. Latest Rolleiflex Brochure post free on request.
With F/4.5 Zeiss Tessar lens £20 0 0
With F/3.8 Zeiss Tessar lens £22 10 0
Made also in a smaller size, 4 x 4 cm., 12 1⅝ x 1⅝ pictures on Standard V.P. Roll Film. With Zeiss Tessar lenses.
F/2.8 £22 10 0 F/3.5 £20 0 0
THE HUNTER SERIES
CELFIX HOUSE, 51 GRAY'S INN ROAD, LONDON, W.C.1.
TELEPHONE: HOLBORN 7311/2
TELEGRAMS: "BUXHUNTER," HOLB., LONDON

at 105 RM, went on sale with a better and brighter f3.8 Triotar lens, in time for Christmas. Such was the demand for this budget professional look-alike Rollei, that 11,000 were sold in 1935, of which 8,200 were exported. Although the art deco model remained in production until January 1936, sales of only 11,600 were achieved. Many were bought as presents and hardly left their boxes, which accounts for the large numbers in excellent condition found in Rollei collections.

Heidecke, from now on, spent his time on improving his current range of cameras and was never to design any further new cameras. Each year would bring fresh modifications and improvements to his stable of T.L.R.s. The stereos were left to slowly fade away with an annual production of around 20,000, until the start of World War II, when the production line was finally laid to rest.

In recent years the Rolleicord camera, although not favoured by collectors, is for some an opportunity of buying a very usable camera at a modest price. Later Cords sported the Schneider Xenar which is similar, or almost identical, to the Tessar lens. The early Rolleicords should be included in any collection of Rollei cameras and would make an ideal Christmas present for your grandson to learn photography from the grass roots and also to be able to hold and handle a piece of equipment so well made and oozing a quality that is so hard to find today.

In the three years prior to World War II the Rolleicord accounted for 44% of Franke & Heidecke production, a total of 58,787 cameras.

CHAPTER 6

ROLLEI'S MODERN NEW FACTORY

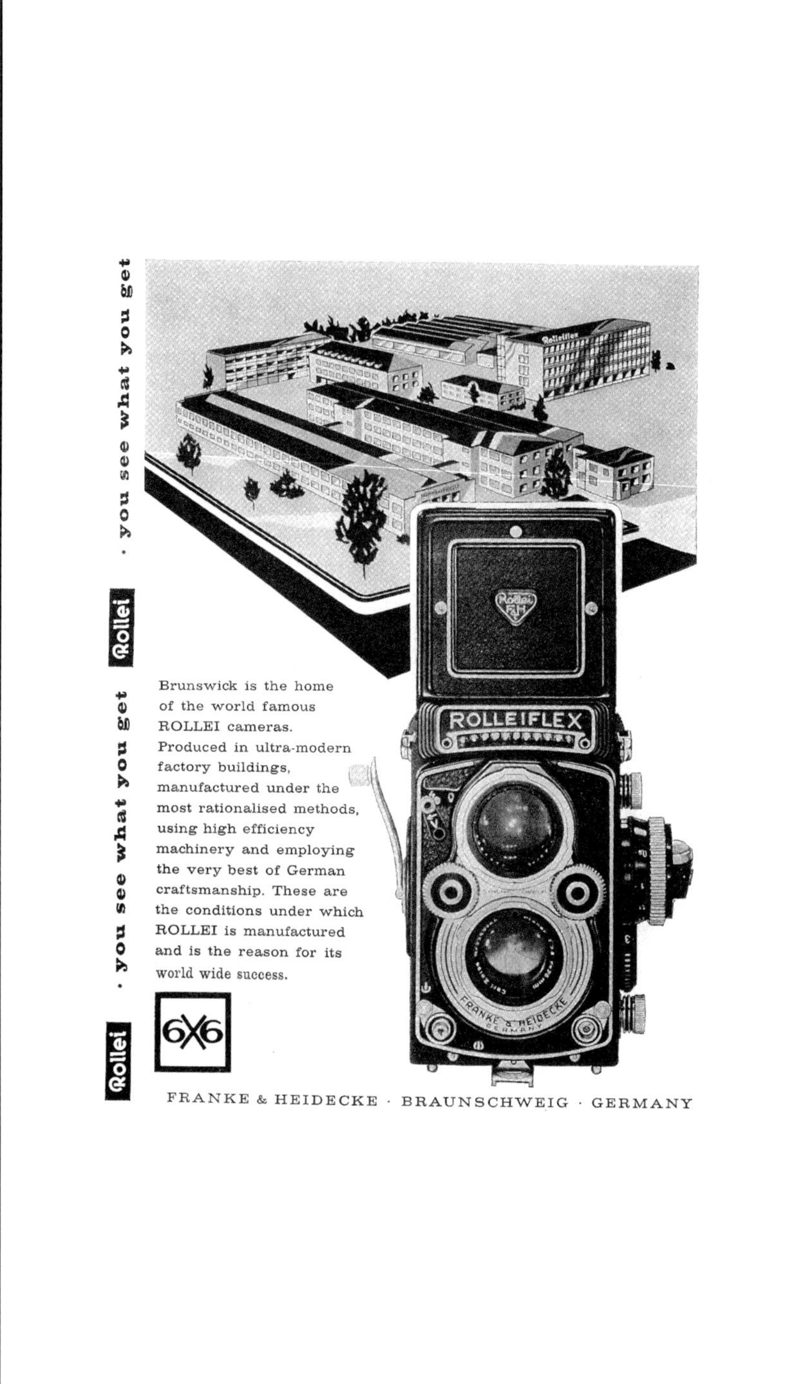
Rollei · you see what you get · you see what you get
Rollei · you see what you get · you see what you get
Brunswick is the home of the world famous ROLLEI cameras. Produced in ultra-modern factory buildings, manufactured under the most rationalised methods, using high efficiency machinery and employing the very best of German craftsmanship. These are the conditions under which ROLLEI is manufactured and is the reason for its world wide success.
6X6
ROLLEIFLEX
FRANKE & HEIDECKE · BRAUNSCHWEIG · GERMANY

ROLLEI'S MODERN NEW FACTORY

In previous chapters we have mentioned the new factory. It was in 1931 that the original 222 employees plus 87 new employees were able to get acquainted with their new home. The factory at Salzdahlumer Straße, which I believed to be only a short walk – a mere hundred metres from the main Braunschweig railway station, I eventually discovered more than three kilometres later.

The No.1 factory buildings, built in 1931, contained some 2000 sq. metres on two floors. The factory, a typical portal-framed 11ft. pitched roof with colt type ventilation for the first floor, ensured ideal working conditions for the work-force, which was soon to grow to just over 500. The centrally placed steam water boiler was to provide central heating and hot water for the various machines, all long since scrapped in favour of individual electric motors and the steam boiler having been replaced by a small hot water boiler.

Immediately after World War II, Paul Franke recalled that a machinery firm agreed to design the factory layout free of charge if they supplied the plant and machinery. Within the design was a steam boiler, located in the centre of the building, so a brick chimney was provided by the builders. Alas, no-one had thought about the storage of coal for the boiler and the disposal of the burnt clinker and ash. Fortunately, the mistake was spotted early on and the order for the steam boiler was cancelled and replaced by a small hot water boiler. Even this arrangement caused some consternation with coal dust. The boiler and chimney were finally removed in 1936 to an adjoining building, constructed for the purpose. Note the chimney on the old factory photograph.

In order to obtain a large number of operatives quickly, Rollei joined the German National Socialist Party whose President, elected in 1920, was Adolf Hitler. Way back in 1931 workers could be militant and becoming a union closed shop had its advantages, probably like paying "protection money". Although the new factory was in a new industrial area and had a good bus service, there were no shops nearby, so a modern works canteen and shop were provided, where the employees could pass their lunch breaks, buy a packet of cigarettes and of course obtain a cooked meal. When the number of employees exceeded 400 the lunch break was staggered, with the ground floor shutting down from 11.30 to 12.30 and the first floor from 12.30 to 1.30. Unlike today, not many took sandwiches, so a family spirit grew between the employees who worked together and played together, with a No.1 first floor football team and No.2 team for the ground floor. The few car-owners, and only about 2% had cars in those days, would collect their colleagues, so cars arriving at the factory could have contained six persons. The front seat in pre-

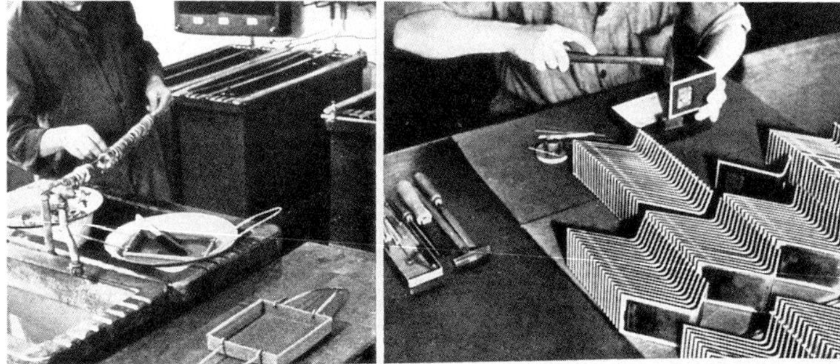

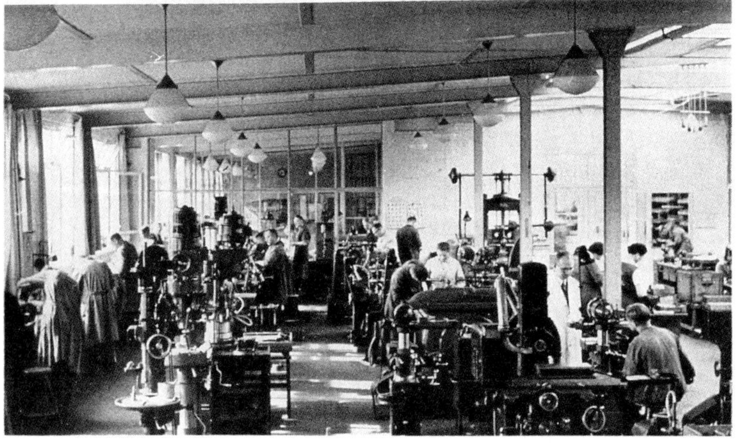

1932, the new factory workshop with plenty of natural light.

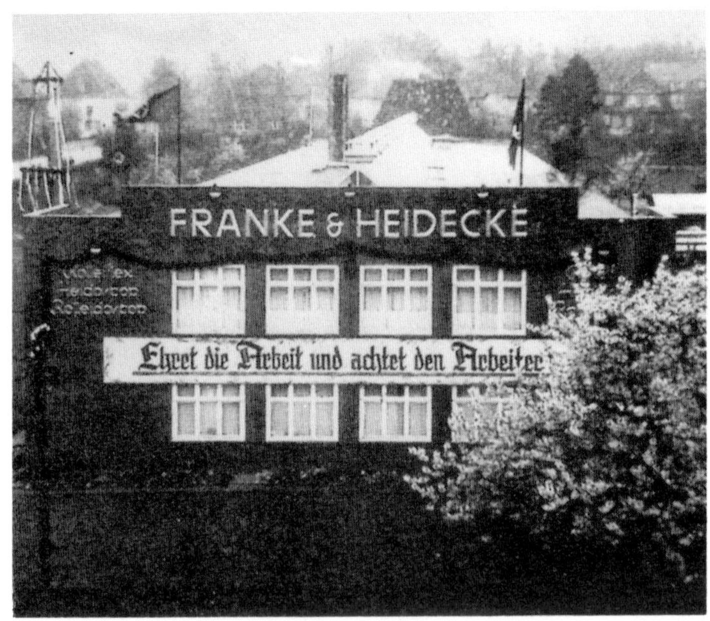

Rollei's new factory. Note the chimney.

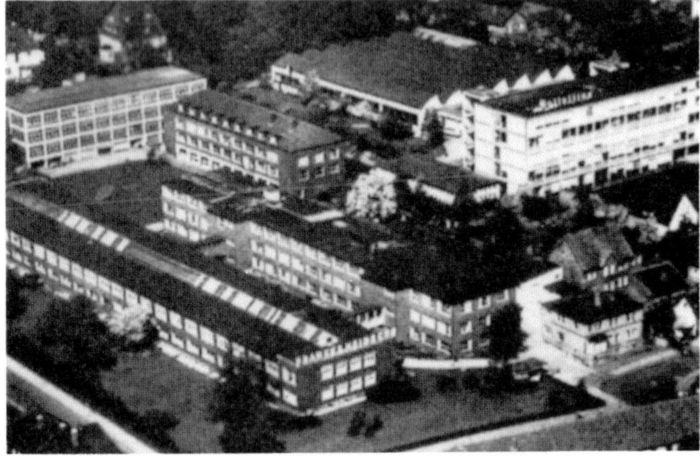

The factory in the 1950s

war cars, before seat belts were thought of, consisted of a bench similar to the back seat, so three in the front was very common. This all helped to keep the employees in their "works family". Many belonged to a works society, whether it was dramatics, choral or meeting in the Bierkeller.

I am often asked when I first became interested in Rollei. I remember it well, way back in 1938 at the age of 11. My mother would not allow me to use her baby Rolleiflex as I had just broken my Woolworth's plastic 1s.6d. (7 1/2 new pence) camera. My mother was so reluctant to part with her camera that it was not until forty years later that she eventually gave it to me. With a school party just before the Easter holidays, we visited the *Daily Mail* newspaper in Fleet Street.

Afterwards, while waiting for the school bus, I spotted a baby Rolleiflex in the shop window of a City Sale and Exchange camera shop. Just like the other schoolboys I had my nose firmly on the glass window with my eyes wide open. I explained that there was a camera just like the one my mother used. My remarks landed on the ears of Erich Vollenweider. He was our school prefect and explained that his father was the shop's manager. We entered this Aladdin's cave, and there I met a rather large Paul Franke who was in London at the time. He knew my mother's parents and arranged for me to correspond with a German pen pal whose father worked for Rollei and was the president of the works stamp club. Until the outbreak of World War II, I corresponded with Vogel and we exchanged stamps.

During the war he was taken prisoner in North Africa, brought to England and gave our address. Later on he was allowed to live with my parents and attended our garden. I will always remember Vogel in his army prisoner of war clothing, looking through my stamp collection as if it was his own. When the war was over, he returned to Germany, but finding his Braunschweig home destroyed he returned to our house in Woodlands Park, Oxted, Surrey. When he arrived he looked like a ghost, was very thin, and had aged considerably. My mother told him that she had the previous day sent off a food parcel to his home in Germany and he replied that this was his home now, he had no home in Germany. After a few weeks my father arranged for Vogel to return to Braunschweig and he was promised a job at Franke & Heidecke. He stayed until 1953 and left to live with his sister in Dresden, East Germany. Sadly, we never heard from him again.

Many of Vogel's recollections have helped the author of this book. His last letter tells us about Heidecke, who in 1951, a year after Franke had died, was at last recognised as a great inventor and technician and a valuable member of society. At the age of 70 he was awarded a degree of Dr.H.C. of the Braunschweig Institute of Technology. Although partly retired, as the business was now run by Paul Franke's son Horst, the now Dr. Reinhold wondered if it was not time to design a new camera. Rollei had at that time no 35mm camera and, although the stereo camera was out of production, he thought why not design a 35mm stereo? With samples of the new Schneider

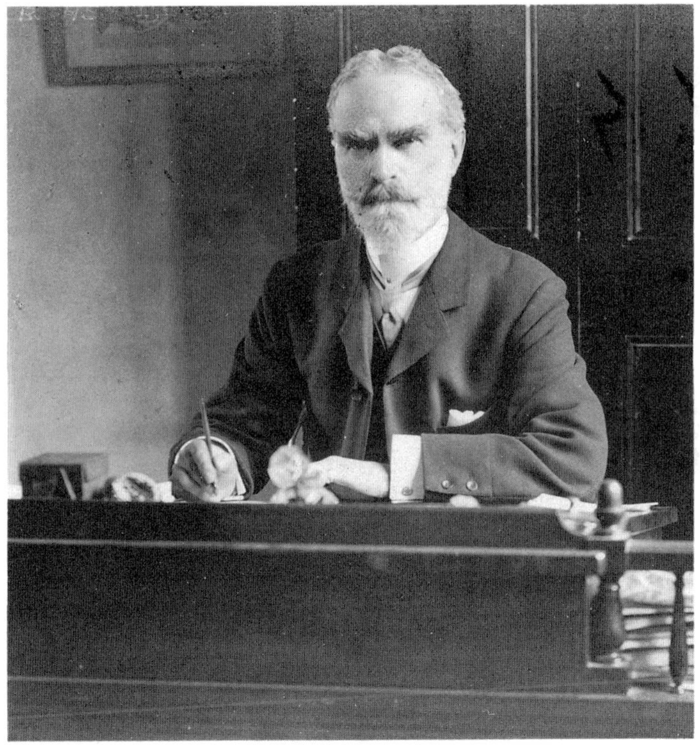

Hans Vollenweider, at his desk at Voigtländer, Paul Franke's boss in 1909. His son Erich joined Franke & Heidecke in November 1927.

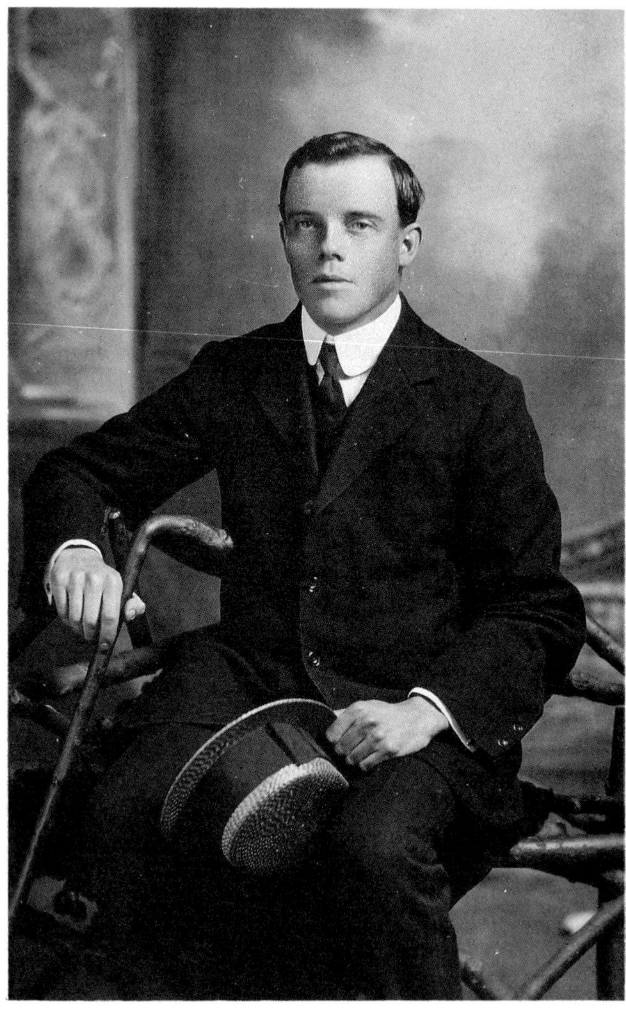

Erich Vollenweider joined the export department of Franke & Heidecke in 1927; in 1933 when the Jews were persecuted Paul Franke arranged for Erich to join City Sale & Camera Exchange in London.

THE Rolleiflex is a combination of the best features of the modern reflex camera and the modern roll-film camera. No focussing is so exact as that on the ground-glass screen, but this has not been possible in conjunction with the use of roll-film until the Rolleiflex came. Rolleiflex permits really serious work with roll film, an advantage to the serious photographer both in the matter of ease of portability and less running costs. With Rolleiflex you can focus as fine as a hair and see your picture (right way up) crystal clear, even at the very moment of exposure. Show the Rolleiflex a subject and it will at once tell you whether it is worth photographing.

YOU can get a ROLLEIFLEX
The 'NO-TROUBLE' CAMERA
with Zeiss Tessar F/4.5 Lens
FOR 38/3 DOWN
and 8 more monthly payments of 38/3,
or £16 : 7 : 6 Cash.

With Zeiss Tessar F/3.8, £18 : 15 : 0 Cash.

We will make the very MAXIMUM ALLOWANCE for your old camera in part exchange for a Rolleiflex.

WALLACE HEATON
LTD.
119, NEW BOND STREET, LONDON
PHONES: MAYFAIR 0924-5-6.
and at 47, BERKELEY STREET, W.1

1930 advertisement for F3.8 and F4.5 Rolleiflex.

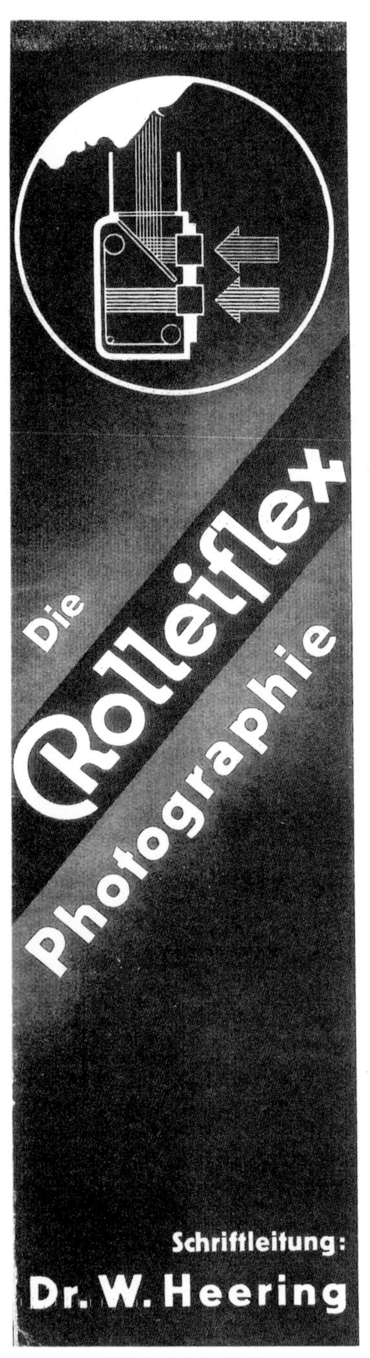

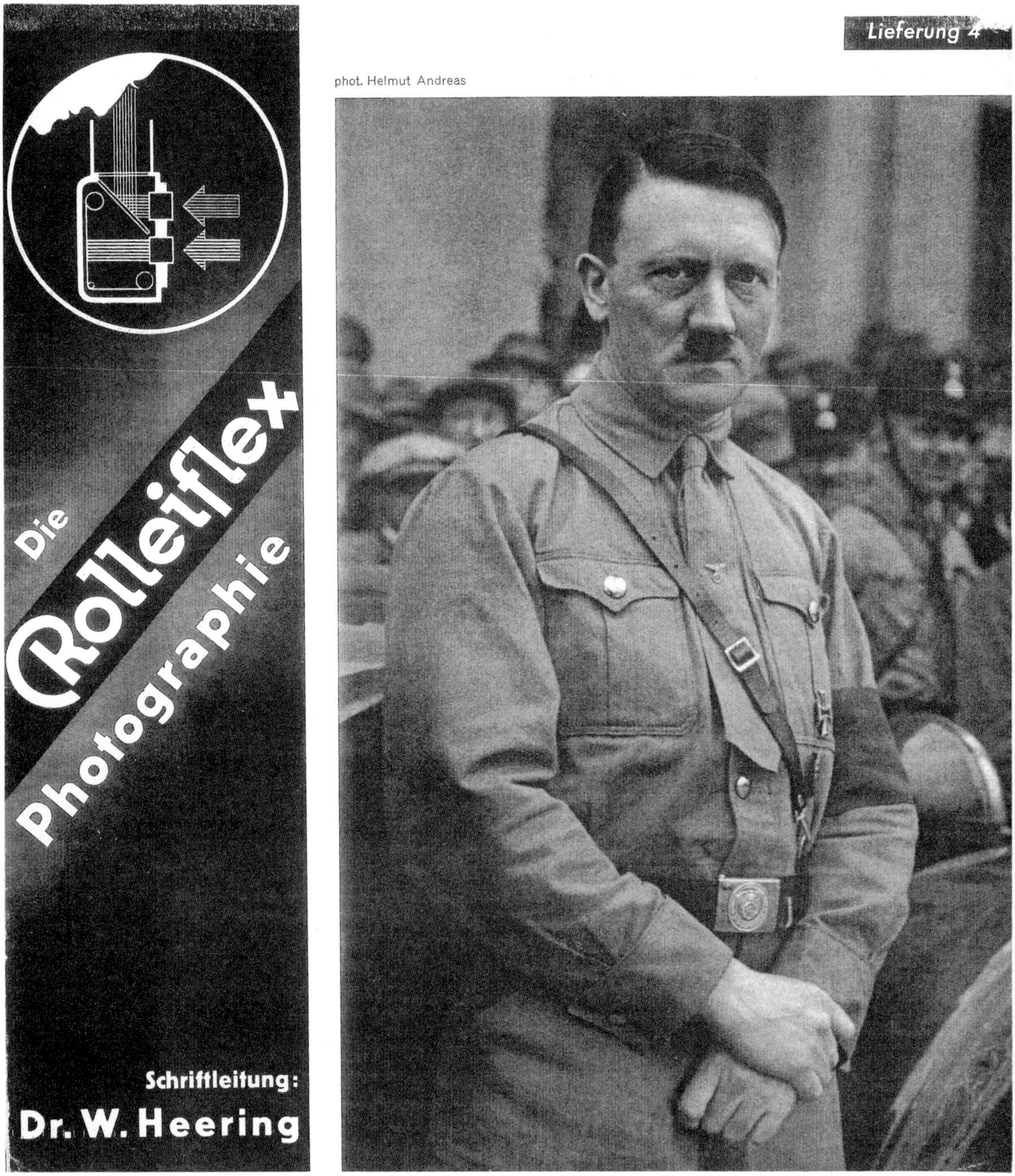

Lieferung 4

phot. Helmut Andreas

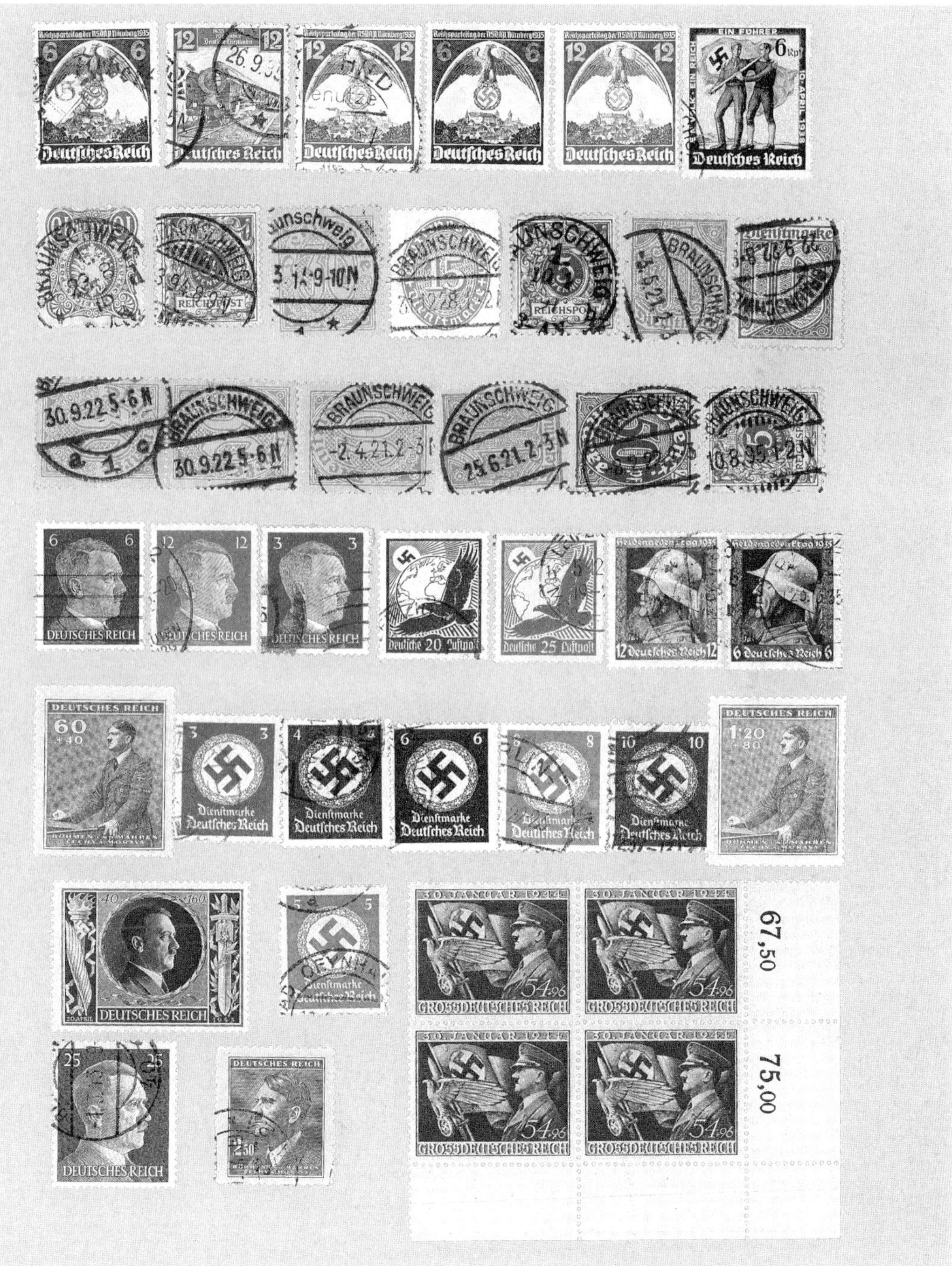

German stamps, dating from the 1920s through to 1944, sent to the author by Karl Vogel.

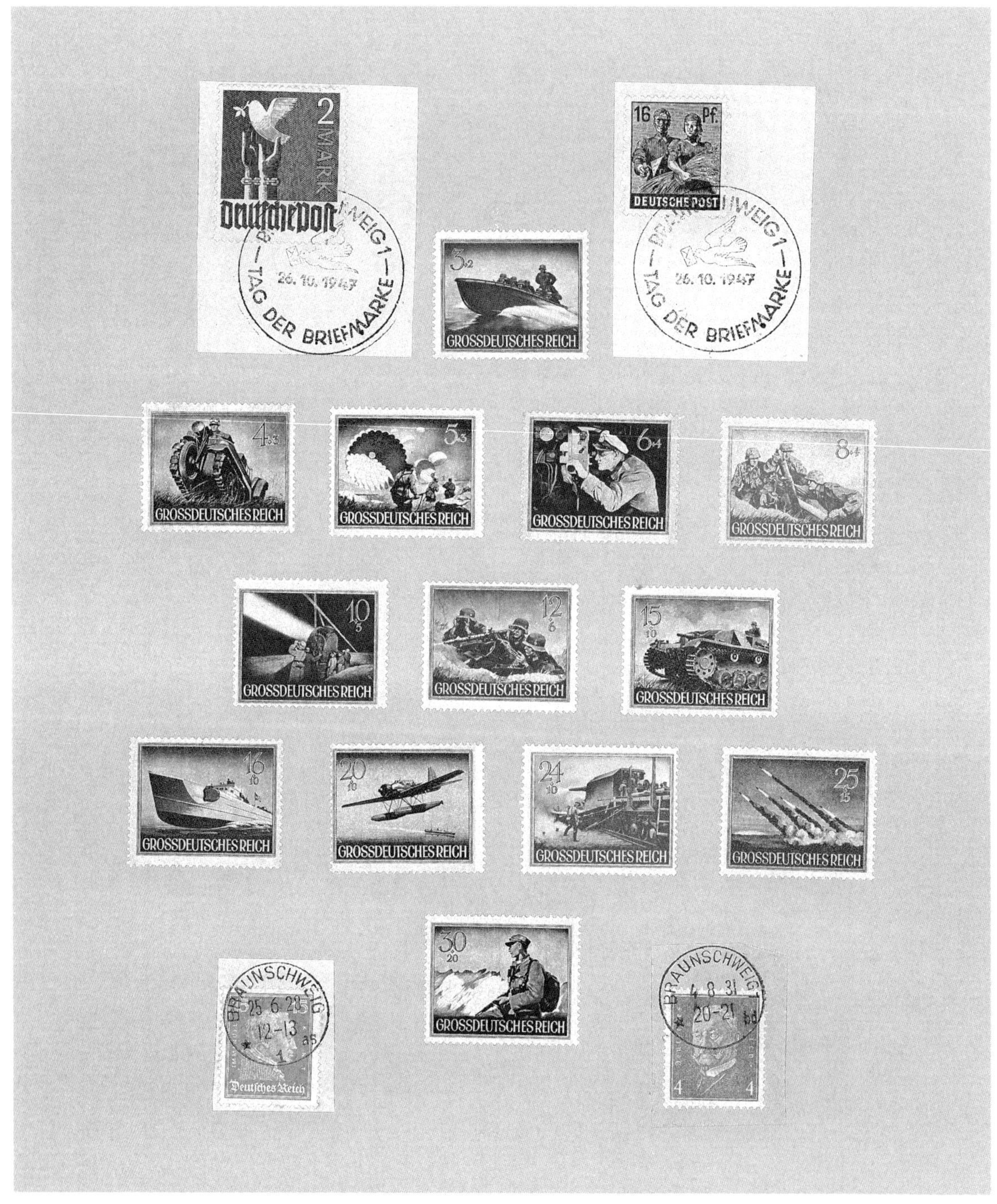

1947 peace stamps (top) and pre-war stamps advertising German military hardware.

Xenon lens, Dr. Reinhold designed his 35mm Xenon stereo camera. A prototype was started in 1953. Dr. Reinhold explained with great enthusiasm that the Xenon lenses were able to converge at close range, whereupon someone named the camera "die Schielen", meaning the squint. After the laughter died down, so did the camera. Later, Rollei-Werke gave me a drawing of the Squint, together with the stereo Automat. Hans Hass, the well-known underwater photographer, asked Rollei to design a 6 x 6 stereo after seeing the Squint in the factory museum. Dr. Reinhold, although not having seen the 007 James Bond films, designed with great enthusiasm two prototypes, one with underwater housing, the other to be used safely on land. By using two Rolleiflex Automats joined together but with only one hood and finder lens the cost of these prototypes must have been horrific and would have demanded a very high price if sold. I wonder where their present home is?

To return to the factory, such was Franke's good fortune in acquiring the Salzdahlumer Strasse factory site of 60,000 sq. metres (approx 15 acres) that the factory now known as Unit No. 1, and built at one side of the site, allowed for another unit to be built only 6 years later still leaving plenty of room for further expansion. This new section, some 3000 sq. metres on three floors completed in 1938, enabled 700 employees to work in very modern conditions and became one of the German Third Reich show factories. It received certificates of good labour working practices from the National-Sozialistischer Musterbetrieb.

1938 was a milestone in Rollei history for the 300,000th camera was sold. Meanwhile in 1937 the Rolleiflex Automat was launched at the Paris World Fair, gaining a major prize. So confident were Franke & Heidecke in January 1937 that they had a sure winner on their hands that they were able to sign the contract for factory extension No. 2. The first Automat No. 568516 finally went on sale in August 1937 with a f3.5 75mm Carl Zeiss Jena Tessar lens and with a cheaper f2.8 finder lens. Full automation of the winding and shutter locking was to say goodbye to accidental multiple exposures and the dominance of Rollei amongst professional and serious amateur photographers was assured for the next twenty years. The new camera looked professionally designed, with all components engineered for their specific job, whereas previously the design had been typical of the small back street engineering works where components are primarily designed using available tools and machine. Heidecke explained that a lot of "zuchtung" (breeding) had gone into the automat and that the design had been prepared first, then the tools were purchased specially for the new camera.

Castings, gears, winding crank, sheet metal work for the hood and knobs were all of good quality and of superlative engineering. I remember being told that Paul Franke, on picking up the Automat at a press call announcing the new Automat in June 1937, accidentally tripped the shutter while demonstrating the camera. For a moment he thought he had forgotten to thread the film under the pressure roller. All you Rolleiflex owners who have actually used your cameras will know the feeling as you wind the film on and

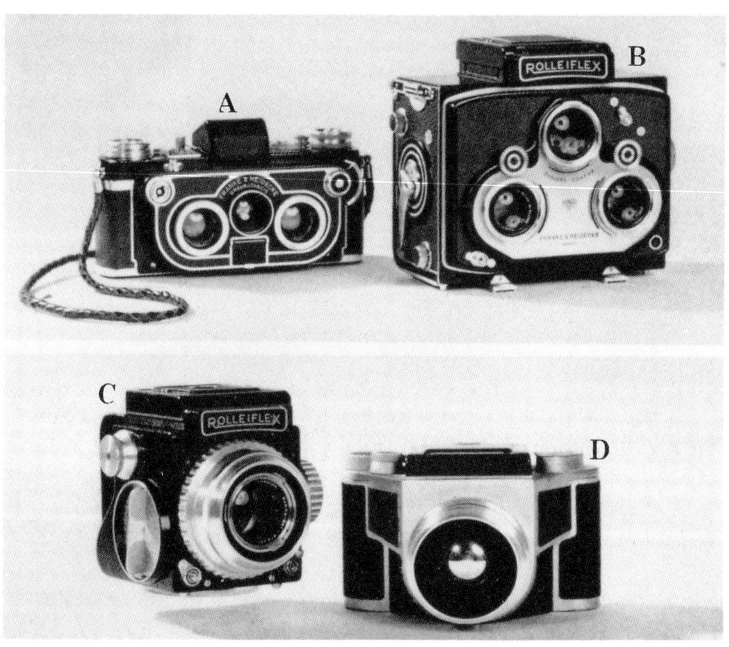

Prototypes

A. 1953 the Rollei Squint
B. 1955 double T.L.R. for stereo
C. Preliminary study for the SL66
D. 1962 a medium format S.L.R.

on without threading under the roller that trips the film counter once the film's attaching tape passes the pressure roller. A safety catch soon appeared on cameras, so you could not accidentally trip the shutter when the camera was not in use. Otherwise the camera had only a few internal modifications to improve production; in 1939, the finder lens was able to accept the taking lens filters, so double bayonets on both lenses were born. The early chrome wheels for aperture and shutter control could easily tarnish in the tropics and were grey-trimmed. Those supplied to Ireland and American markets in 1941 had synchronisation with a top speed of 1/25 for use by press photographers with their large press 25 bulb flash guns.

From 1937 to 1950 the Automat sold in large numbers, with few modifications. After World War II the camera became available with the f3.5 Schneider Xenar lens or Zeiss Tessar factory-coated lens. In 1949 the camera was redesigned with X synchronisation on the bottom right-hand corner. A newly designed hood where a filter could be stored, a new large magnifier plus built-in frame sports finder and a few other modifications gave the camera a further six years until the introduction of the 3.5E.

Our next chapter will take the reader through the war years, recalling how those left at Rollei survived, but first perhaps a few words on the other German camera manufacturers are in order.

Ernst Leitz, as we all know, manufactured the precision 35mm Leica camera. Leitz of Wetzlar, West Germany, was an optical firm. Oskar Barnack who invented the Leica first worked in Jena, dare we say Carl Zeiss. Leitz had three factories, each one far larger than Rollei's 1938 factory. Leitz, founded in 1849, had an enormous background of optical experience and employed many thousands. Oscar Barnack was employed to design lenses for the fast-growing cinema industry and this sparked the idea to make a 35mm camera. His first prototype, the UR-Leica, was made in 1913 and became one of the World War I casualties, to be resurrected in 1924. Production began in 1925. As with Rollei, in the early days only a few cameras were actually delivered. In 1926 a worthwhile 1654 were produced. In 1927 the figure was 3000 and in 1930 a staggering 38,000 were produced. Just prior to World War II, between 30 and 35 thousand Leicas were produced anually. Of all the German camera manufacturers, Leica probably produced more books, magazines, catalogues, leaflets and advertised their products more than anyone else. Rollei, prior to World War II, were producing in their small (by comparison) works over 50,000 cameras per annum, although admittedly lenses and shutters were bought in from Zeiss. When, in 1940, Rollei's camera sales reached 400,000, Leica sales totalled 367,000.

It was not until 1934 that 35mm roll-film could be bought in disposable cassettes. Previously, film was bought in bulk. My wife remembers well when, under our bedclothes, cassettes were loaded with Ilford FP4, bought in bulk for my old Leica, which left bits of sharp film cuttings to stick into her every time she turned over. Yes, I did have a Leica and I still sometimes take my early model IID on holiday, complete with Tessar look-alike f3.5 5cm Elmar lens.

Zeiss Ikon was formed when Carl Zeiss brought together Contessar-Nettel, Erneman, Goerz and Ica Aktiengesellschaft after World War I. Ikon, Greek for image, was selected by Zeiss as the name of this group. Unfairly maybe, the only name to survive this ill-fated group is Contax, now owned and manufactured in Japan by Yashica. For those Contax devotees about to commit hara-kiri, let me tell you that Cambridge Instruments of Milton Keynes, U.K., bought Leitz in August 1989, so Leica became a British company, to be sold again in 1991.

Zeiss suffered from World War II in that their business was divided between East and West Germany. With no family feeling or succession and no management direction Zeiss Ikon continued until 1972 to churn out 104 different models, all regrettably outdated and manufactured in similar obsolescent factories. Zeiss Ikon Contarex cameras had superb lenses and, with more thought on their design and weight reduction, might well have survived, but this was left to the Yashica Contax which, although an excellent camera, is now seldom seen in the shops.

Voigtländer, prior to World War II, like Zeiss Ikon, had a large range of nothing special. During World War II, Karl Pritschow decided in 1941 that the feud between the two Braunschweig firms should end. Reinhold, now aged 60, agreed that with their reduced labour force they should help each other. After World War II Voigtländer specialised in 35mm cameras and later, in the 1970s their design and research department was way ahead of their competitors. Whether they would have survived within the auto-focus field, I would not like to speculate, but survive they did, only to be taken over by Rollei. The prize was the design section that were responsible for the birth of the Rollei 2000/3000 series of 35mm cameras with interchangeable backs. With the video style side grip 3003 users are often mistaken for owning a wonderful new miniature camcorder.

Rollei have now sold the trade name of Voigtländer to a photo store group, leaving Rollei and Leica the only main West German camera manufacturers. At the turn of the century, almost 100 years ago, there were said to be almost 200 different camera manufacturers. Today, there are just two. To survive in today's market you either compete in the mass market or you seek the small niche for specialised products, a respected name helps to ensure repeat business. Today, in the 1990s Rollei are ahead of the world's medium format cameras.

CHAPTER 7

THE STUDIO CAMERA

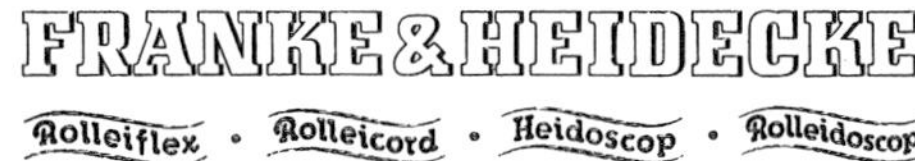

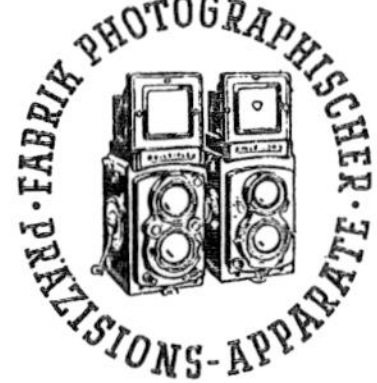

Dear ROLLEI Friend:

We wish you great pleasure in the use and ownership of your new ROLLEI. Countless successes and achievements by ROLLEI photographers throughout the world indicate that your results will be equally wonderful.

The name ROLLEI guarantees that the selection of materials, manufacture, assembly and inspection has been carried out with infinite care. Therefore, you possess in ROLLEI a precision camera fully dependable in all situations.

Operation of the camera and accessories is extremely convenient but please consult the enclosed literature before you try the camera for the first time. Your photo dealer, our representatives or we ourselves stand ready to serve you cheerfully should you be in need of further technical information.

If some of your pictures should turn out exceptionally well or even win prizes in photographic contests, we should like to share a small measure of your pleasure. Please write us a short note and remember, if you are interested, that we continually buy better than average ROLLEI shots for our advertising picture file.

Wishing you every success, we are

Very cordially yours,

F r a n k e & H e i d e c k e
Fabrik photogr. Präzisions-Apparate

Dr. Heidecke H. Franke

THE STUDIO CAMERA

The Rollei Studio Camera 9 x 9. Was there such a camera? Was it a 6 x 9? Many have attempted to find the truth. Firstly, Robert Pins, the American Shutterbug columnist and Rollei collector, ran an advertisement offering $1000 reward for information leading to one. There were no replies to his advertisement. The Rollei Collector's Club, together with many photographic journals have all asked the same question. Did Rollei, in the 1930s build and sell a large studio camera? The answer is yes.

The secrecy surrounding the mystery is simple to understand. In 1932 the proprietor of the famous Berlin studio, Kardas, near to Paul Franke's photographic store, asked whether they could supply a camera that would take a roll-film or cut- film size 9 x 12 (3 3/8" x 4 1/2") for taking portraits. Salomon Kahn, the studio proprietor, explained to Paul Franke that many of his clients wanted the negative, not glass plates which were difficult to store, but a film negative that would last forever. At that time photographic paper was inclined to curl and many people thought that the life expectancy of a paper image was of short duration. It later transpired that the real reason for this enquiry was to enable Herr Kahn to continue to take portraits, not in his studio, but at the houses of his clients, so he wanted a portable camera. Once the film was developed he could make contact prints which he could sell. Also he would sell the negative to his client for making contact prints. This latter reason he did not divulge.

Paul Franke spoke to Heidecke, now in the new factory and looking at additional formats for his T.L.R. The baby had been launched the previous year and it seemed a good idea to construct a professional studio camera. The camera was a scaled-up replica of the 1932 6 x 6 with lever wind. One of the cameras had a f3.8 105mm Tessar lens, the other a f4.5 100mm. In December 1932 two prototypes were shown to Salomon Kahn and he selected the 100mm lens camera and a special price of 250 RM was agreed, with delivery in February 1933. Franke and Heidecke thought that there would be a great future for the camera and even thought up a slogan: "you see what you get".

Studio cameras in the early 1930s usually required a black cloth over the photographer's head, and bending down is not one of the best positions to take a photograph, as well as being a difficult position from which to direct the sitter. However, with a portrait Rolleiflex, giving a picture size of 3 3/8 x 3 3/8, the photographer could direct the model and could quickly glance down to take a picture without having to put a cloth over his head, by which time the sitter could have moved or altered their expression.

In 1921, Studio Kardas were using the Mentor Studio reflex camera, made in Dresden. The two-fold lens movement permitted considerable selec-

THE NEW MENTOR STUDIO REFLEX CAMERA

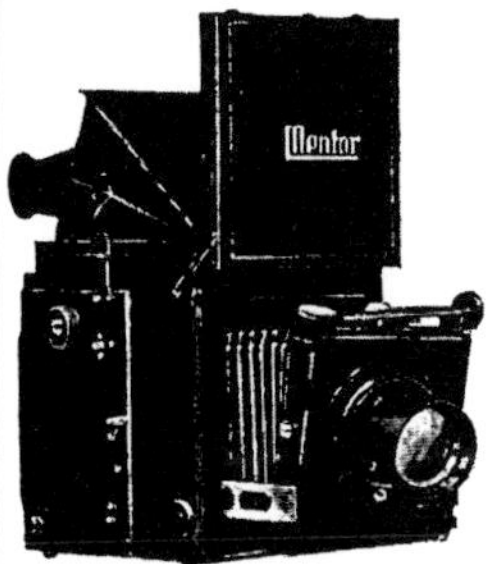

Two-fold Lens Movement permitting of considerable selective focussing.

Additional mirror and hood — subject can be viewed and focussed at eye-level.

Mentor Self-Capping Focal Plane Shutter.

Adjustable Focussing Screen.

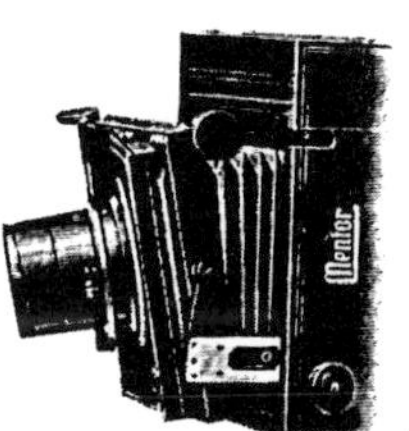

Size.		Camera.	Price, including 3 Double Dark Slides, Metal Release and Strap.	R.M.
Inch.	Cm.	No.		
3¼×4¼	9×12	211	With Extension from about 8¼ to 14 in.	750
—	12×12	212	,, ,, ,, 8¼ to 14 ,, ...	750
5 ×7	13×18	213	,, ,, ,, 10 to 18 ,, ...	870
5 ×7	13×18	214	,, ,, ,, 12 to 21½ in.	990

THE NEW MENTOR STANDARD REFLEX

A REFLEX CAMERA OF SPLENDID FINISH AND RELIABILITY.

Specially adapted for Telephoto work. Extreme durability. Self-capping Focal-plane Shutter. Vibrationless. Easily handled. Perfect and Unfailing Action. With and Without Reversing Back.

With Reversing Back for Upright and Oblong.

Sizes		With Zeiss Tessar F/4.5			With Zeiss Tessar F/3.5			With Zeiss Tessar F/2.8		
Inch	Cm.	Camera No.	Lens Focus	R.M.	Camera No.	Lens Focus	R.M.	Camera No.	Lens Focus	R.M.
2½×3½	6.5×9	153	5¼	**423**	5153	5¼	**468**	0153	5¼	**567**
3¼×4¼	8×10.5	201	6½	**516**	5201	6½	**597**	0201	6½	**669**
—	9×12	203	7	**534**	5203	8¼	**705**	0203	6½	**669**
3½×5½	10×15	204	8¼	**639**	5204	8¼	**765**	—	—	—
4¾×6½	12×16.5	206	8¼	**699**	5206	8¼	**825**	—	—	—
5 ×7	13×18	208	8¼	**699**	5208	8¼	**825**	—	—	—
5 ×7	13×18	210	10	**828**	5210	10	**960**	—	—	—
Without Reversing Back for Oblong.										
2½×3½	6.5×9	151	4⅛	**357**	5151	4⅛	**381**	0151	5½	**507**
3¼×4¼	8×10.5	161	6	**432**	5161	6	**495**	0161	6½	**609**
—	9×12	163	6	**432**	5163	6	**495**	0163	6½	**609**
3½×5½	10×15	164	6½	**516**	5164	6½	**597**	—	—	—
4¾×6½	12×16.5	166	8¼	**639**	5166	8¼	**765**	—	—	—
5 ×7	13×18	168	8¼	**639**	5168	8¼	**765**	—	—	—
Stereo	4.5×10.7	181	3	**447**	—	—	—	—	—	—
Stereo	6×13	182	3½	**477**	5182	4⅛	**531**	0182	5½	**822**

Prices in Reichsmark ex Dresden, including 3 Double Slides, Cable Release and Strap.

MENTOR CAMERA WORKS, DRESDEN, 50

1932 Mentor Studio reflex camera
Europe's most common studio camera

tive focussing and, with an additional mirror and hood, could be used in the same way as today's Rollei 35mm 2000/3000 series. The Mentor range of cameras were very advanced for that period and could be found in many German studios. The sports version was very popular for outdoors photographs and was used for the German 1933 commemorative stamps.

The Mentor Camera Co., originally the Goltz & Breutmann Kamera Co. of Berlin, started to manufacture Reflex Strut cameras in 1898 and, with Graflex of America, produced around 80% of the world's studio cameras in the late 1920s. For a studio as famous as Kardas, Franke & Heidecke thought that here was an opportunity to widen their range of Rollei cameras. At that time the Mentor Camera Co. still had works in Berlin and Mr. Taylor, who supervised the sales of Rollei cameras for the U.K. importer R.F. Hunter, was told by Paul Franke that, when he visited the Mentor Camera Co. and looked at their range of cameras, he could find no 9 x 9 film camera, the largest being a size 6 x 9.

Mr. Taylor of R.F. Hunter was also told of Salomon Kahn of Berlin who wanted a 9 x 9 studio film camera, and had said that Adolf Hitler had agreed to be photographed with this camera, whereby he obtained publicity and helped Franke & Heidecke, who at that time were ardent supporters of the Third Reich. Paul Franke asked whether George V, King of Great Britain, would agree to be photographed as this would publicise the camera in G.B. Although Mr. Taylor approached several studios he was unable to obtain a picture which was clearly being done for advertising and Mr. Hunter, the importer, wrote to the Mentor Camera Co. to find out more about studio cameras. The Mentor Camera Co. had just released a new portable reflex camera, very similar to today's medium format S.L.R., with a fixed Tessar lens and Compur shutter costing 198 RM, whereas the larger Rolleiflex was to be sold for 250 RM. With Rolleiflex cameras already selling at a premium it should sell well thought Messrs. Hunter and Taylor. Paul Franke, pleased by the response, decided that 14 cameras should be built, all with 100mm f4.5 Tessars, the same lens already used on the Mentor camera, and respected by studio photographers. The first camera would be sent to Salomon Kahn to take the photograph of Hitler and postage stamp illustrations – that would see a large donation going from Franke & Heidecke to the Nationalist Socialist Party funds – good P.R. on both sides. The camera, together with the photographs, would appear at the Berlin Photographic Fair, which they did.

In the autumn of 1932 Kahn received the prototype which he successfully tried. In February 1933 the production cameras were ready for dispatch. They were sent in pairs, one on loan to a studio for evaluation, the other retained by the importer for demonstrations. These cameras were constructed as prototypes, without a large amount of tooling, to establish whether in fact there was a market. Remember that Heidecke's wife had suggested a baby Rolleiflex and sales for this camera had not come up to expectations. When the cameras were ready four were sent to America and two to England. Paul Franke was personally taking two cameras to Hamburg for Herr Saal at his photo shop. However, the Rolleiflex studio camera met its death in an unusual and sad way. Perhaps this story is best left untold, but the history of Rollei would not be complete without giving the reasons for the demise of what might have been another chapter in Rollei's history. Even today there may well be a place for a 9 x 9 T.L.R. or S.L.R. roll-film camera.

Some years ago in the late 1950s I was asked by an American journalist for the story behind the studio camera. I replied that I was not at liberty to enlighten him, as some of the people concerned were still alive. Some years later, when Robert Pins was writing the Rollei story for the American journal *Popular Photography* he again asked for information on this camera. The editor added a postscript : "In the 50s I visited the Franke & Heidecke Rollei Werke in Braunschweig as the guest of Horst Franke, son of one of the co-founders of the company. I mentioned to Franke that I had heard about the 9 x 9 Rollei and what was the story. Franke became very flustered and spluttered that only one camera had been made. I tactfully dropped the subject – Editor" *American Popular Photography.*

The sad story was that Salomon Kahn was a Jew. He wanted the camera badly. The landlord of his studio had been told that he was unwise to allow a Jew in his building. He cut off the water and while Kahn was able to take pictures he had to process them at home. Kahn spoked to Paul Franke at his photo shop, which was also on the Kurfürstendamm in Berlin. He reasoned that if he had a larger version of the Rolleiflex he could visit clients' homes, take the photograph and make contact prints. Film rolls would be easier to carry around than glass plate negatives. He could not tell Franke the true reason for wanting the camera in case he told his landlord.

The firm Franke & Heidecke were ardent and proud supporters of Hitler's National Socialist party and I would quickly hasten to add that many other German industrialists also supported Hitler, and with large sums of money. In January, 1933 Hitler became Chancellor of the German Reich. In February a mysterious fire gutted the German Reichstag and the Communists were blamed. A Dutchman, Marinus van de Lubbe, admitted to a Leipzig court that he had set fire to the building. In the show trial, maps of the building were shown. They excluded the underground tunnel linking the building to the home of Hermann Goering, the president and chief minister to Adolf Hitler's party.

Salomon Kahn was a Jew, so Franke & Heidecke were in a difficult position. A Jew had taken Adolf Hitler's official portrait to be used for the definitive stamp issues for 1933/34. The National Socialist Party imposed conditions on Jews, as we now know. On Saturday the 11th March 1933 all Jewish-owned department stores in Braunschweig were looted and on the following Monday all Jewish lawyers and judges were expelled from the Courts. Many Jewish families lost relatives that weekend. On the 9th March Salomon Kahn had left his studio early as was his custom on Thursdays. He was seized by stormtroopers who beat him, and he was ultimately sent to

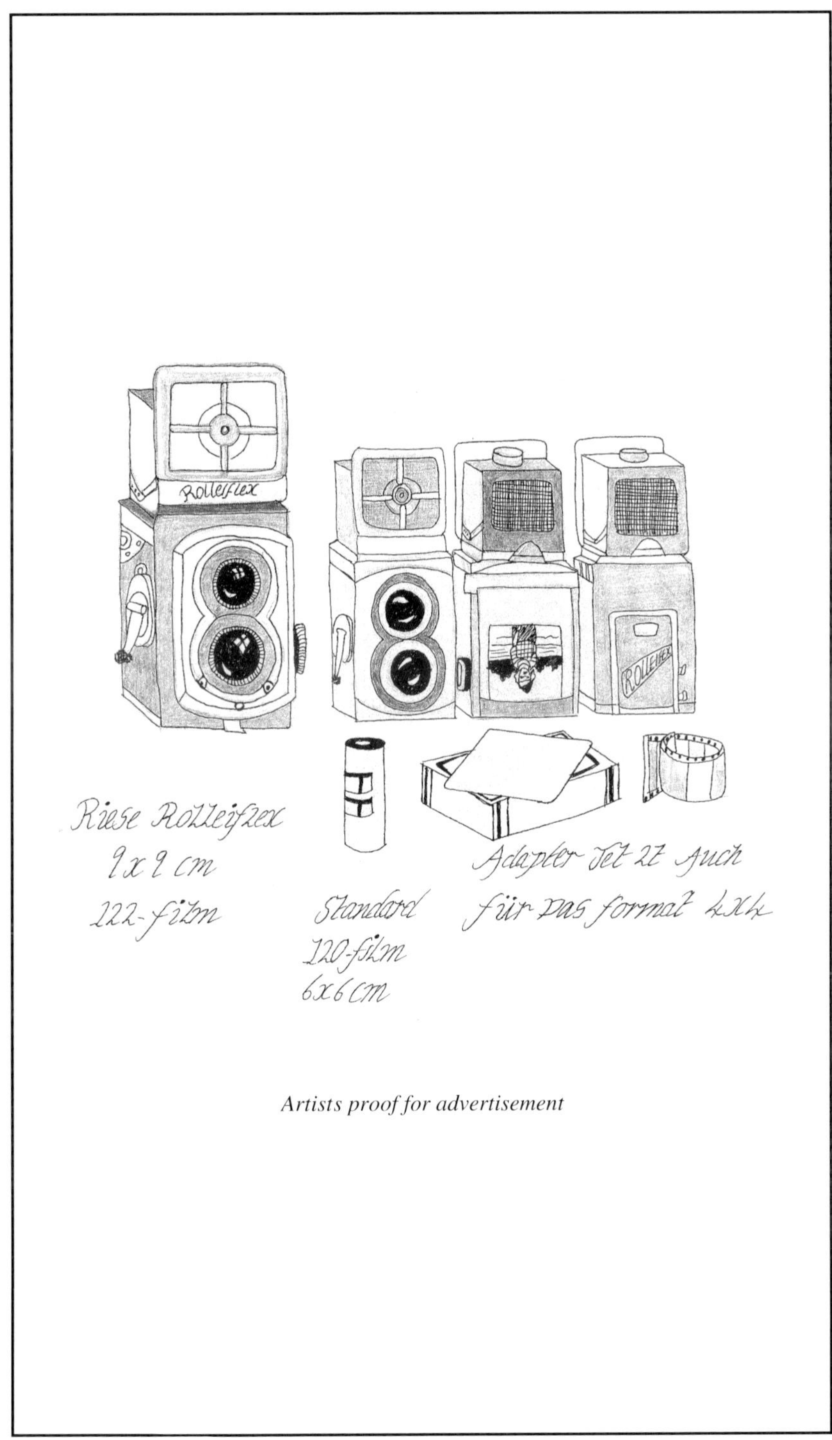

Artists proof for advertisement

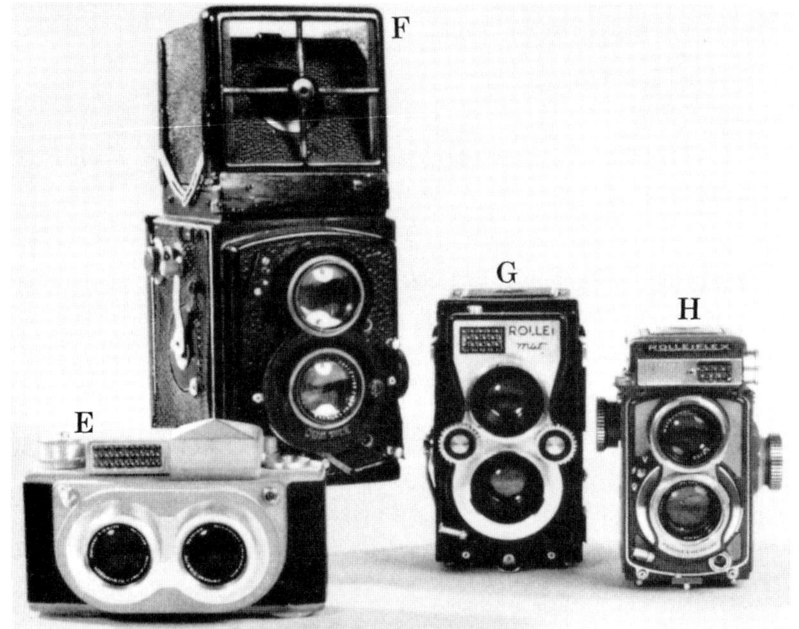

More Prototypes:
E. 1954 twin lens 35mm Rollei
F. 1933 9 x 9cm studio Rollei, 100mm, f3.5 Tessar
G. 1959 Rolleimat for Rollei Magic
H. 1959 4 x 4 with exposure meter

Dachau concentration camp with others from Braunschweig. Altogether 5000 Jews arrived that month at Dachau, a long train journey via Munich. They were never to be seen again. Did Paul Franke witness Salomon Kahn being taken by the stormtroopers? We will never know for sure.

We do know that Paul Franke continued to sell the idea of the camera to distributors and suggested they approached a well-known studio to try out the camera and obtain photographs for advertising. Hoyningen-Huene, the American film studio fashion photographer and master of lighting employed Horst and Schenker, who were both well-known photographers; they were asked if they would try out the cameras. Then suddenly without warning, the English and American distributors both received cabled messages that the camera was withdrawn, and could they hold their samples until production problems were sorted out. Hoyningen-Huene, on asking Burleigh Brooks Inc., the American distributors, when the camera would be delivered and possibly thinking about a fee, was told that they had instructions to hold the cameras as Franke & Heidecke were worried about the Jewish problem in Germany, and they could obtain no further information.

What became of the camera? The Städtisches Museum in Braunschweig has the two original 1933 prototypes and another made by Heidecke in 1955. The other prototype was used by the production team as a template. The four cameras sent to America must still be in the U.S.A. but could well have been discarded as old valueless junk. The two cameras sent to R.F. Hunter, the English distributors, were thought to be lost during the war when their premises in Grays Inn Road suffered bomb damage. The only information R.F. Hunter could give Alec Pearlman were the notes and brochures from Mentor Camera Co. which were still in their files. The remaining four in Germany were kept in a cupboard in No. 1 factory unit, together with the original prototype, camera components and old press tools. Robert Pins, who was a New York press reporter, wrote in his article *The Rollei Story Part V* : When the Queen Mary arrived in New York soon after the end of World War II with a shipload of returning Canadian soldiers, I was the only New York reporter able to get aboard to interview them. One of the returning soldiers, a Canadian sergeant, said he had something to show me. He went to his bunk and returned with a 9 x 9 Rollei. I asked him how much he wanted for the camera, but he would not part with it. A few months later I was offered a 9 x 9 Rollei for more than $300 by a returning soldier. I borrowed the camera and actually took some photographs.".

The Americans who were first into Braunschweig were no doubt looking for souvenirs. There is no doubt that all cameras ready for dispatch, completed or almost completed, vanished. Captain Cullum Brown of the English 21st Army reported that any stock that gave the impression of being worth any money had gone. When he took over responsibility of Rollei Works he had to sign that there was no stock of finished cameras. Such are the fortunes of war. From Robert Pins we now learn that two of the four German cameras must be in the U.S.A. or Canada. The two sent to Ponder & Best, Rollei's West Coast distributors in Los Angeles, and the two seen in the showroom of Burleigh Brooks, Englewood, New Jersey in 1964 must surely be somewhere, but where?

Reinhold Heidecke thought of the T.L.R. idea by accident as a camera was needed for the trenches in World War I, and it seems as if Salomon Kahn realised the need for a portrait camera because of the onset of World War II. Perhaps there is a demand today for a 9 x 9 roll-film camera. Possibly Polaroid would be the ideal film, who knows?

The Berlin Photographic Exhibition was a great success. The large photograph of Hitler and two smaller photographs of the stamps were shown. In 1939 Vogel, the author's pen pal who also collected stamps, was given by his father, who worked for Rollei, the photograph of the Berlin stand and the set of stamps on a cover to advertise Rollei. We often exchanged stamps, but these particular ones he gave me would not fit into my album so I soaked them off and today still have the stamps and the photo of the stand showing four cameras and a wooden mock-up camera. Going through my collection of stamps later with Vogel, he told me how Salomon Kahn had taken the photographs and when they found out the photographs had been taken by a Jew there was a lot of trouble. At first Paul Franke was very upset at what happened to Kahn but visitors to the Berlin Exhibition learnt that Kahn had taken the photographs and that it had been his idea to construct a studio camera in the first place and later, when rumours of Kahn's disappearance became known, the mainly Jewish dealers were horrified. Paul Franke was worried that the Americans would boycott Rollei products, should the news cross the Atlantic.

When Hitler's publicity men heard about the incident and the damage it could cause overseas, the whole studio camera project was scuttled and Rollei were forbidden to use the photographs taken by Kahn for advertising. The brochures were destroyed, as was the advertising cover with the stamps that was going to be sent out to studios. And to think I removed the stamps from my stamp album.

In 1950 I was invited to visit Kodak at Harrow, north-west London. At lunch I sat next to Alec Pearlman and a representative of Hunter's, the English Rollei importers. Alec Pearlman was interested in some research I was doing for a book on the life of Lawrence of Arabia and told me about his book *The Rollei Manual*. He was surprised when he discovered my knowledge on Rollei cameras. Lunch over and our tour round Kodak completed, together with Hunter's representative we all went back to Pearlman's Harrow photo shop in St. Ann's Road. On being shown his collection of Rollei cameras, I remarked that there was one model missing. Pearlman replied that he knew he had no stereos and he only collected the T.L.R. I asked "Where is the large studio camera?" Neither Alec Pearlman, nor Hunter's were aware that there was a 9 x 9 studio camera, but I knew where I could find my photograph of the Berlin Rollei exhibition stand.

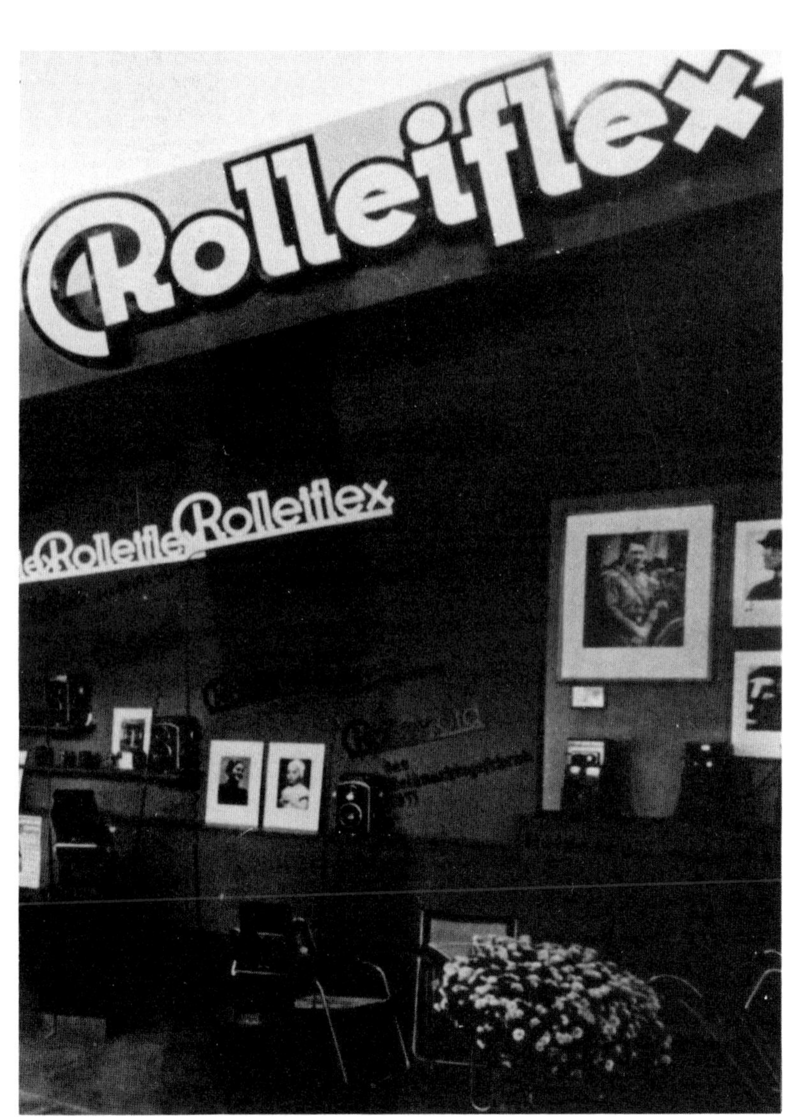

1933 Berlin exhibition with 3 studio cameras under the Nazi photographs.

FRANKE & HEIDECKE
BRAUNSCHWEIG

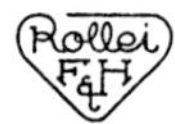

ROLLEIFLEX
ROLLEICORD
HEIDOSCOP
ROLLEIDOSCOP

FABRIK PHOTOGR. PRÄZISIONS-APPARATE

Postanschrift des Absenders:
Franke & Heidecke, Braunschweig, Salzdahlumer Straße 196

Drahtwort: Rolleiflex Fernsprecher: Sammel-Nr. 5010 Geschäftszeit: 7–17
Sonn.: 7–12

Herrn

Direktor Karl Pritschow
i.Hs. Voigtländer & Sohn

B r a u n s c h w e i g

Campestraße

Ihre Zeichen: Ihre Nachricht vom: Unsere Nachricht vom: Unser Hausruf: Unsere Zeichen:

BRAUNSCHWEIG
Salzdahlumer Straße 196
22.7.1941

Betreff:

Sehr geehrter Herr Pritschow!

Für die freundliche Übersendung Ihres Sonderdruckes über das Petzval-Voigtländer-Objektiv danke ich Ihnen verbindlichst. Besonders gefreut habe ich mich über die Widmung, die mir zeigt, daß auch Sie sich gern noch unserer gemeinsamen Arbeit erinnern.

Für den Fachmann ist es immer wieder reizvoll und lehrreich, die Arbeiten seines Fachgebietes bis in ihre frühesten Anfänge zurückzuverfolgen, und es ist m.E. ein großes Verdienst, wenn der heutigen Generation durch Abhandlungen wie die Ihre über das Petzval-Objektiv solche frühen Pionierleistungen nahegebracht werden und das Verständnis dafür gefördert wird.x

In diesem Sinne danke ich Ihnen nochmals bestens und verbleibe mit verbindlichen Grüßen und

Heil Hitler!
Ihr

x „Ganz allein durdh Aufklärung der Vergangenheit lässt sich die Gegenwart begreifen."

G o e t h e, Tag- und Jahreshefte 1811

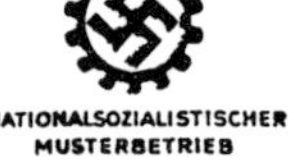

NATIONALSOZIALISTISCHER
MUSTERBETRIEB

Postscheckkonto: Hannover 40606
Bankkonten: Reichsbank-Girokonto 82 Braunschweig, Deutsche Bank Fil. Braunschweig, Braunschw. Staatsbank, Braunschweig

A L0. Vieweg

24. JUL. 1941

The firms Voigtländer and Franke & Heidecke were pleased to be working together during the war.

Some weeks later I saw Alec Pearlman, who had obtained from Hunter's various letters, notes and the cable and wireless message asking for the withdrawal of the camera. After looking at Vogel's letters and the photographs, Alec Pearlman asked if I would be interested in helping him with his book *The History of Rollei.* So with all good intentions I spent many an evening with Alec collating the information he gathered for his book.

I must confess I was more interested in the removal of stamps from discarded envelopes as I carefully brought some order to boxes of letters, literature and catalogues. My stamp collection, I remember, required an extra album, so I felt well rewarded for my considerable time.

At that period Rollei cameras were still in very short supply. As my interest in Rollei grew, I started to collect Rollei cameras, now helped by my mother, aunts and uncles, who all contributed. Good specimens coming into Alec Pearlman's shop soon found their way to my house. It is not everyone who has an understanding girlfriend, later to become my wife, and who some 40 years later will lovingly dust my precious collection and will allow her "other half" to spend 120% of their income on "unessential cameras". In 1953 on our honeymoon we acquired a new Rolleiflex in Gibraltar which absorbed nearly all of our spending money, but I am getting carried away. I soon learnt that Alec Pearlman obtained most of his information from Erich Vollenweider before World War II, the same person who introduced me to Paul Franke and arranged my pen pal Vogel.

The fate of Salomon Kahn as related by Herr Vollenweider, also a Jew, was why the latter came to England. With Vogel's story, together with notes that Mr. Taylor had written in 1933 which were obtained from Hunter's, the true story then emerged. So upset was Alec Pearlman that he could not continue with his book *The History of Rollei.* Thereafter Alec wrote about his love of print quality, water and snow scenes and used to love visiting camera clubs, giving talks and showing his favourite prints. Alec continued to update his *Rollei Manual.*

After my marriage in 1953 I lived in Wimbledon. We moved in 1957 to Dorking, then I started the book that Alec should have written, but without his help the project was put to one side. Many of Alec Pearlman's Rollei collection, in particular those unusual accessories which are hard to find today, can be seen in the Jersey Photographic Museum. Our German au pair girl, who helped in the translations some thirty years ago, married into a famous photographic family which became a Carl Zeiss subsidiary in 1956 and Rollei in 1973 .... her married name, Sonia Voigtländer.

Postcript 1991

I have tried to visit the Braunschweig Städtisches Museum that holds the original factory collection of Rollei cameras. In 1981 when Rollei went into receivership due to losses in the Singapore plant the liquidator gave the considerable collection of Rollei prototypes, production cameras etc. to the local museum.

On each occasion I have endeavoured to pay a visit, the museum has suddenly closed – for cleaning! They have a studio camera 9 x 9 production model, the one that was hidden away in the lower cupboard that was Dr. Heidecke's office. The museum claim that this camera was a 1934 pre-war prototype.

Two of our Club Rollei members have been able to see the camera at the museum. They confirm that this camera had no sports finder within the hood, but a finder on the side. The Rolleiflex's name was of 1929 – 1936 vintage with a Schneider Xenotar lens, Compur shutter. The hood has a round Franke & Heidecke logo used by Rollei from September 1933 to October 1935.

Curiously the Xenotar lens was first offered on the T.L.R. 2.8C in 1953. Possibly this was Heidecke's new studio camera 6 x 9cm and he experimented with a Xenotar. This camera we think was made in 1954 just six years before Heidecke died. The appearance we are told was excellent.

We are informed that the Braunschweig Städtisches Museum has two other studio cameras, both with no name. One camera was previously owned by David Ohlson who worked for the American Rollei distributor and sold the camera back to Rollei. This camera has a lever film wind and requires restoration. This was one of the original prototypes. The other camera is in mint condition with knob film wind and was the pre-production model that was in Heidecke's office. Both camera used 9 x 9cm film with Carl Zeiss Tessar lens.

Today in the 1990s Rollei do manufacture a large format camera. The LFC uses normal aerial film giving a usable image format of 230 x 230cm (just over 9 x 9 inches), its main market being industrial surveying.

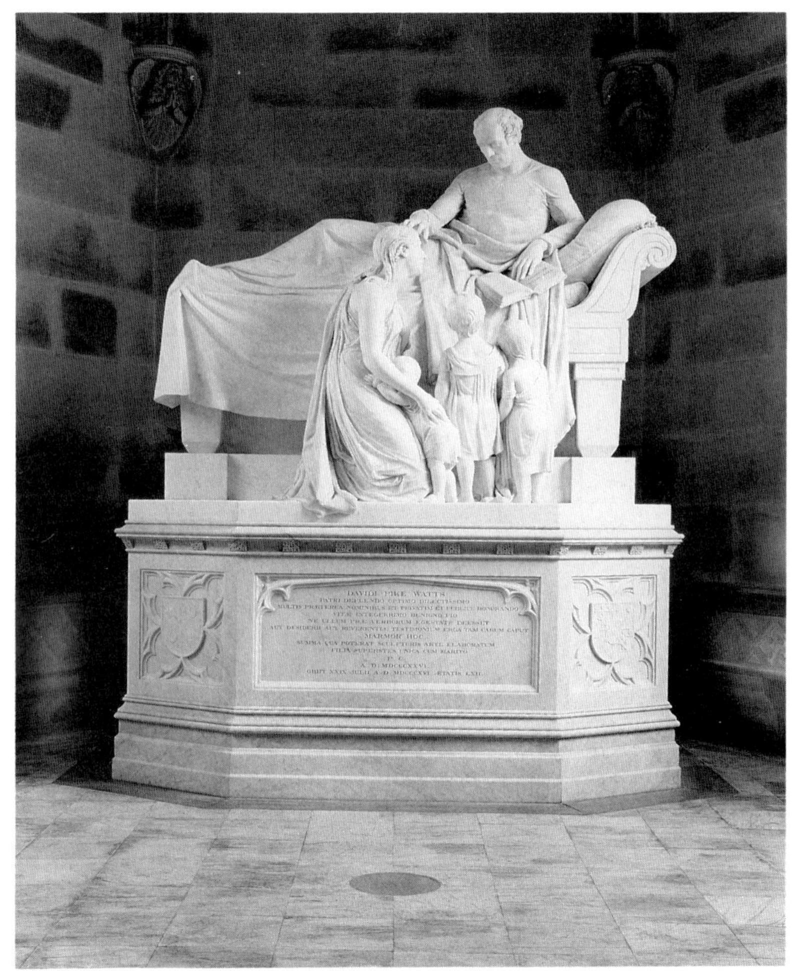

Memorial to Pike Watts. Another fine example taken with a f3.5 Tessar on a Rollei T T.L.R. Photo: W.T. Harrison A.R.P.S.

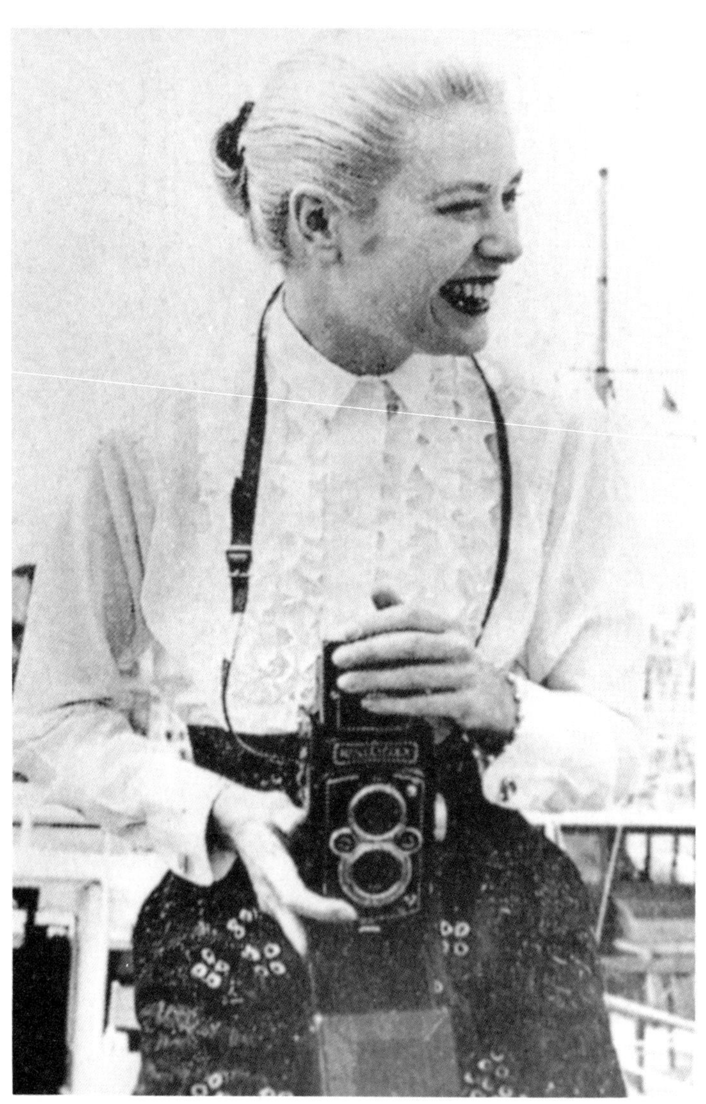

Grace Kelly at Port Galere with the author's 1956 Rolleiflex 2.8D.

CHAPTER 8

THE PRODUCTION MACHINERY

FRANKE & HEIDECKE
Rolleiflex · Rolleicord · Heidoscop · Rolleidoscop
BRAUNSCHWEIG

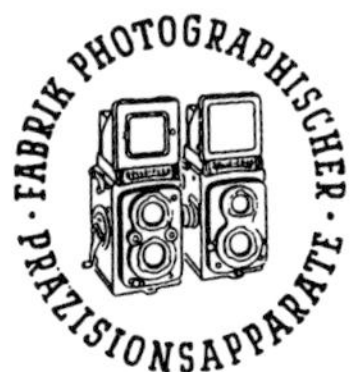

PREISLISTE

Code	Rolleiflex und Rolleicord mit Zubehör	DM
Aulux	Rolleiflex-Automat, Modell 1950, Tessar 3,5 mit Antireflexbelag	435.00
Auxen	Rolleiflex-Automat, Modell 1950, Xenar 3,5 mit Antireflexbelag	398.00
Coxen	Rolleicord II, Xenar 3,5 mit Antireflexbelag	238.00
Berau	Bereitschaftstasche für Rolleiflex-Automat, Modell 1950	33.00
Berin	Bereitschaftstasche für Rolleiflex-Automat 1950 und Rolleikin	35.50
Tabef	Bereitschaftstasche für Rolleiflex-Automat, bisheriges Modell	27.50
Tacin	Bereitschaftstasche für Rolleiflex-Automat u. Rolleikin, bish. Modell	30.00
Corbe	Bereitschaftstasche für Rolleicord	24.50
Cocin	Bereitschaftstasche für Rolleicord und Rolleikin	27.00
Baobe	Sonnenblende in Bajonettfassung	10.00
Baspo	Rollei-Sportfilter in Bajonettfassung (Faktor 1,5)	10.00
Baihe	Rollei-Gelbfilter hell in Bajonettfassung (2 x)	10.00
Baimi	Rollei-Gelbfilter mittel in Bajonettfassung (3 x)	10.00
Balin	Rollei-Hellgrünfilter in Bajonettfassung (2 x)	10.00
Baeen	Rollei-Grünfilter in Bajonettfassung (3 x)	10.00
Baora	Rollei-Orangefilter in Bajonettfassung (6 x)	10.00
Baubi	Rollei-Hellrotfilter in Bajonettfassung (8 x)	10.00
Babla	Rollei-Hellblaufilter in Bajonettfassung (1,5 x)	10.00
Basky	Rollei-U. V. Filter in Bajonettfassung (1,5 x)	10.00
Bapun	Rolleinare, Satz I (100-45 cm)	29.60
Baodo	Rolleinare, Satz II (50-31 cm)	29.60
Baken	Rolleiparkeil I	13.60
Bakdu	Rolleiparkeil II	13.60
Lekoe	1 Lederköcher, enthaltend: 2 Satz Rolleinare mit dazugehörigen Rolleiparkeilen und 5 Filtern nach Wahl	136.40
Foapt	Plattenadapter 6/6	17.20
Fosli	Neusilberkassette 6/6	10.80
Fofoc	Mattscheibenkassette 6/6	9.80
Fopla	Planfilmeinlage	0.50
Focom	Komplette Plattenadapter-Einrichtung, bestehend aus: 1 Plattenadapter, 3 Neusilberkassetten, 1 Mattscheibenkassette	59.40
Rorsp	Kinefilmeinrichtung „Rolleikin"	56.00
Foead	Panoramakopf	16.00
Blika	Anschlußkabel für Blitzlichteinrichtung	2.60

Die obigen Preise verstehen sich freibleibend.

1950 Price List

THE PRODUCTION MACHINERY

P.W.Harris was sent over by the British Government to report on the camera industry in Germany and how the 21st Army Group was helping the local population to return to life in peacetime after the military style they knew so well; many, feeling lost and unwanted, regretted the outcome of the war.

Mr. Harris's report makes interesting reading. He stated: "Gone are the Nazi flag and uniform so prominent in the Franke & Heidecke advertising I had studied before my visit. I had expected to find an old-established business, founded over 100 years ago as the brochure had stated. On being introduced to Paul Franke, the co-founder, I remarked that he was wearing well for someone over 100 years of age! Herr Franke was very surprised; when I showed him the advertisement he replied, 'Do not believe all the advertisements you read'. However he was greatly amused so I got on very well and was shown around the works and report:-

"The British 21st Army are well liked and have helped Franke & Heidecke to start a new life. The basis of the firm's products are the Rolleiflex and cheaper Rolleicord cameras, both of which are beautifully designed and extremely well-made by pressure diecasting in aluminium alloy, with special tools for this costing 6000 RM, about £600. In spite of the high finish, when the casting leaves the press there are still 160 milling and drilling operations required, and these are done by hand.

"The pressure diecastings are made by a specialist firm, Roders of Soltay. The other aluminium pressings are done on the premises, including the camera back and work on the main body. The very smooth focussing movement of the Rolleiflex is achieved by parts of two opposed cams, with spring-loaded followers. These followers carry the front plate of the camera, which in turn carries the focussing and taking lenses. These followers and their associated cams are very precise pieces of engineering. The cams are blanked by a special tool, then machined on the periphery to exact size and shape in relation to their orientation on the focussing spindle. The followers are stamped in steel and are shaped to move back and forward in a parallel bearing.

"The front plate carrying the lenses must be exactly 90° to these parallel faces and therefore it is important to have the front face of the follower exactly square with the two bearing faces. This is done in another special purpose grinder designed and made by Franke & Heidecke."

"The black finish on Rollei cameras is supplied by outside firms, and is roughly inspected for quality. All aluminium is acid-dipped before finishing. Some of the brightest beading on the Rollei cameras is achieved by grinding after blacking; ingenuity was seen in the application of dual grinding heads for finishing the edges of certain parts. Many parts were ground and burnished. The usual high standard of attention to detail in polishing to plating was noticed. The camera exhibited a wide diversity of finishes – nickel, chrome, polished aluminium etc. – and care was evident at all stages. The hobbing of knurled control wheels was again seen.

"Leather was used for covering the body of the camera. The lenses were Tessars made by Zeiss and shutters were Compur by Deckel. In this connection it should be noted that, as a result of the Russian occupation of the Zeiss factory, Franke & Heidecke were going over to Schneider lenses. The business is essentially a partnership concern, built up over a long period. Loans and assistance from Zeiss were refused in order to maintain independence. Profits for many years are reported to have been ploughed back, and the balance sheets indicate a flourishing state of affairs. There was a wide range of war equipment manufactured without additional plant or extension. This firm is an excellent example of the best type of a German precision engineering factory. Its standards are of the highest in every sphere of its activities and the result is a series of absolutely first-class photographic instruments.

"The factory itself is well laid out, well lighted and ideally equipped to carry out the production of high class work. The proprietors took an active interest in the work of the factory and appear to be men with an expert knowledge of the business. The plant is good, well looked after, and in excellent condition and the employees appeared to be proud to work for the company. Pride of achievement and of workmanship were apparent everywhere and profit did not appear to be the only motive that kept Franke & Heidecke moving.

"Herr Franke considered there were no manufacturing secrets in making precision cameras other than good jigging, special purpose tooling and concentration on a standardised limited range with, he added, the provision of 25 years' experience!"

Mr. Harris mentioned in his report, which was most thorough, that Paul Franke was very jovial, considered he was the grandfather, and was very proud of his employees and the entire business. While having lunch on the second day of his visit in the works canteen, he met the older Reinhold Heidecke, who was most uncooperative and resented the British occupation of his works. Capt. Cullum Brown, sensing an argument was about to break out, quickly pointed out that they all had their orders to carry out whether they liked it or not and life would be so much easier if they all accepted the position.

Mr. Harris spoke about other German factories he had visited where prisoners taken by the Germans were working as slaves. Had not the British allowed the workers to remain, and prisoners of war been allowed to return home, and how many residents of Braunschweig had been deported to England? Heidecke had to agree that now the war was over the British had been very kind and apologised for his earlier behaviour. Later Heidecke asked Mr. Harris if he could, on his return to England, arrange to send some English and American photographic journals so he could see what progress had been made over the last five years outside Germany, and in turn Heidecke gave Mr Harris a VAG, the last camera he had designed while working with Voigtländer.

Some weeks later, Heidecke was surprised when an army lorry arrived at the works and the driver asked for a signature for a large tea chest addressed "My Friend Reinhold Heidecke". Before accepting the chest Heidecke wanted it opened and true to his word Mr. Harris had sent the chest, filled with many photographic magazines and books. The army corporal and driver who had come from Hanover were promptly given lunch as Heidecke arranged for a new Rolleiflex to be boxed up, together with a letter of thanks for all the magazines that Mr. Harris had sent.

Just as the army lorry was departing, Paul Franke arrived to see his partner enthusiastically waving "auf Wiedersehen" to the soldiers. Heidecke took Franke to his office and showed him the contents of the chest. Franke looked at the black printed address label on the lid and remarked, "My friend – and you nearly set the watch dogs on him!". With enthusiasm Franke collected a number of magazines and was about to leave the office, recalled Paul's son Horst, who had come to see what all the fuss was about. At the bottom of the chest was a box which he opened revealing a letter from F.W. Harris addressed to his friend. It read, "As promised I have, to my wife's delight, sent you this pile of photographic magazines which was accumulating dust in our house. On leaving Germany I also paid a short visit to America and thought you might like this gift of an American Rolleiflex copy". The camera was a "Marvel-Flex" 6 x 6 T.L.R. with Wollensak f4.5 83mm lens made by Seroco. Sears Roebuck, the American department store group, unable to obtain supplies of Rollei cameras, had in 1941 started to make their own. Neither Paul Franke, his son Horst, nor Heidecke had seen or heard of this camera. Heidecke did not think much of the camera and together with the letter kept the camera in his office in case Mr. Harris returned, so he could quickly place the camera on the mantelpiece. Paul Franke was very surprised at this generosity of the British Government inspector and this gift removed any further animosity towards the British occupational army who were seen as friends doing their duty. Well done Mr. Harris. Horst Franke suggested that they send Mr. Harris one of their Rolleicords. Paul said, "Yes that's a good idea, son, we will send a Rolleiflex". Heidecke replied that he had already sent a letter of thanks with a Rolleiflex.

The first five years after World War II were not easy with war clouds briefly appearing and problems with the divided Berlin. With Rollei, however, it was business as usual and during 1949 new production lines were being prepared for the launch of a much expanded range of products. In 1949 the accumulated production of all Rollei cameras exceeded 1/2 million.

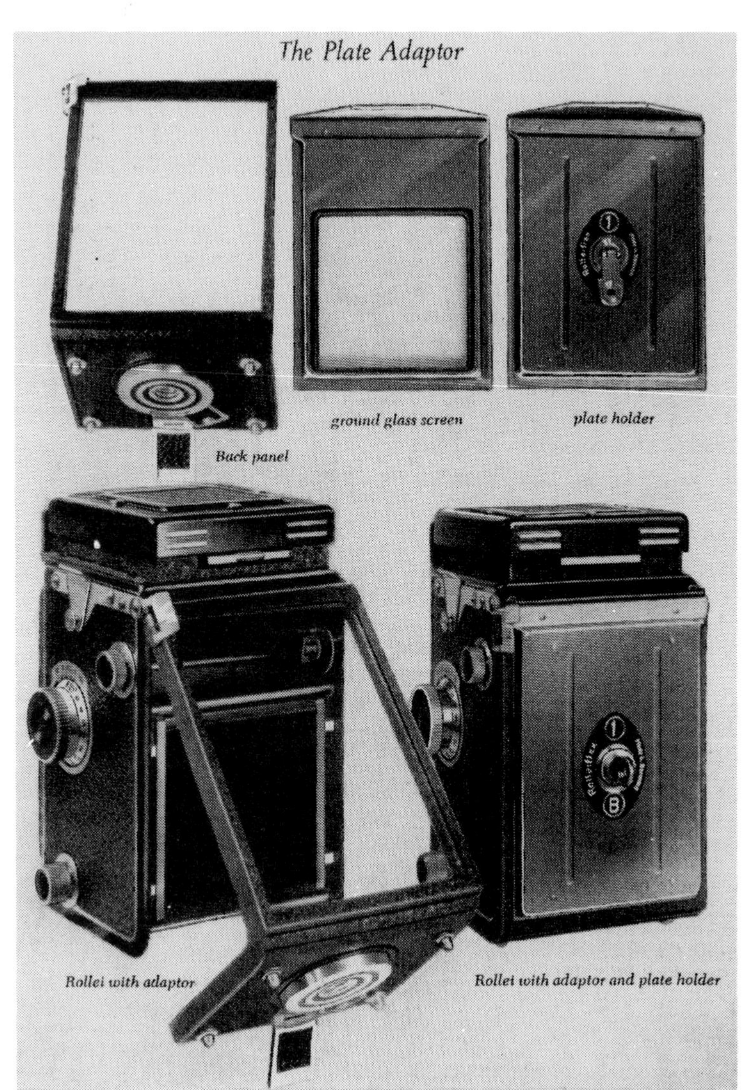

Most Rolleiflex and Rolleicord T.L.R. cameras accept the plate adaptor.

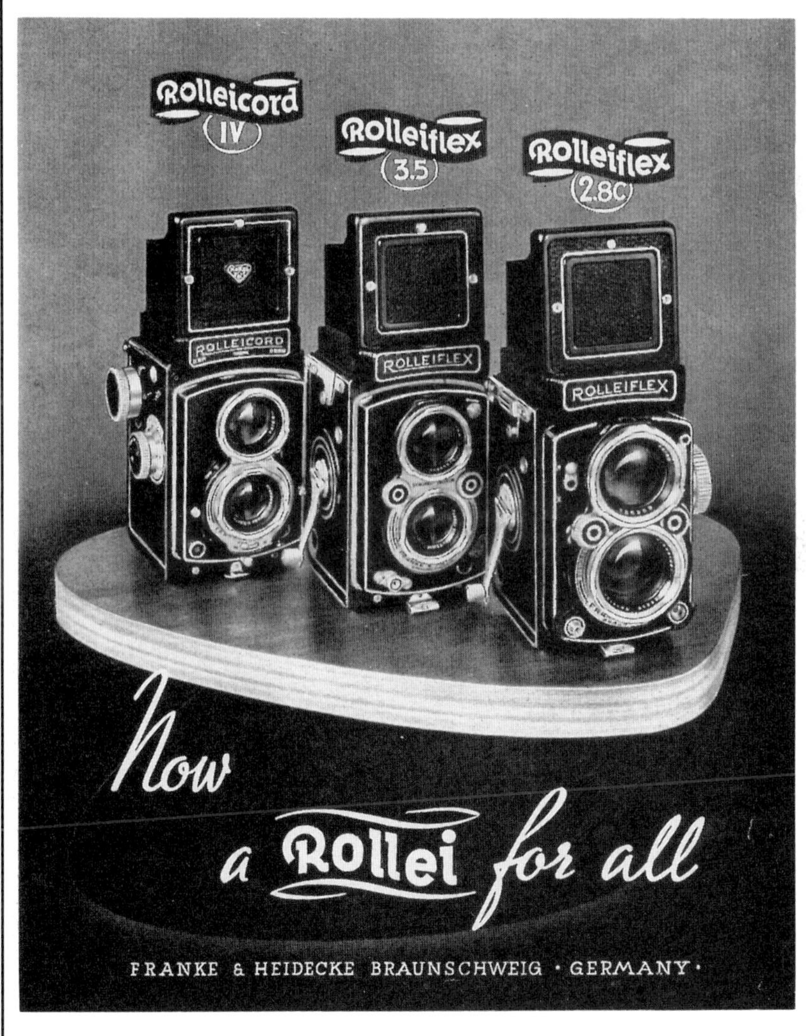
Rolleicord
IV
Rolleiflex
3.5
Rolleiflex
2.8C
ROLLEICORD
ROLLEIFLEX
ROLLEIFLEX
Now
a Rollei for all
FRANKE & HEIDECKE BRAUNSCHWEIG · GERMANY ·

INVENTORY OF PATENTS HELD BY FRANKE & HEIDECKE

Prepared by Capt. Cullum Brown, 21st Army Infantry Brigade.

German Patent Number	Title
527'348	Opening and release device for objects and a release lever.
519'590	Device for indicating the diaphragm and speed setting in cameras.
604'896	Film guide for roll-film cameras.
526'509	Photographic camera with carrier strap.
558'913	Roll-film guide device particularly for small cameras.
598'348	Camera with adjustable focussing device.
562'876	Container for photographic apparatus.
602'571	Roll-film camera.
614'967	Film tripping device for roll film cameras.
657'611	Roll-film camera back with film tachometer.
604'952	Photographic camera.
602'293	Roll-film camera.
614'425	Iris diaphragm.
604'847	Adjusting device for objectives.
616'158	Device for determining the exposure time by focussing device and diaphragm on photographic apparatus.
647'410	Roll-film camera with film tripping device.
614'807	Device for equalising parallel axes on photographic apparatus having a plurality of objective lenses.

621'420	Film tripping device for roll-film.
616'159	Photographic camera having a collapsible light protection passage adapted to screen a focussed image area.
614'848	Adjusting device for photographic camera objectives.
648'956	Roll-film camera.
625'306	Film tripping device for roll-film cameras.
641'855	Opening and release device for objective shutters.
662'617	Focussing light passage for photographic cameras.
614'340	Light passage for photographic camera focussing device.
698'482	Roll-film camera.
644'611	Camera with pre-indicator.
697'247	Film tripping device for roll-film cameras.
708'549	Film tripping device for roll-film cameras.
685'301	Film tripping device for roll-film cameras.
666'364	Photographic camera with carrier strap.
678'052	Device on photographic cameras for securing screening elements.
675'225	Device on photographic cameras for securing screening elements.
727'236	Film tripping device for roll-film cameras.
729'306	Film winder device for roll-film cameras.

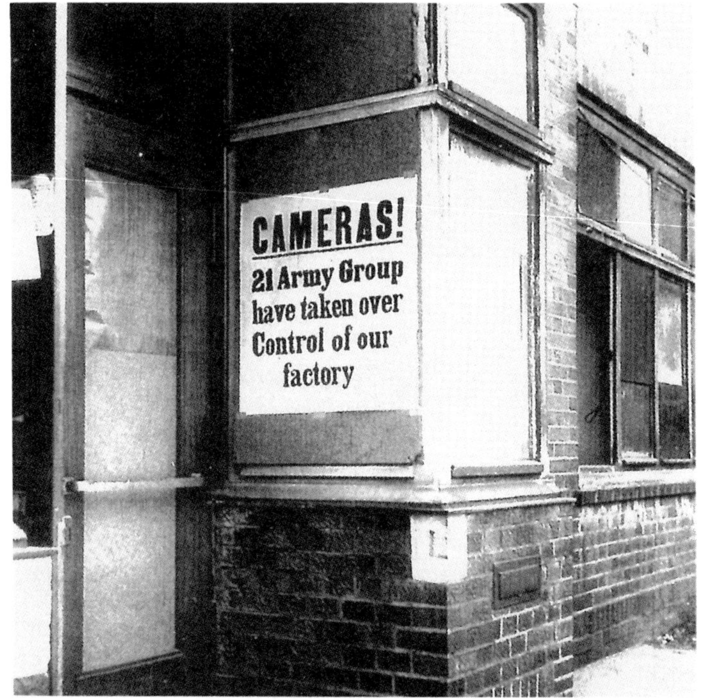

The British Army 21st Group were responsible for the changeover to peacetime activities. This included education and the Rollei factory, but at first this was not appreciated.

The old models were still selling extremely well due to the world shortage of Rollei cameras. The 1950s were considered the golden years of the T.L.R. with many manufacturers jumping on the bandwagon. How many different T.L.R. 6 x 6 cameras could be bought in the 1950s I do not know. Collating all known T.L.R.s took me many months. Somehow I managed to lose the list. The number exceeded a staggering 500 with 294 made in Japan alone. Nearly all the cameras had, I remember, an f3.5 lens with only 22 with the f2.8.

The Rollei 2.8A utilised the Tessar lens, which yielded soft pictures, possibly good for portraits but not for landscapes or pictures requiring enlargements. The camera was naturally the cause for great concern at Rollei as the opposition were producing f2.8 cameras in the 6 x 6 format. The first Hasselblad in 1948 used a Kodak Ektar f2.8 80mm lens. It had four elements, in a three component triplet with the same angle of view as the 80mm Planar.

Surprisingly, from 1953 Hasselblad changed to the 2.8 Tessar! Then in 1957 to the Planar. The Rolleiflex first introduced the Zeiss 2.8 Planar in 1952 with the 2.8C version.

Rollei bought their lenses from Carl Zeiss, who also manufactured cameras under the Zeiss Ikon label in Dresden. In 1934 they produced a T.L.R., not a threat to Rollei, who were well established by now, but in 1939 they marketed the Ikoflex III T.L.R. with a f2.8 Tessar. Production ceased with the onslaught of World War II. The f3.5 version of the Ikoflex continued after the war. This included some variations. It ceased production in 1960.

It was the surplus pre-war lenses that Rollei used in their first attempt at a f2.8 T.L.R. which unfortunately gave poor results. After recalling the ill-fated cameras for a lens change, the adverse publicity affected future sales. Fortunately the f3.5 Tessar lens was held in such high esteem that sales of the 3.5 Automat, either with Tessar or Schneider Xenar, continued and by 1954 750,000 Rolleis had been sold. Which model camera was the one to reach this number is not known. From a sales and marketing point of view, it depended on which country you lived in.

1954, Rolleiflex's Silver Jubilee Year, saw an international photographic competition organised, which helped many photographers to experiment. Many of the entries, although off-beat, did have the advantage of launching a number of young hopefuls into fashion photography, and helped to publicise Rolleiflex cameras. One interesting development from this competition was brought about by Hans Hass, who wanted to take underwater photographs. Hass and Heidecke jointly designed the now famous underwater housing whereby the Rolleiflex camera could photograph marine life at a depth of up to 300ft, which was not previously possible. So successful was the Rollei Marine housing that several types were made, including a prototype for the new grey baby 4 x 4 Rollei, but was never marketed.

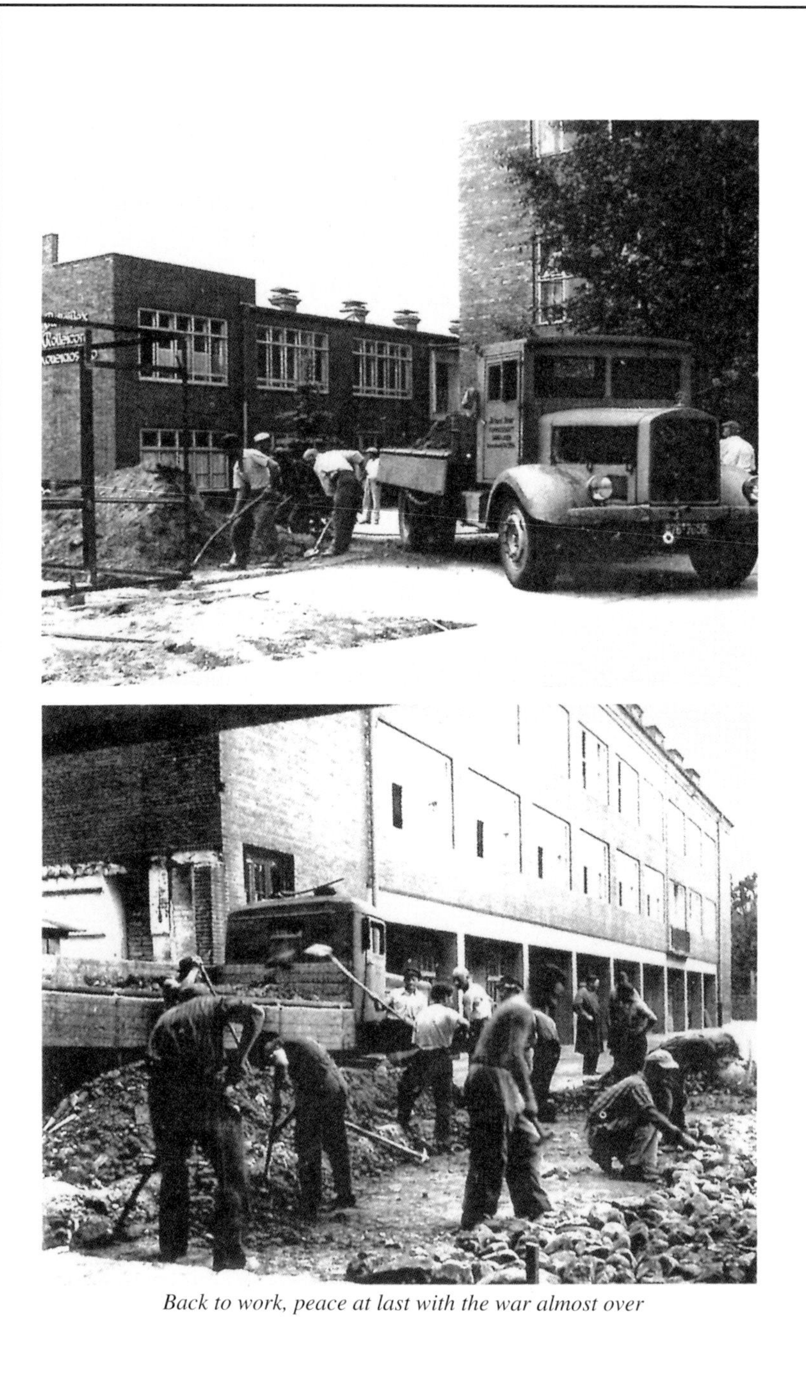

Back to work, peace at last with the war almost over

1956 saw the millionth Rollei sold, 600,000 of which had been constructed since 1940. The factory continued to expand and the number of employees now numbered 1600. By the following year a further 500 employees had been added to the payroll. Voigtländer, with 2600 employees, whose factory was also in Braunschweig, brought the total number of employees engaged in photographic manufacture to over 5000, to become the city's main employer. Today the photographic industry in Braunschweig employs around 1150, including 450 in Leica's projector factory. Audi Volkswagen Garages are now the largest employers, their main factory some 22km from Braunschweig employing over 52,000.

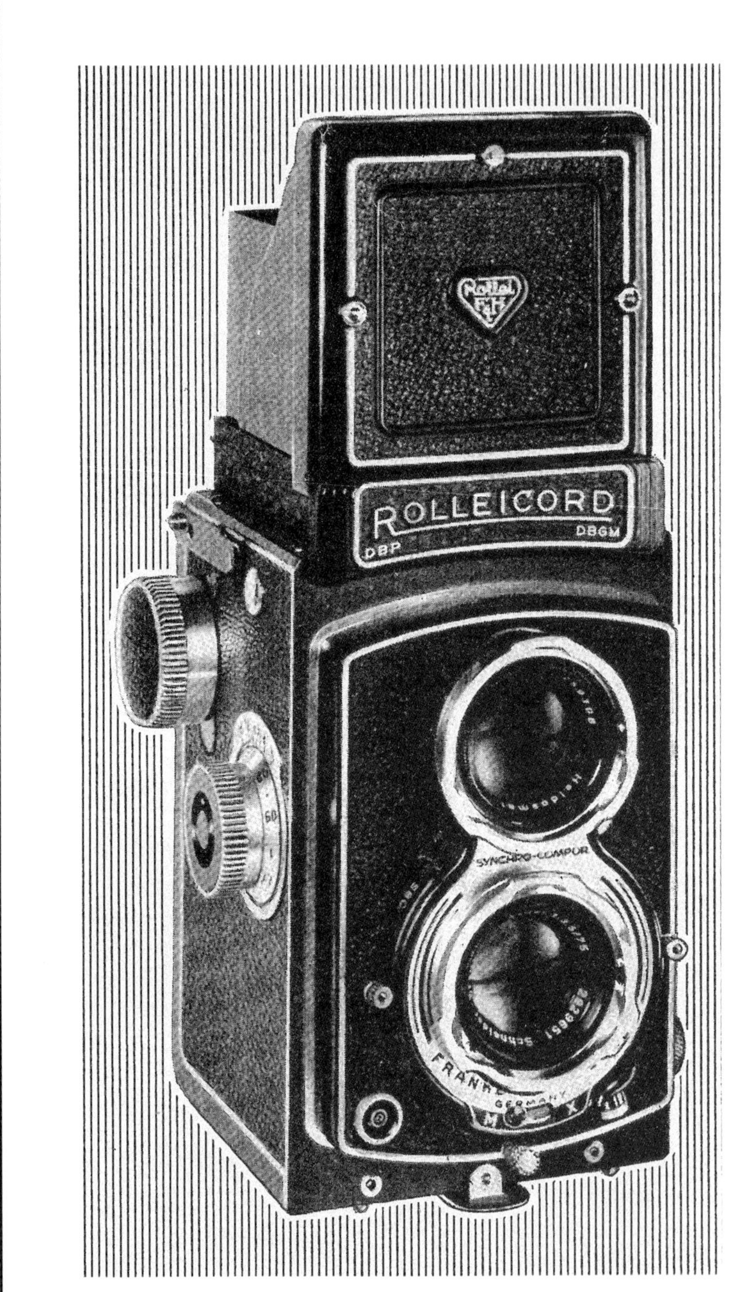

1953 Rolleicord IV with Schneider Xenar lens.

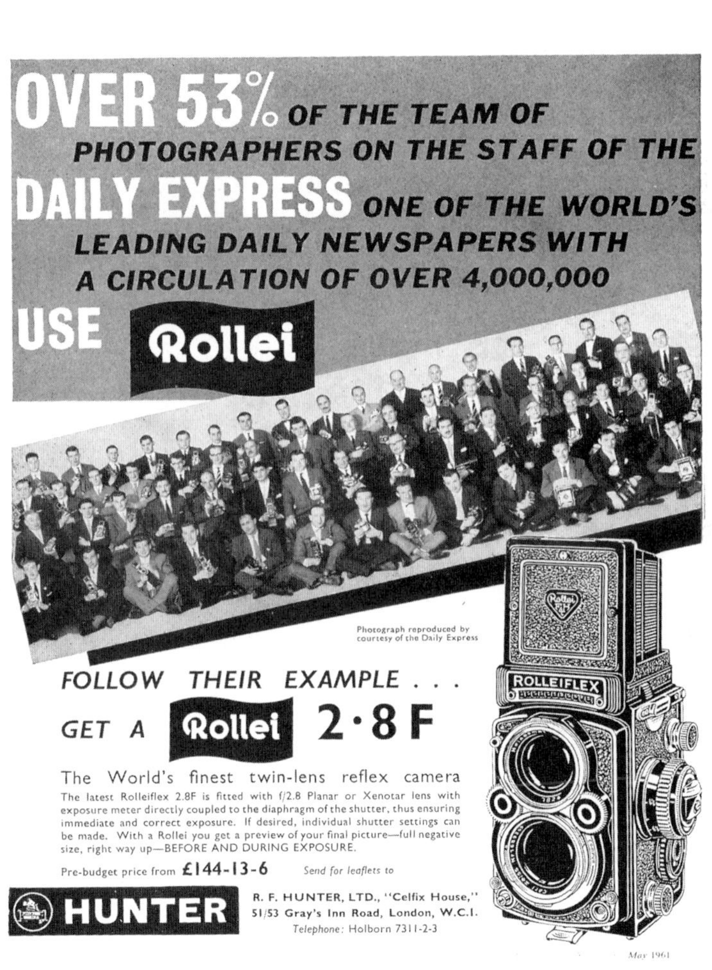
OVER 53% OF THE TEAM OF PHOTOGRAPHERS ON THE STAFF OF THE
DAILY EXPRESS ONE OF THE WORLD'S LEADING DAILY NEWSPAPERS WITH A CIRCULATION OF OVER 4,000,000
USE Rollei
Photograph reproduced by courtesy of the Daily Express
FOLLOW THEIR EXAMPLE . . .
GET A Rollei 2·8F
The World's finest twin-lens reflex camera
The latest Rolleiflex 2.8F is fitted with f/2.8 Planar or Xenotar lens with exposure meter directly coupled to the diaphragm of the shutter, thus ensuring immediate and correct exposure. If desired, individual shutter settings can be made. With a Rollei you get a preview of your final picture—full negative size, right way up—BEFORE AND DURING EXPOSURE.
Pre-budget price from £144-13-6
Send for leaflets to
HUNTER
R. F. HUNTER, LTD., "Celfix House,"
51/53 Gray's Inn Road, London, W.C.1.
Telephone: Holborn 7311-2-3
ROLLEIFLEX
May 1961

men who make ROLLEI . . .

The men who make Rollei never "make do." They make *sure*. Every Rollei part, however small, has to be just right. It even has to *feel* right. The most modern machines in the world produce the parts for the Rollei, and many of the more intricate machines are made by the craftsmen inside the factory to their own exacting requirements. Science is called in to test them. But it's the 30 years of concentrated craftsmanship in the hands of the men that really *makes* a Rollei. To such hands precision is a habit; perfection is second nature. Under such hands Rollei comes almost alive . . . every one an ideal picture-making instrument. Photography owes a lot to Rollei—and to the craftsmen who build them.

Here is a special machine built to ensure the most exact focus setting at infinity.

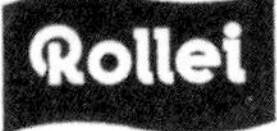

THE CAMERA WITH CRAFTSMAN-BUILT RELIABILITY

Illustrated is the Rolleicord Va, the wonderful "ALL PURPOSE" camera, with Synchro Compur Shutter and Schneider f/3.5 Xenar lens. With the use of the exposure counter assemblies five different negative sizes can be obtained, a great advantage when taking colour. **£48.13.0**

Exposure counter assemblies (4×4 and 4×5.5cm) (24×36mm and Bantam). **£3.6.10** each

E.R. case **£4.16.6.**

FULL LITERATURE ON ROLLEI CAMERAS FROM YOUR DEALER OR 3d. IN STAMPS FROM SOLE IMPORTERS:—

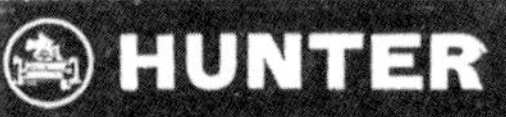

R. F. HUNTER LTD.

CELFIX HOUSE, 51-53, GRAY'S INN ROAD, LONDON, W.C.1.
Tel. Holborn 7311-2-3.

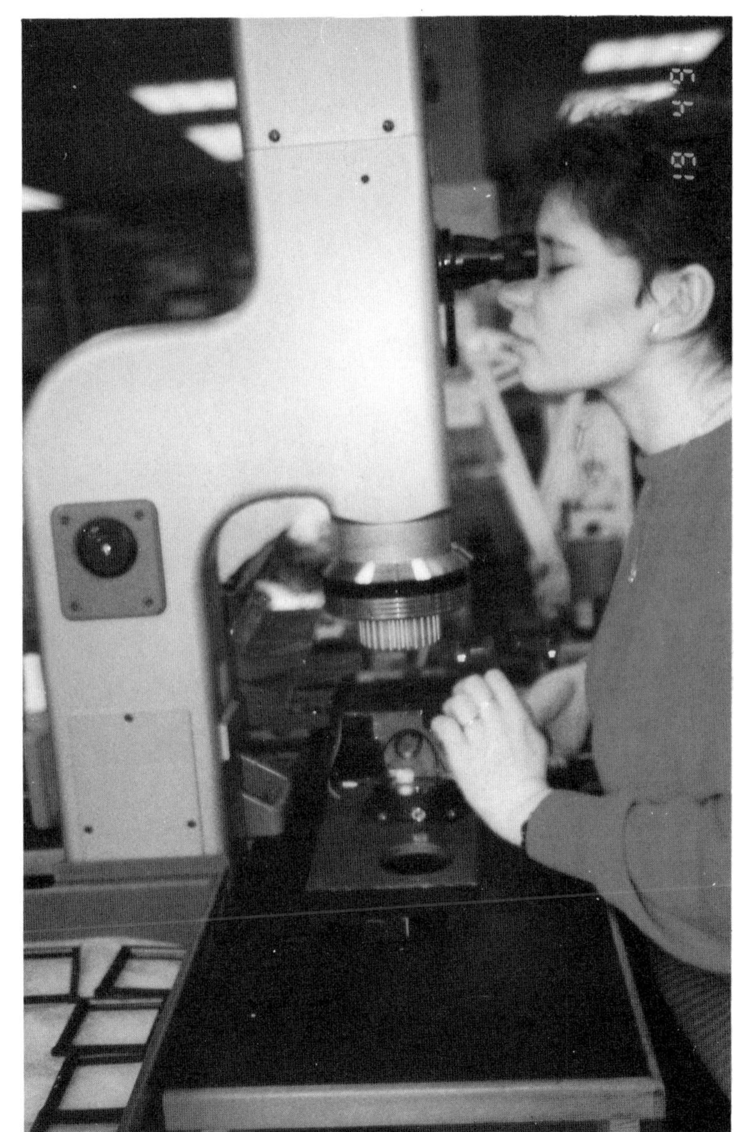

Today many women have taken over the work of their male colleagues within the factory

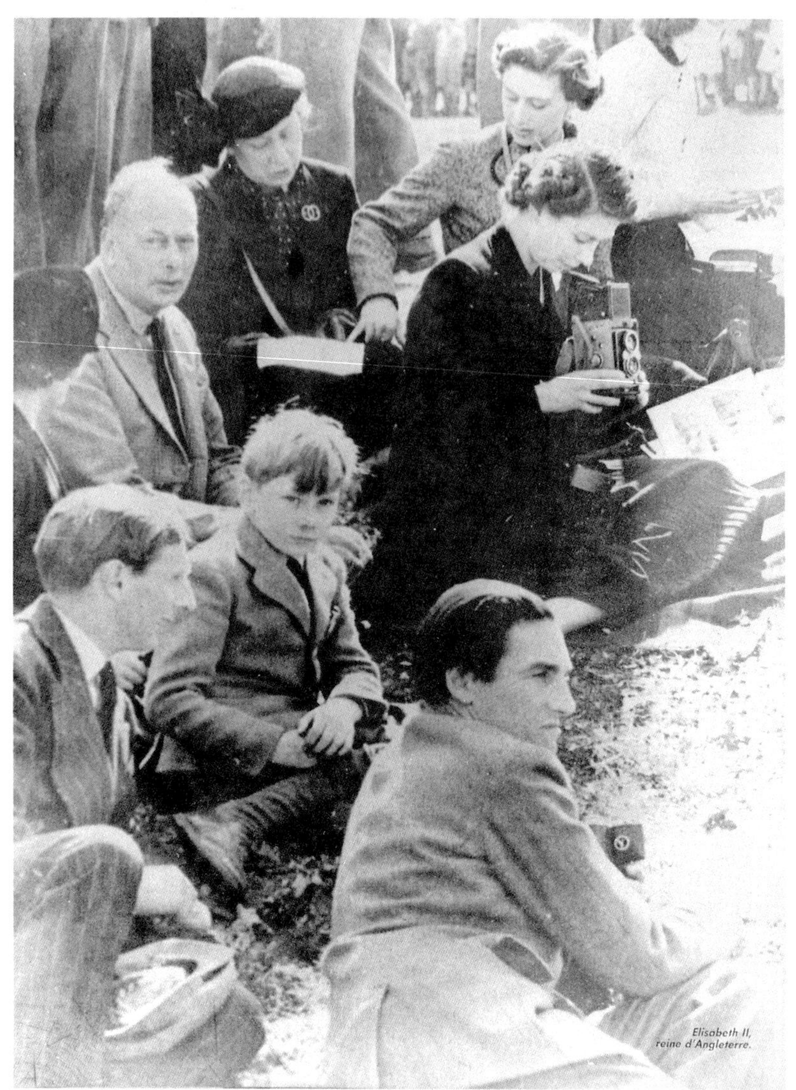

Queen Elizabeth II with Cecil Beaton's Rolleiflex Automat.

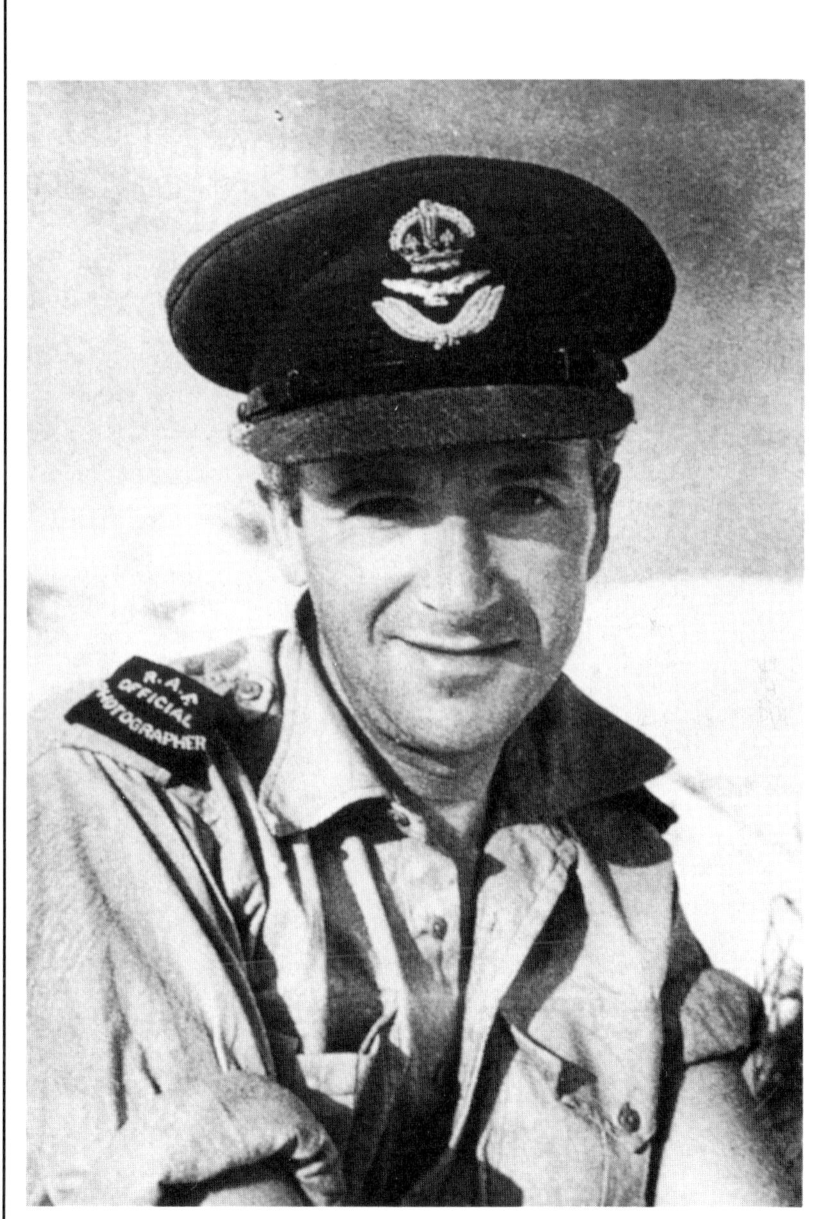

Cecil Beaton in the R.A.F.

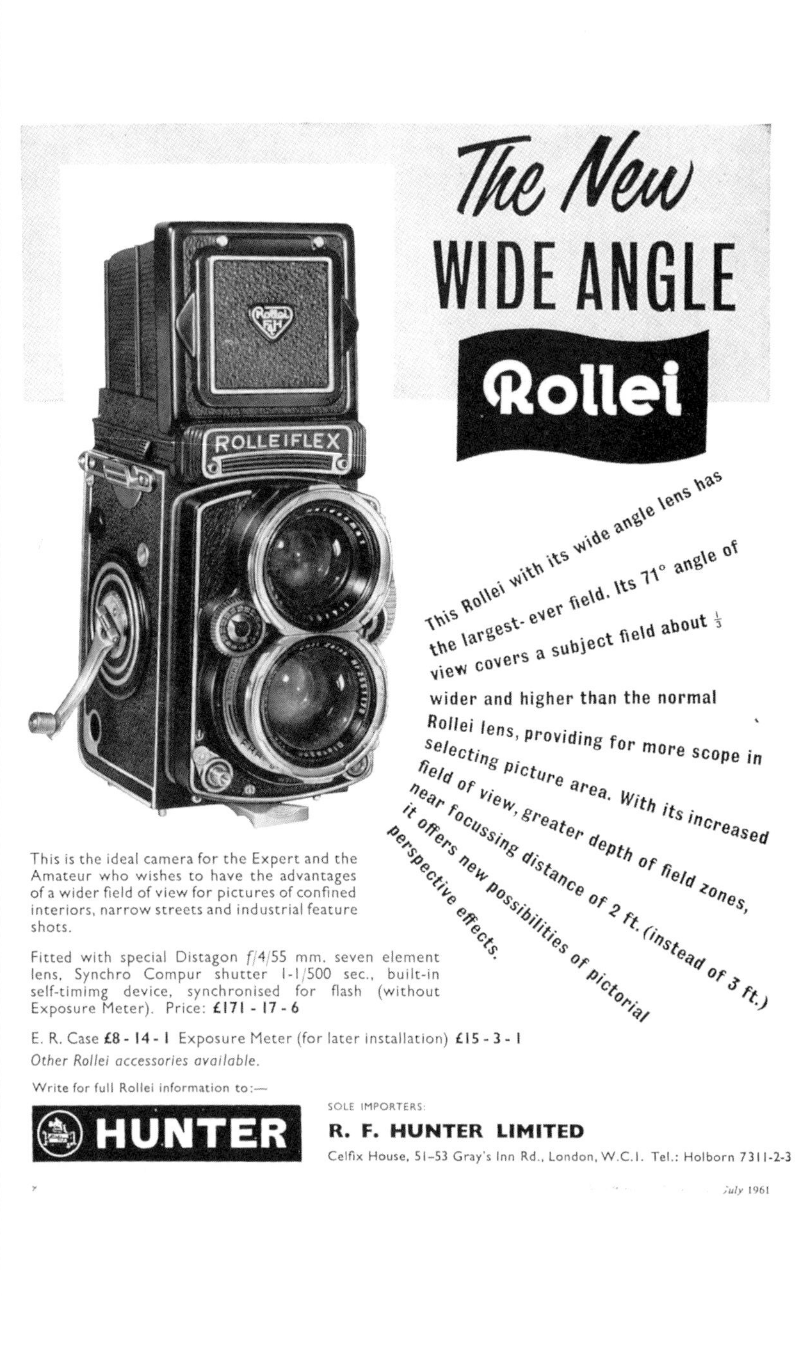
The New
WIDE ANGLE
Rollei
ROLLEIFLEX
This Rollei with its wide angle lens has the largest-ever field. Its 71° angle of view covers a subject field about 1/3 wider and higher than the normal Rollei lens, providing for more scope in selecting picture area. With its increased field of view, greater depth of field zones, near focussing distance of 2 ft. (instead of 3 ft.) it offers new possibilities of pictorial perspective effects.
This is the ideal camera for the Expert and the Amateur who wishes to have the advantages of a wider field of view for pictures of confined interiors, narrow streets and industrial feature shots.
Fitted with special Distagon f/4/55 mm. seven element lens, Synchro Compur shutter 1-1/500 sec., built-in self-timimg device, synchronised for flash (without Exposure Meter). Price: £171 - 17 - 6
E. R. Case £8 - 14 - 1 Exposure Meter (for later installation) £15 - 3 - 1
Other Rollei accessories available.
Write for full Rollei information to:—
HUNTER
SOLE IMPORTERS:
R. F. HUNTER LIMITED
Celfix House, 51–53 Gray's Inn Rd., London, W.C.1. Tel.: Holborn 7311-2-3
July 1961

CHAPTER 9

ROLLEI T

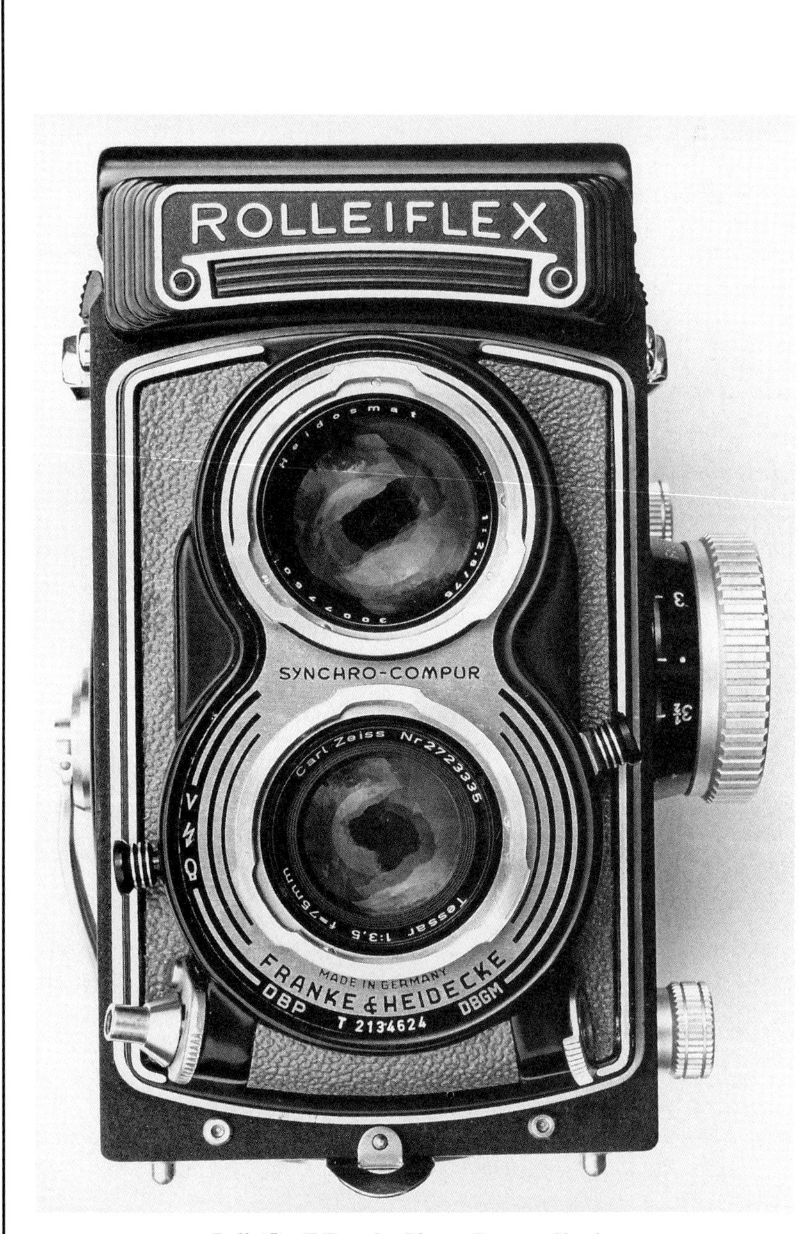

Rolleiflex T Type I   Photo: Terence Sheehy

ROLLEI T

Of all the Rollei T.L.R. cameras, the T is today the camera most often still being used by professional photographers. To own this budget-priced camera was to the budding amateur-cum-weekend-wedding photographer the "visiting card". The mothers of most brides had heard that the Queen had a Rolleiflex, as did Grace Kelly, Cecil Beaton, Norman Parkinson, Terence Donovan, David Bailey, Lord Snowdon and Lord Lichfield. Whether the Rolleiflex was a 2.8F, a 3.5F or 6008 did not matter. Rolleiflexes could be seen the world over at weddings. In 1992 the struggling semi-pro could buy a T for around £250. Today, the smart vendor would ask £300 or more for a black T with meter. Why was the T so popular? Price alone would not have ensured this popularity.

The T has become another classic Rolleiflex from which virtually all other cameras of this type are derived, with a focussing screen that always shows the full size picture upright as it will appear on the negative, again using the popular 120 size film. Unfortunately a 220 size could not be constructed due to limitations of space within the camera. After all, this was a budget camera costing £75.85 in 1960 with meter, against the 3.5F at £110 again with meter. Was the additional cost worth the additional de luxe features found on the 3.5F? Way back in 1958, when the Rollei T first appeared, the average male office worker was earning around £12 a week. After paying his rent, food etc. he may well have had a surplus of £1 per week, so the saving would be considerable. In 1958 a weekly photographic journal cost 5p. Today the same journal costs £1.20. The same increase on the Rollei T would equate to £2,086. Interesting, as today's Rollei 2.8GX costs £1,250 and the specification is greatly improved.

The T, for Tessar, was stripped of a number of features, but still retained outstanding German precision workmanship to keep its accuracy over many years. The T accepted the bayonet I filters for the four-element Zeiss Tessar taking lenses, whereas the 3.5F has the five- or six-element Planar and takes bayonet II filters. Otherwise the two cameras are similar in so far as they both use 120 film, take a range of accessories and carry the name "Rolleiflex". How did the Rollei come about? The simple answer is competition. With so many T.L.R.s flooding the market at a cheaper price than the Rollei product, something had to be done. Future sales of T.L.R. had peaked with many amateurs switching to 35mm S.L.R. cameras. Furthermore it was not possible to reduce the high labour content of the 3.5E introduced in 1956. At a directors' meeting they discussed a survey on all the available T.L.R. cameras that could be considered serious competition in the U.K. market, where information was readily available. The survey revealed 31 different models available from just one dealer's shop, with an average selling price of £57. The research

Rolleicord Vb now £62,* 100% Rollei quality, 20% price reduction!

It's a fact! the regular price of the Rollei Vb is down £15. Now you can own a TLR that's hand built made by Rollei—for only £62/6/6. All the advantages of the TLR—better colour, less enlarging, picture-size 2¼in. square viewing—plus all the quality and reliability of Rollei! Schneider Xenar f/3.5 4-element taking lens, Synchro-Compur X synchronised shutter, 1–1/500 sec. with B and self-timer. Bright Rollei clear split-image focusing screen. Detachable focusing hood—so you can use it at eye level with Rollei Pentaprism . . . and if you want to shoot on 35 mm. as well you can do it with a Rolleikin attachment.

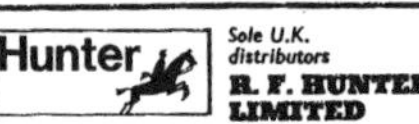

Sole U.K. distributors
R. F. HUNTER LIMITED
51/53 Gray's Inn Rd., London, W.C.1
Tel: HOL 7311/2/3, HOL 8866/7/8

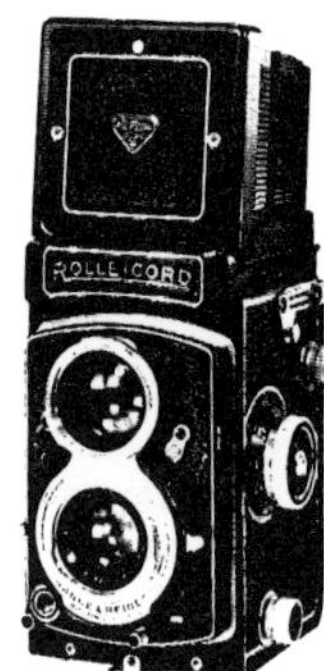

Rolleicord Vb is not only an excellent camera—beside giving you years of good photography it will maintain a high resale or trade-in value—it's a good investment too! Go to a Rollei authorised dealer—a man who really knows his Rolleis—and see a Rolleicord Vb. A wonderful photographic investment at £62/6/6.

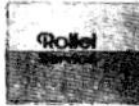

For expert advice and information visit the authorised Rollei dealer who displays this sign.

* Any Rollei Authorised Dealer will arrange extended credit and fair part-exchange prices on your old camera.

and design team were requested to find a more economic camera than the Rolleicord which, although an extremely good camera, was only bought by amateurs who were now changing to 35mm. Incidentally, the selling price of the Rolleicord at £48.50 was well below the average T.L.R. and, although very popular at this price, did not make a large contribution to the firm's bottom line (profits).

1957 found annual sales continuing to rise. A further 100 employees were recruited. The directors considered their position. After all, the public were buying all the cameras they could construct. The millionth Rollei had been sold the previous year with the 2.8D available with either Zeiss Planar or Schneider Xenotar lens. Why launch a budget Rolleiflex when we are selling all the cameras we can construct, reasoned the bank's representative who often attended directors' meetings. Another Rolleicord was considered. Finally, in blizzard conditions, at a February directors' meeting nothing was agreed except a cosmetic change for the Rolleicord V and the R & D agreed to look into ways of reducing the production costs of the Cord V, while providing cosmetic changes to existing models.

In April 1957 the Rolleicord Va went on sale. Employees now totalled over 2000. A young university undergraduate by the name of Theodore Uhl had started the previous September. He had studied commercial plastics for automobile engines. Deciding not to join Volkswagen, also in Braunschweig, he started at Rollei. One of his ideas was incorporating plastic parts within the Rolleicord Va, well hidden from prying eyes. The following year two friends, also from university, studying P.T.F.E. and related plastics, joined Theodore in the research and design section of Rollei. Their expertise in the use of modern materials was brought to the attention of the elderly Reinhold Heidecke, who always wanted to know what was happening. The graduates pointed out that by using methods and materials they had acquired at university they could show considerable savings on the current 3.5E Rolleiflex.

The full directors' meeting held after the summer recess had to confirm the Rollei booking for the Photokina exhibition in October the following year, and they had to make a decision which products would be shown. So began the design for the budget Rollei T, for Theodore, as the camera was quickly nicknamed. This was very quickly changed when the management realised that T did not stand for Tessar. So Theodore, for reasons unknown, departed from Rollei. The main savings from the production point of view were the use of levers to control shutter speed and aperture instead of wheels as on the Rolleicord, and using plastic knobs which later reverted to metal on the Mark II version. The new camera would use grey leather with black trim and would therefore be easily identified and not mistaken for the more expensive black brother the 3.5F. Another departure, which may partly account for the camera's popularity today, was the feature whereby multiple picture sizes could be taken with the aid of an automatic switchable counter for 12 size 6 x 6cm or 16 size 4x4 and 4 x 6cm exposures. At first 35mm Rolleikin adapters could not be used, but this was soon rectified.

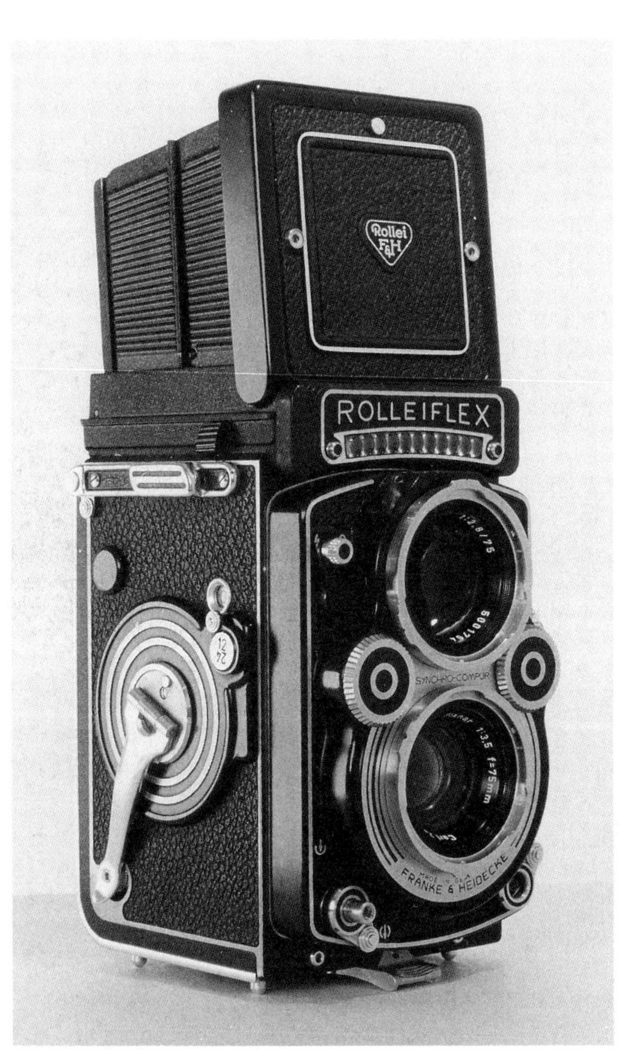

Possibly the most favoured Rolleiflex; the 3.5F with 120/220 facility. Camera No.2838261. Photo: John G. Banks L.R.P.S.

It was the T that aroused the most interest at Photokina. The other camera, the new 3.5F with coupled exposure meter, looked like the previous exhibition's 3.5E. I remember working on the stand demonstrating the range of Rollei products and was surprised at the large amount of accolades the grey T received, until someone asked whether the camera actually took good pictures, as his 2.8A with Tessar lens seemed to take pictures out of focus. I quickly suggested that perhaps the viewfinder magnifier glass should be changed to suit his eyesight. Surprise, surprise when I received a letter from Malcolm Thomson thanking me for my advice. I mention this as, with age creeping up on many, an eyesight correction lens can be obtained cheaply for most cameras, including nearly all Rollei cameras, and exchanged for the magnifier glass.

The Rollei is probably the only post-war camera that has been incorrectly documented. Briefly, production on the T started on the 12th August 1958. Fortunately for Rollei, employees in those days were only entitled to two weeks holiday, whereas today the norm is four weeks. The first production batch of 1000 cameras was scheduled to be completed in two weeks, then the next month 2000 cameras. By the 4th November, 1000 cameras were ready for dispatch and every other week a further 1000 cameras went into boxes ready for the Christmas trade. By the end of the year 13,000 cameras had either left the factory or were waiting for final assembly.

1959 was a good year, with 26,000 cameras coming off the production line with the optional black T available from No.2136000. In 1960 with a carry forward of unsold stocks, output was reduced to 13,000 and the following year increased to 16,000. By 11th November 1966, when the camera was updated, a total of 99,000 cameras had been constructed, an average of 14,143 over the previous seven years. The second variant was fitted with the Synchro-Compur X shutter. The arms, now metal, on the speed and aperture levers had replaced the black plastic, and most of the Mk II versions were black. Identifying the earlier Mk I is quite simple, with the logo under the taking lens "Franke & Heidecke". However, "Synchro-Compur" between the lens may not be so easily remembered, similarly the "Synchro-Compur X" on the Mk II, whereas the "Rollei-Werke" logo under the taking lens should not prove difficult.

The Mk II version from Nos. 22000000 commenced on 11th September 1966 until 2228999 was reached in July 1968. Various numbers, 2242000/2249999, 2310000/2314999, were allocated to cameras constructed in 1968/70, making a total of 22,000 Mk II Rollei T. There was a possible order for the British Ministry of Defence for 5000 cameras, with a stipulation that the sync lead was able to withstand misuse and not drop out as in the Rolleicord. Although the Rollei T was out of production this was the most suitable camera which met the specification required. An order was eventually placed for 5000 cameras for delivery during late 1971 at the rate of 500 in the first year, 1500 in the second year and 1000 each in the third and fourth years. "Rollei-Werke Franke & Heidecke", Rollei's official name at the time, was

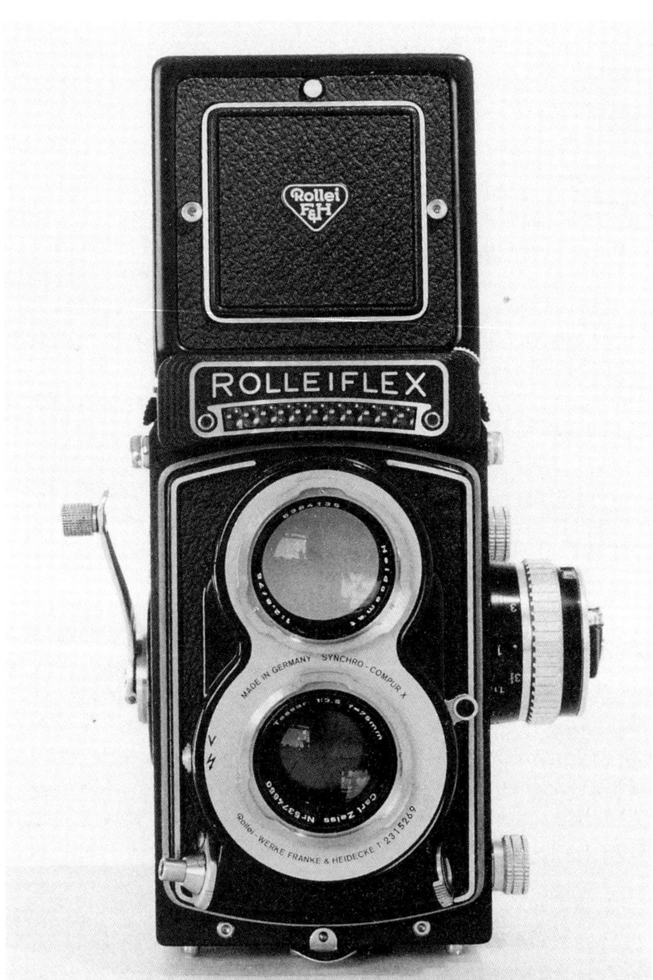

Rolleiflex T Type III with white face front from the collection of John G. Banks

used as the logo beneath the taking lens and between the lens "Made in Germany-Synchro-Compur X".

This lens panel is an immediate aid to recognition, as no longer could a camera be stolen or misappropriated and the number changed as the lens panel could not be removed or altered. Thus was born the "White Faced" lens panel not available on any other Rollei camera at that time, but which can be found on the last Rolleicord Vb and Rolleiflex 3.5F and 2.8F cameras of 1980/82. The same logo was also to be found on the gold Aurum of 1983 and the 1986 Platin edition.

Such an order, fortunate as it was, brought a few problems. Rollei could only just find 3500 Tessar lenses. Further supplies were not available. To overcome the problem the Ministry of Defence agreed that Schneider Xenar, as used in the Rolleicord V already bought by the Ministry of Defence, could be substituted. So the Rolleiflex X, was born. But wait a minute, the 1950 Rollei was an X, so the Xenar became the T Mk III version. Altogether 6000 cameras were constructed with approximately 2500 with Xenar lenses. Their numbers range from 2315000 (1971 Sept) to T231999 (1975 June), giving a final production of 126,000 T cameras. In 1987 the Ministry of Defence recalled over 2000 of these cameras which went to auction. Many dealers, never having seen such a camera, bid high prices of around £160 each for the Xenar version with the Tessar auction price around £88, the original cost paid by the British Ministry of Defence. In 1988 shops were advertising Xenar Mk III Rollei at £230. Today the mint version would fetch over £350.

The Ministry of Defence cameras were distributed throughout the British armed forces. Most went to the Royal Navy and some were engraved above the Rolleiflex nameplate, like the example in the Jersey Photographic Museum "MoD 763/127 R.N.". On camera No. T 2316630, which was part of the consignment constructed in 1972, and which was allocated to the Royal Navy Advanced School of Photography, H.M.S. Excellent, Portsmouth, the Ministry of Defence engraved number shows contract No.763 and date of draw-off. The life span of the camera before disposal was 15 years. How many cameras today would last this length of time in everyday school use? The replacement camera selected was an S.L.R., also using Carl Zeiss lenses made in Germany. The body, made outside the E.E.C., has proved troublesome, needing considerable servicing through the short life of some gear wheels, unlike the Rolleiflex T which required mimimal servicing and showed little signs of wear. Such are today's cameras, made to sell, to scrap and to replace. Gone, I am afraid, are the days when we all lovingly admired our new Rolleiflex or Leica and contentedly savoured the excellent workmanship. So, the last Rolleiflex T, the budget-priced camera, first thought of by Theodore Uhl, was completed on the 12th May 1976.

The last batch of Rollei T cameras, some 300, ended with number 2,320,300 which had Heidosmat f2.8 75mm viewing lens No. 4115358 and a Schneider Xenar f3.5 75mm taking lens No. 11863983 in a Synchro-Compur

X shutter and factory-fitted exposure meter. The other Rollei Ts in this last batch purchased by the British Ministry of Defence were similarly equipped.

After the termination of the Rollei T.L.R. T in 1976 there remained the 2.8F that continued until 1976, with the special 2.8F Aurum in 1981 with a production of 1250 and a further 1500 in 1983, followed by the 2.8F Platin in 1986, the Aurum Platin in 1989 with a small production run of 99.

1976 saw the last of the Rollei T and the Rolleicord Vb T.L.R. budget-priced cameras; the 3.5F also went out of production leaving the 2.8F that was available with either a Zeiss Planar lens or the Schneider Xenotar. In 1987 the 2.8GX went into production and is still being manufactured in modest numbers of around 2000 units per annum.

Today's firm of Rollei Fototechnic is very much alive, expanding into new and exciting technology with an assured future led by Wolfgang Sass who has inherited the qualities of both Paul Franke and Reinhold Heidecke. Long may the name of Rollei continue to delight both the amateur and professional photographers throughout the world.

ROLLEIFLEX T

BAYONET SIZE I

The finest twin-lens reflex in its price class, the Rolleiflex T is designed to give the economy-minded photographer a true Rolleiflex at a modest price. A multi-format camera, the Rolleiflex T offers 12 standard 2¼x2¼ pictures or optional use of the 16 Exposure Mask Set. This permits taking 16 1⅝"x2⅛" pictures or 16 1⅝"x1⅝" Super Slide Size pictures on No. 120 film—all with full parallax correction and automatic counting.

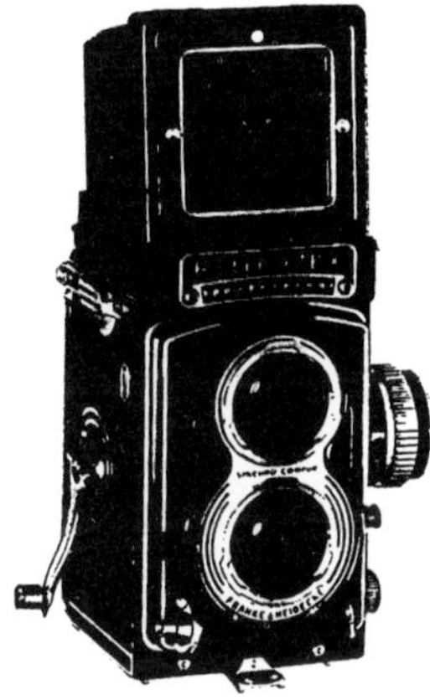

ROLLEIFLEX T with Exposure Meter Kit T (accessory) installed. Bayonet Size I

- Brilliant Rolleiclear focusing screen with rangefinder wedge
- Detachable flat-folding focusing hood with interchangeable 2.5x top magnifier
- Single-lever adjustment of EV and stop/speed selection
- Rapid-action crank transports film, cocks shutter and advances film counter
- Optional use of Rolleikin 2 for 35mm film (above camera No. 2,151,000)
- Exposure counter automatically switches from 12 to 16 when 16 Exposure Mask is inserted
- Pre-wired for owner-installation of dual-range Exposure Meter Kit T, or use with Rolleilux (combination lens hood and exposure meter attached to taking lens bayonet)
- Synchro-Compur MXV shutter; B, 1 to 1/500 sec.
- Zeiss Tessar f/3.5 75mm lens of improved construction and performance

ADDITIONAL SPECIFICATIONS

f/2.8 Heidosmat viewing lens; delayed-action timer; time indications up to 60 sec.; automatic prevention of double exposure; full-field magnifier, eye-level sports finder; depth-of-field indicator; film speed reminder dial; wt. approx. 36 oz.

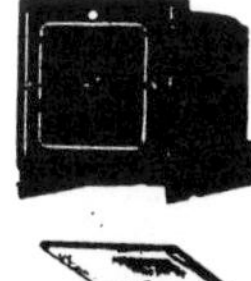

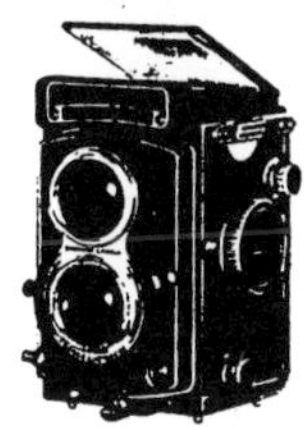

REMOVABLE FOCUSING HOOD
HINGED FOCUSING SCREEN FRAME

Cat. No.		**ROLLEIFLEX T**
1012	With Tessar f/3.5 75mm lens, less meter. Includes lens cap, carrying strap and cable release .... 1-2 ...	**$190.30**
	3-6 ...	**186.84**
	over 6 ...	**181.65**
1013	Case, deluxe Eveready with detachable front	**$ 20.16**
1503	Exposure Meter Kit T—dual range; owner installed	**$ 28.96**
1533	16 Exposure Mask Set, for 16 1⅝"x2⅛" or Super Slide exposures on No. 120 film. Including all masks	**$ 6.24**

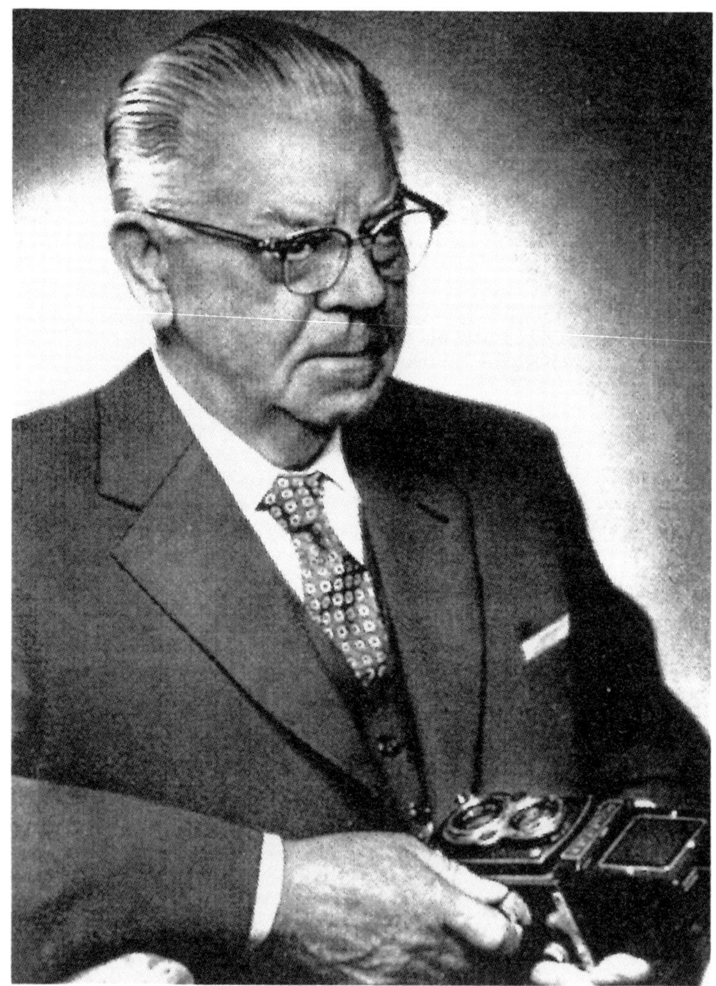

Reinhold Heidecke with the Rolleiflex Automat

CHAPTER 10

ROLLEI LENSES

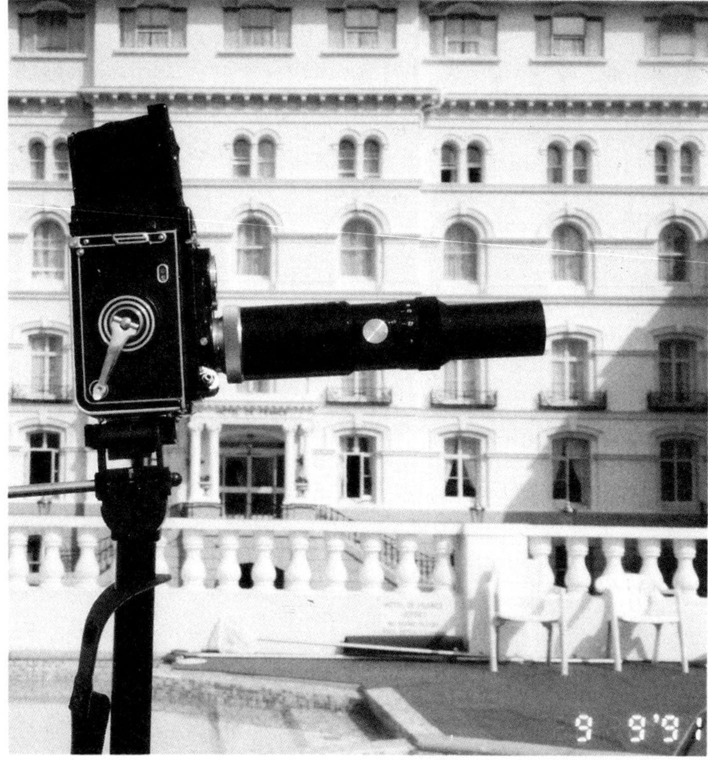

Rollei T with Carl Zeiss Magnar 4X photographed with Rollei A/F Prego outside The Hotel De France, Jersey home of Club Rollei and the Jersey Photographic Museum

ROLLEI LENSES

From the very beginning Reinhold Heidecke used Carl Zeiss lenses and shutters. Today, Carl Zeiss is located in north-east and western Germany, and once was joined together as one firm. Heidecke's choice in selecting Carl Zeiss lenses was very fortunate as Zeiss lenses are still available worldwide and therefore help in the marketing of Rollei cameras where brand loyalty can mean so much.

After World War II, with the uncertainty of obtaining Zeiss lenses, Rollei looked for an alternative lens supplier within West Germany. From October 1945 the first lenses were received from Jos. Schneider works at Bad Kreuznach, West Germany. Their Xenar first appeared in the automatic Rolleiflex, starting at serial number 999,999 in 1945. This lens was almost identical in design to the Zeiss Tessar, both with four elements. The father of this type of lens was the Cooke Triplet lens designed in 1893 by Dennis Taylor, of Taylor & Hobson fame.

The best-known and respected lens was the Tessar, known truly throughout the world. The lens gave sharp results, capable of large enlargements. Today, the Tessar has been replaced by the Zeiss Planar or Schneider Xenotar. As Grandpa used a Zeiss, many consider the Zeiss the superior product. In fact the Xenotar is equally good and even under a microscope it is difficult to say with any certainty which delivers the best results. Usually the Schneider T.L.R. is harder to sell and the collectors certainly prefer and pay a considerable premium for those cameras with Zeiss lenses. Both companies have strict quality control so a dud lens should be most unlikely.

Rollei enthusiasts will be totally familiar with Carl Zeiss Jena as producers of the finest camera lenses in the world; even Nikon's early pre-war cameras were fitted with Carl Zeiss lenses. They have often been copied the world over, but never to the exacting tolerances of their original concept, by optical manufacturers from the Far East, the European countries and the USSR. Carl Zeiss is also known throughout the world as the leading manufacturers of high quality research microscopes. Indeed, from the very beginning in 1846, when Carl Zeiss made his very first microscope, this important aspect of the Carl Zeiss origin of optical construction was to continue to the present time with the continued manufacture of the world's best range of optical microscopes now produced by the two Zeiss foundations: Carl Zeiss West Germany and Carl Zeiss Jena. They are two totally separate companies, in fact "Foundations", although disputed many times in the courts of the western world, split by the Second World War, now with no connection except their pre-1945 joint pedigree. This is a great pity for Europe and the world, as one Zeiss would have combined effort to compete against the Orient with such a great force with its many fine optical products.

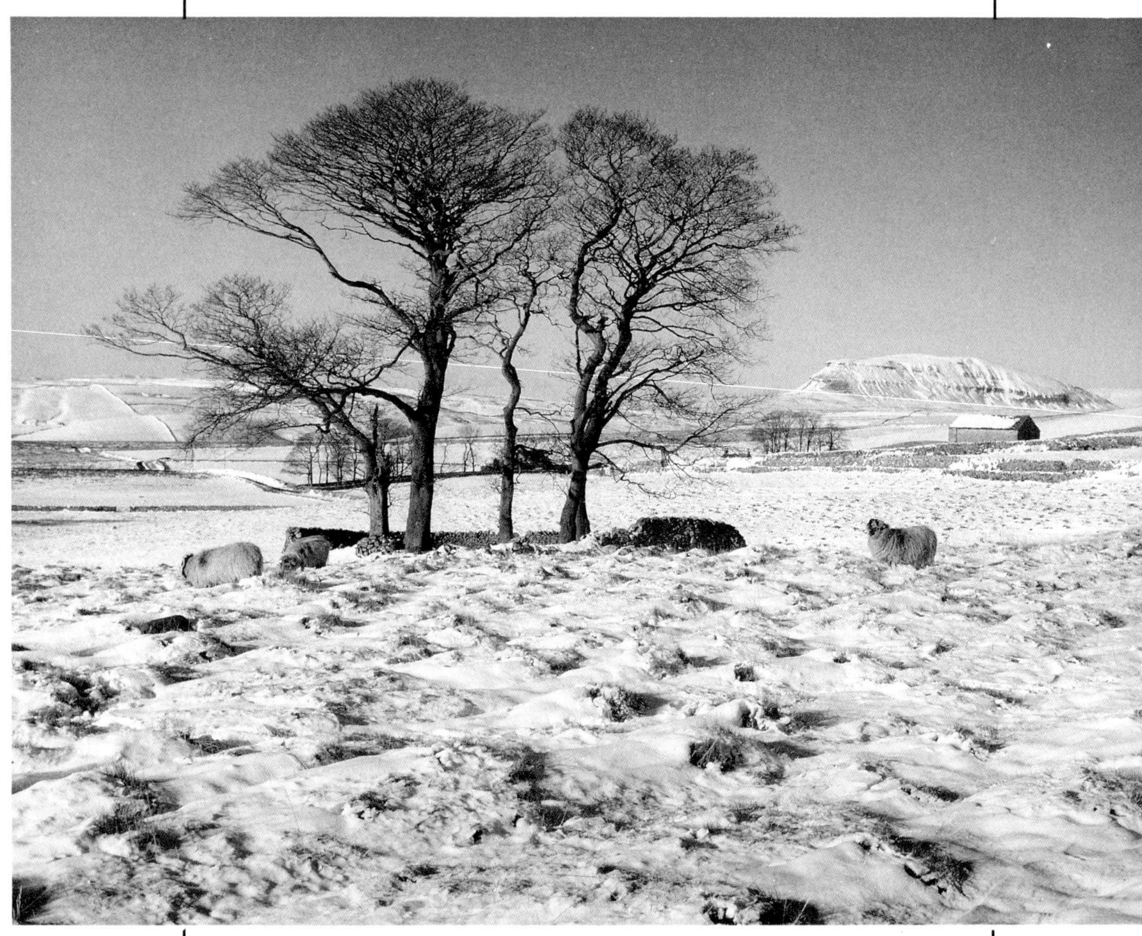

The First Fall. Photo: Dennis Parker A.P.P.S. Taken with a Rolleiflex 3.5F with a 6-element f3.5 Planar. The additional element was included as a rear filter colour correction for the lens. It was easier for a production line to continue as previously and add an additional element than coat the existing elements. Performance for black and white negatives was not affected but colour was improved, especially the removal of a blue cast on transparencies.

We owe a lot to Carl Zeiss (1816-1888) and the democratic foundation formed a year after his death, in 1889, by Professor Ernst Abbe, his partner for many years. The foundation, named in Zeiss' memory, was to form the basis for the modern Zeiss optical manufacturers.

The workshops for precision engineering and optics were first established in 1846 by the thirty-year-old Carl Zeiss, then a university mechanic in Jena, Prussia. Dr. (later Professor) Ernst Abbe was to join him here to form a partnership in 1866. Dr. Otto Schott established contact with Abbe in 1879 and was able to provide detailed advances in glass manufacture, by stipulating strictly scientific rules for its composition. From this early partnership in 1884, the Glastechnisches Laboratorium, later to become Jenaer Glaswerk Schott & Gen, was formed by Otto Schott, Carl Zeiss, Ernst Abbe and Roderich Zeiss (Carl Zeiss's son). They received considerable financial assistance from the Prussian state.

A year after the formation of the Carl Zeiss Stiftung in 1889, the first Zeiss camera lenses (Anastigmats) with the new Schott glass types were manufactured. These Concentric lenses were evolved from the Rapid Rectilinear design (Steinheil) and owed much to the new Schott glass production for their performance. The name of the lens: the Carl Zeiss Jena Protar. Within the basis of the establishment of the new Carl Zeiss Foundation, there was a special relationship between new enterprises and employees, with participation in the decision-making initiatives and the encouragement to produce the best possible product with the tooling available together with the raw materials and the theory that science, technology and economics serve man, not vice versa. From 1900 the company introduced the working of an eight-hour day.

Dr. Paul Rudolph joined Otto Schott at the Glastechnisches Laboratorium as the Chief Camera Lens Designer shortly after its formation and was responsible for the commercial production of the Carl Zeiss Jena Protar as defined above as a member of Ernst Abbe's research staff. He then went on to produce the design for the Carl Zeiss Planar as a five-element construction in 1896. Most Club Rollei members will know that, on paper, the Planar was a perfect lens design. However, the first prototypes produced a very soft image caused by the air gaps providing much internal reflection. Because of this, the design was shelved until the Second World War. It was then first produced for the Luftwaffe as an aircraft camera lens for air to ground photography because of its high resolution and incredible definition. The camera industry, however, had to wait until 1954 for the improved G. Lange design.

Dr. Rudolph's best-known design was the Carl Zeiss Tessar invented in 1902, inferior in design to the Planar, but able to produce high resolution, together with very good contrast and the lack of flare, without any coating. The Tessar was very similar in construction to the Taylor Cook Triplet of 1893, but vastly superior, due to the four elements (three elements, with the rear element split into negative-positive components) together with the use of

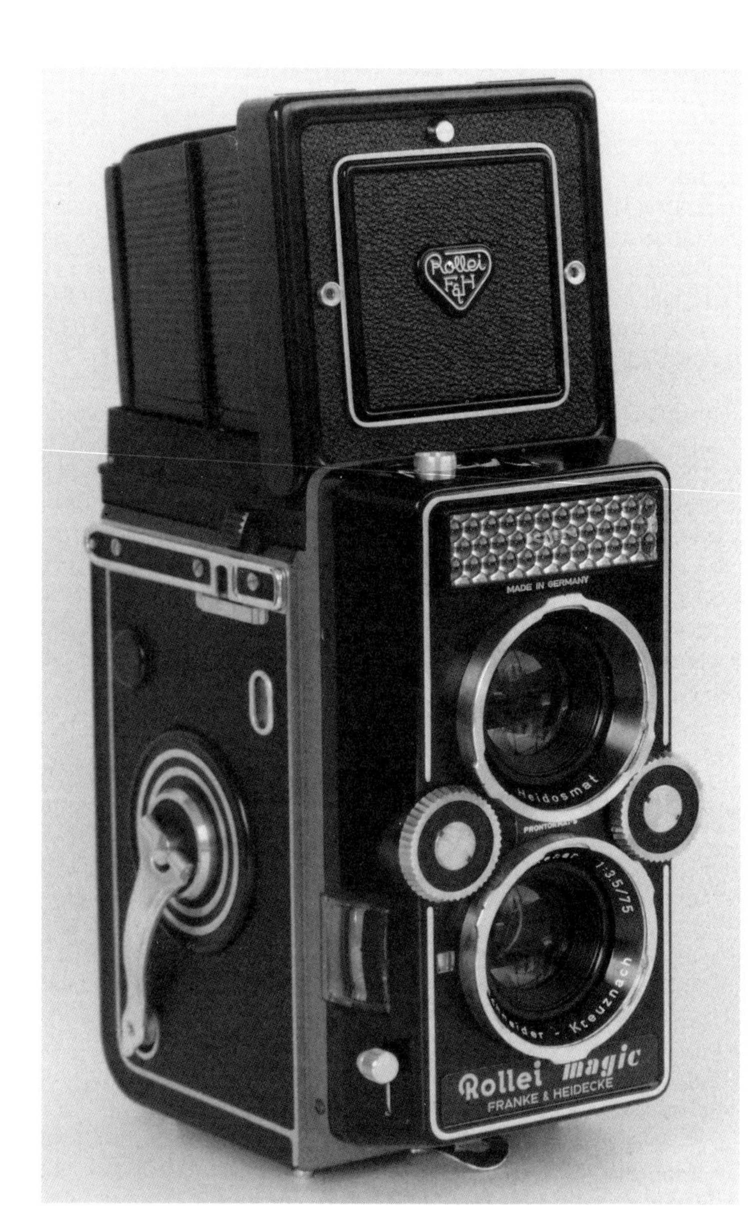

Rollei Magic I with Schneider f3.5 Xenar from the collection of Terence Sheehy.

the new Schott glass types. This was the lens to be associated with the Rolleiflex cameras for nearly all their production life. Indeed Dr. Heidecke's first prototype in 1908 was the first of the long line of Tessars to be used by the company, with the 1928 Rolleiflex fitted with a f4.5 Tessar. To the present day Rolleiflex 6000 series cameras still use the high power Tele-Tessars.

Another milestone in the history of the Carl Zeiss Tessar was set in 1908/9 when Mr. E. Wandersleb of the Zeiss research team demonstrated a method of constructing Tessar lenses with interchangeable front elements which makes it possible to obtain different focal lengths with the same camera extension. This was the forerunner of the modern convertible lens. In 1923 the Apo-Tessar was introduced, later to become the most widely used lens for photo processing work.

Otto Schott, the main architect of optical manufacture, was to transfer his share of the glassworks to the Carl Zeiss Stiftung in 1919, making it the whole owner. He was then sixty-eight years of age and played little part from then on. He died in 1935. Professor Ernst Abbe, born in 1840, was active until his death in 1905. He would have been most impressed with the continued work of the Stiftung but of course saddened by the division of the company that followed at the end of the Second World War. He was a brilliant designer of microscopes and is mainly remembered for these and the fact that his fine microscopes greatly assisted the struggle against infectious diseases, to bring a marked improvement to human living

A further landmark in optical design was to take place during the 1930s. In 1926 Mr. L.Bertele transferred to the Carl Zeiss Jena design team, when Ernemann Cameras of Dresden merged into the Carl Zeiss Foundation. He was responsible prior to this, in 1924 with August Klughardt, for the design of the six-element f1.8 Ernostar anastigmat, a lens of extreme wide aperture for the time which quickly made history. Mr. L.Bertele and his design team worked hard to produce the Carl Zeiss Jena Sonnar, a lens based on the Tessar type having only three air-spaced elements, with the first and last acting as converging lenses and the central element being a meniscus, curving towards the object. It took Bertele and two other people three years to calculate the Sonnar design, producing a three-foot high pile of papers, totally covered with figures and consisting of 3200 pages. The Carl Zeiss Sonnar was the fastest available lens at its time with an aperture of f1.5. Fitted to the 1921 Zeiss Ikon Contax I it was also available with an aperture of f2, at a slightly lower price and stopping down to f16. The f1.5 only reached f11 prior to coating. The design is still used as one of the world's best telephoto lens constructions and, as Club Rollei members will be aware, is found on the 135mm Tele-Rolleiflex and now the current Rolleiflex 3000 and 6000 series cameras as well as Hasselblad and Contax.

Other important milestones in the history of pre-1939 Carl Zeiss Jena lenses include: Dr. Rudolph and Professor Abbe in 1897, constructing anamorphotic lenses with the aid of cylindrical glasses and Brewster prisms; 1929 the introduction of the Biotar lens designed by Mr. Merte with extreme aperture of f1 and f0.85, intended for special photographic purposes; 1934, the first fast and distortion-free lens with an angle of view of 90°. This lens was to revolutionise the technique of aerial photography and was called the Carl Zeiss Topogon, followed by the Pleon designed for similar tasks but an angle of view of 140°, a few years later.

The last important discovery of the 1930s was the process for coating lenses with the object of reducing flare and reflections on the optical surfaces. This was developed by the Zeiss works and patented, although not introduced until after the war. It was adopted in the mass-production of optical systems and enabled the optical designer unrestricted opportunity in not keeping the number of air-to-glass components to the minimum.

One of the most important developments in pre-war camera production took place during 1926, when the Zeiss-Ikon Aktiengesellschaft was founded at Dresden by the Carl Zeiss Stiftung. This was an amalgamation of four of the leading German camera makers: Contessa-Nettel of Stuttgart; Ernemann of Dresden; Goerz of Berlin; and Ica (a Zeiss company) also of Dresden. These companies combined to produce the most complete camera technology of the time (pre-Rolleiflex). From this we have seen the famous Contax and Contaflex designs produced in the Dresden works and the Stuttgart factory producing many of the pre-war Zeiss folding camera models.

CHAPTER 11

1950 – A SAD LOSS

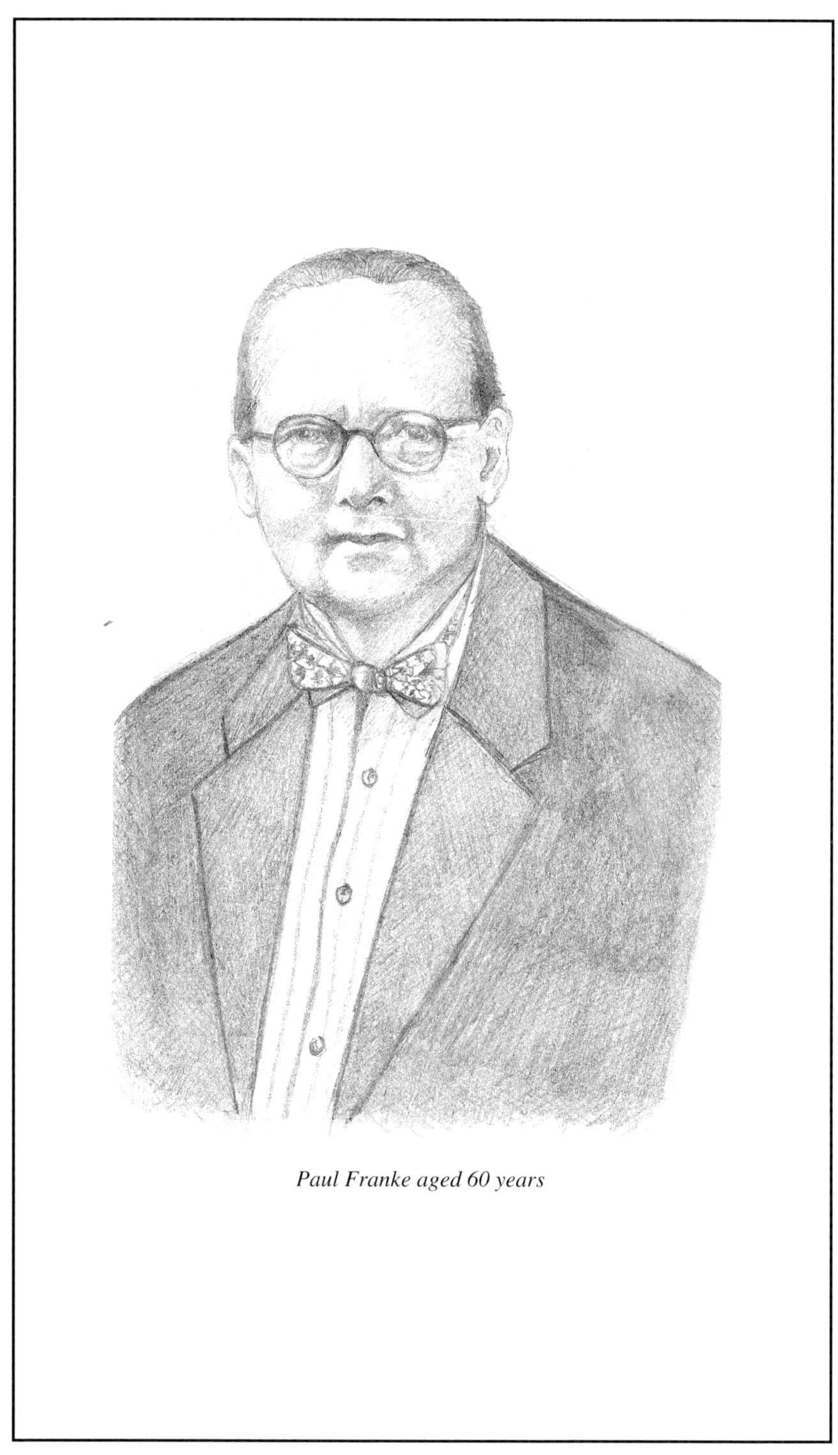

Paul Franke aged 60 years

1950 – A SAD LOSS

Paul Franke died on the 18th March 1950. He lived to see the firm he began in 1920 with his partner, each with a 50% share, grow to become one of the most respected names in the photographic business worldwide. From a modest start employing twelve staff in the first year, Rollei now had over 1000 employees. They also now had many models and the 2.8A on the drawing board. Sadly, Paul Franke died just at the beginning of Rollei's "golden years". Franke had loved meeting people, taking his buyer "friends" proudly around the works and later to dinner. Equally, he loved a large meal and a glass or two. Maybe it was the German celebrations over "Silvesterabend", a traditional German New Year celebration, that proved too much for his heart and led to his death at only 62.

A keen gardener, he was to be seen cutting the grass at the weekends or, before World War II, riding his horse. Paul Franke enjoyed the life of the country gentleman. As a salesman he was typical of the pre-war breed, well dressed with a flower in his buttonhole and always acting the father figure. His visits to the English importers were eagerly awaited by some of the staff. He brought chocolates from Germany for some of the typists, some monetary reward to someone in the service department and the commissionaire on the main entrance to R.F. Hunter's in Grays Inn Road. It was a pleasure to do business with Paul Franke, and this approach achieved very much more than expensive advertising. Today, sales personalities have vanished. I can recall many such as Paul Franke, and I for one regret their passing.

Paul Franke's son Horst succeeded him, to begin with very successfully. After all, these were the golden years of the twin lens reflex cameras. To begin with world markets could not be satisfied. 79 different Japanese companies started to market their own Rolleiflex/Rolleicord clone copy. Today, only six are still making cameras, none a T.L.R., and today only Rollei the originator manufactures a T.L.R., the Rolleiflex 2.8GX and the grey leather-covered special edition 2.8GX.

Horst knew the workings of Rollei, the camera, production and the commercially important part of the overall business. Being keen and eager to make his own mark, the firm prospered and he was able to exploit the demand for T.L.R.s so that new models could be added. In 1953 Horst came to London and I acted as a chauffeur, taking him to see Alec Pearlman and then on to Northolt Airport, on the outskirts of London, for his return to Hanover. I asked about the studio camera and he said that his father had been very remorseful about the whole affair. At one time his father had considered moving to England, but thought that it was not far enough away and wondered about America. He went on to explain that his father had been trapped. The majority of the firms he did business with belonged to Jews. If he moved to

America, and they joined in the war, he would be held prisoner and if not, would be unable to do any business. Jews could do nothing to save themselves in Germany. Horst admitted that at the time he thought Hitler was doing the right thing, but he now saw things in a different light.

It was the British, Horst went on to say, that he resented when they first took control of the factory, but he bore no grudge, they were very good with the children, glad the war was over and helped us to get back into production, he said. They had even obtained some lenses for them from the Russian zone. His father had thought that the British Army would dismantle the factory and set it up in England, as Germany had done in Poland.

Paul Franke's son Horst was not a financial juggler like his father. He only knew the words "expansion" and "profits". When the market was saturated with T.L.R.s and the vogue had changed to 35mm S.L.R. he could not cope. The now ageing Dr. Reinhold, although in his seventies, still took an active part in the business. He died in 1960, almost ten years to the day after Paul Franke had died, and in the best traditions of Dr. Reinhold, more and more new designs came from the drawing office and an ever increasing debt was mounting to pay for new tooling and the launch of the wide angle, Rollei Magic T.L.R.s and a range of projectors.

Paul Franke would have seen the writing on the wall and would, as in World War II, have cut his labour force and bank debt. The last time I spoke to Horst he said his army of employees was growing and he had to sell more and more cameras to conquer new markets. Unlike World War II he was not fighting a military battle, but a commercial battle with the Japanese!

So ended the ties of the Franke & Heidecke "family". In 1962 the name was changed to Rollei-Werke Franke & Heidecke. Two years later the position was so bad that the company was completely reorganised, with many management changes. Dr. H. Peesel became managing director and Rollei started to fight for survival. The new management team reduced the work force to 1624 and Dr. Peesel carried out a total reorganisation of all domestic and foreign distributors and a range of new models were launched at the 1966 Photokina. A worldwide sensation was achieved with the baby 35mm, the 35T, the smallest full-frame viewfinder camera, size 24 x 36 with Tessar f3.5, which joined the 16S ultra miniature launched the previous year. The book's author, having considerable experience within the textile trade, faced similar problems. His factories in Manchester and Northern Ireland suffered through the Far East imports as did Rollei. He chose to consolidate, with the capital obtained by closing factories to re-equip with modern machinery those factories remaining, to introduce round-the-clock working and to specialise in a superior product to that being imported into the U.K. In this manner a lean, highly automated business, ahead of its competitors, increased its market share. Those textile firms in the mid 1960s and early 1970s faced with the then current tax position of 95% and high interest rates prevailing resorted to reduction in employees, as turnover declined, and eventual closure. Those who

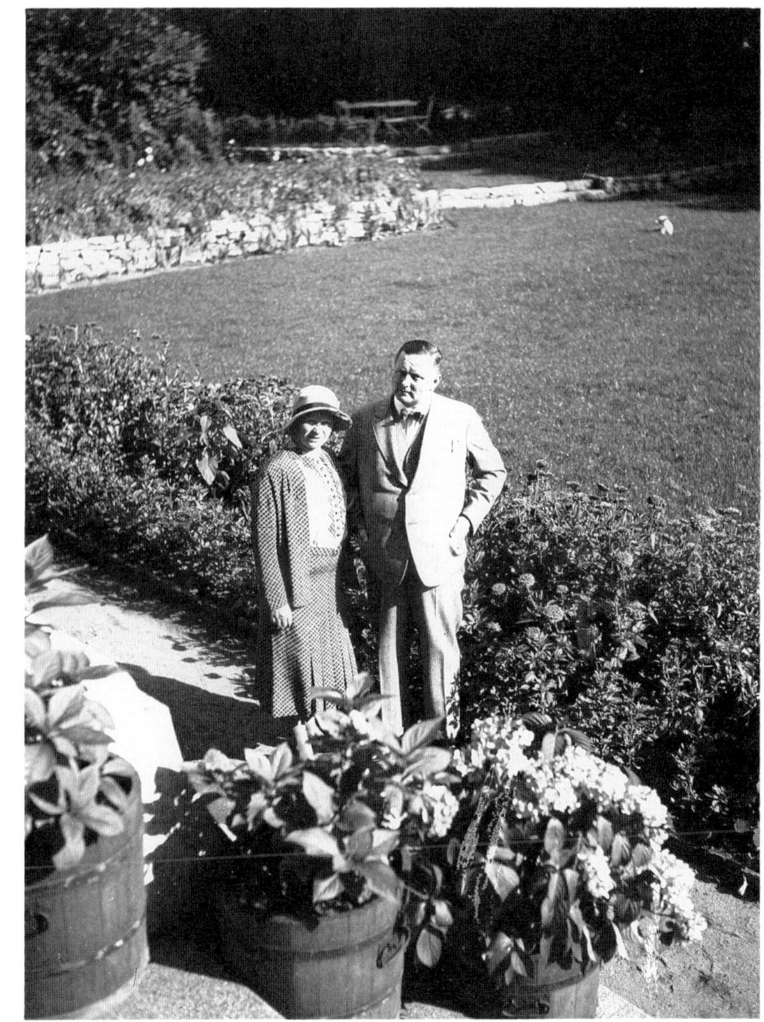

Paul Franke with his wife Ella in the garden he so loved
August 1949

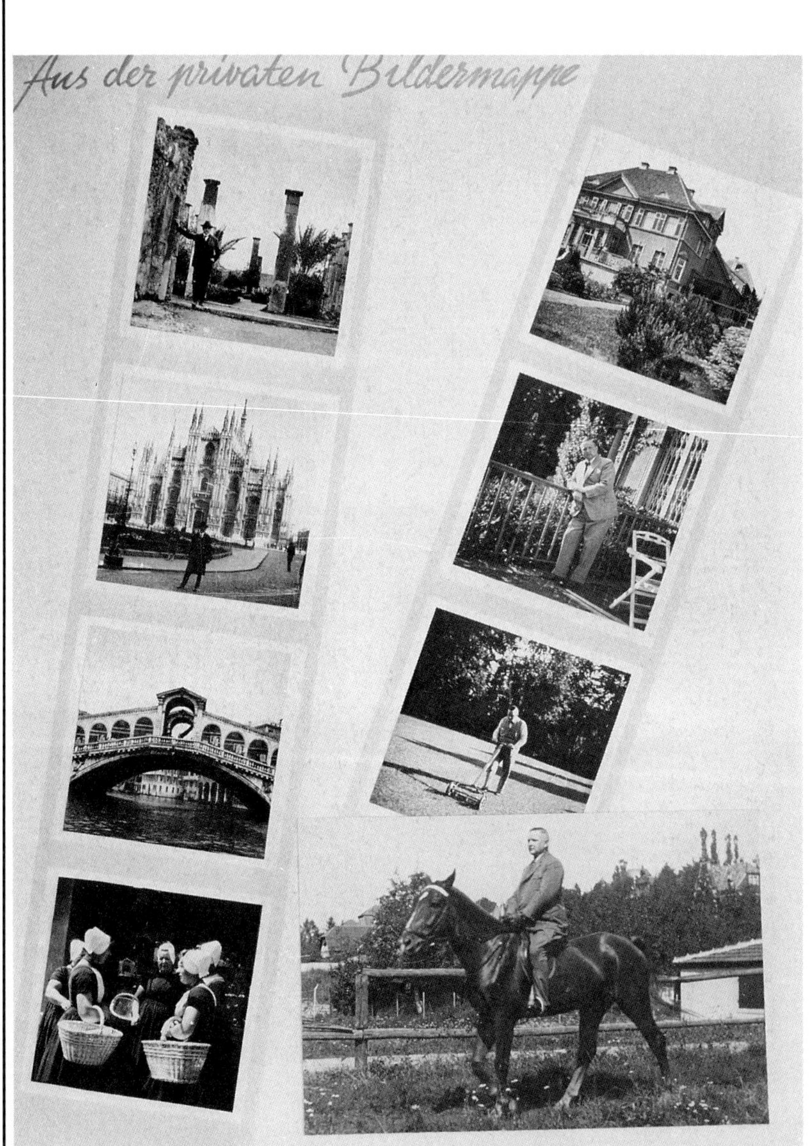

Paul Franke on his travels, in his garden and on his horse.

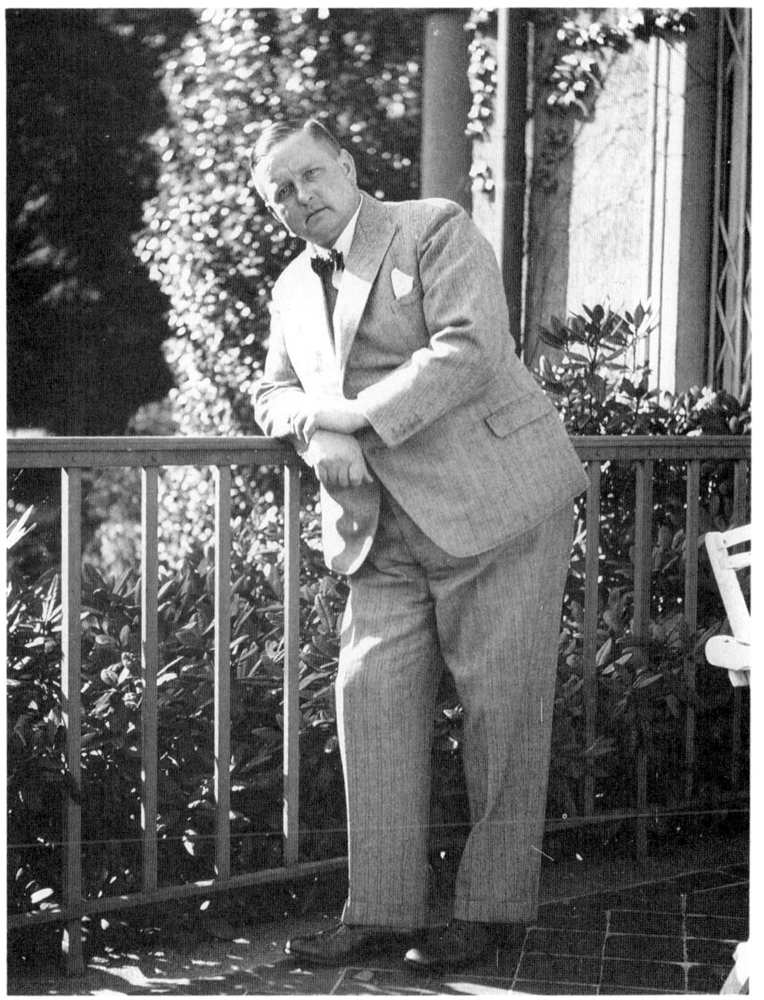

Paul Franke

started on new products to retain turnover soon found out that marketing unfamiliar lines was not a soft option and sales were only obtained at below cost. Hence the well-known phrase "Cannon Fodder for the Mill" for those orders showing no profit.

I mention this analogy because in 1963 if Rollei had decided to specialise in the medium format market and put all their R & D into the SL66 S.L.R. with interchangeable lenses and tilting lens board etc., there would have been sufficient orders for this model alone to keep the business independent of banks and financiers at least into the 1990s or the next century. The SL66 was finally launched in 1966 to compete with the Hasselblad, Pentagon, Zenith and Bronica. The Hasselblad first appeared in 1948. The 1600F suffered from a shutter defect and lacked the quality of today's Hasselblads. Try and find a working model. The 1000F in 1952, still with focal plane shutter and a reduced speed, overcame these problems. Most cameras seen today have an inoperative shutter.

The 1957 500C adopted an innovative Compur front shutter copied from the Zeiss Ikon post-war Contaflex and it remained in production until 1970 when the current 500cm became available. Today the most advanced mechanical and reliable medium format camera without any doubt is the current Rollei SL66SE with spot metering. Whereas the RB67 is the repairers' bread and butter, they seldom see a SL66 in for repair and you would be surprised at how many professionals prefer this versatile and dependable workhorse.

It is interesting to read old photographic journals. The camera preferred by their editors are (1) the cheapie plastic which they know will last a short time, to be replaced by another model with the possibility of a launch, and of course the advertising that goes with it. (2) the manufacturer or importer who provides a camera or cheaper product for a competition or press release in return for a free feature, thus reducing the journal's payout to contributing journalists. Hasselblad and Leica have certainly been masters of this craft. Many feel strongly that, although the SL66 cost over twice as much as the 2.8f Rollei T.L.R., with a little more thought this camera would have been a winner. Even Rollei's advertising at that time was targeted on the new breed of compacts in various formats.

Who says that the Germans blindly go to war having collated information from many sources on their enemy's strength and ability to stem their armies? In 1970 Rollei decided to conquer the Japanese photographic trade. They set up a factory in Singapore with the assistance of the Hessische Landesbank, who became shareholders, and by 1974 Rollei employees in Braunschweig numbered 1648, in Lüneburg Heath, West Germany, 316 and in Singapore 5696. This gamble failed and Dr.Peesel resigned and was succeeded by Peter C.J.Peperzak. With the company in receivership many thought that was the end of Rollei but not so. The company was saved by the U.K. British United Scientific Holdings who bought the original German section of the business

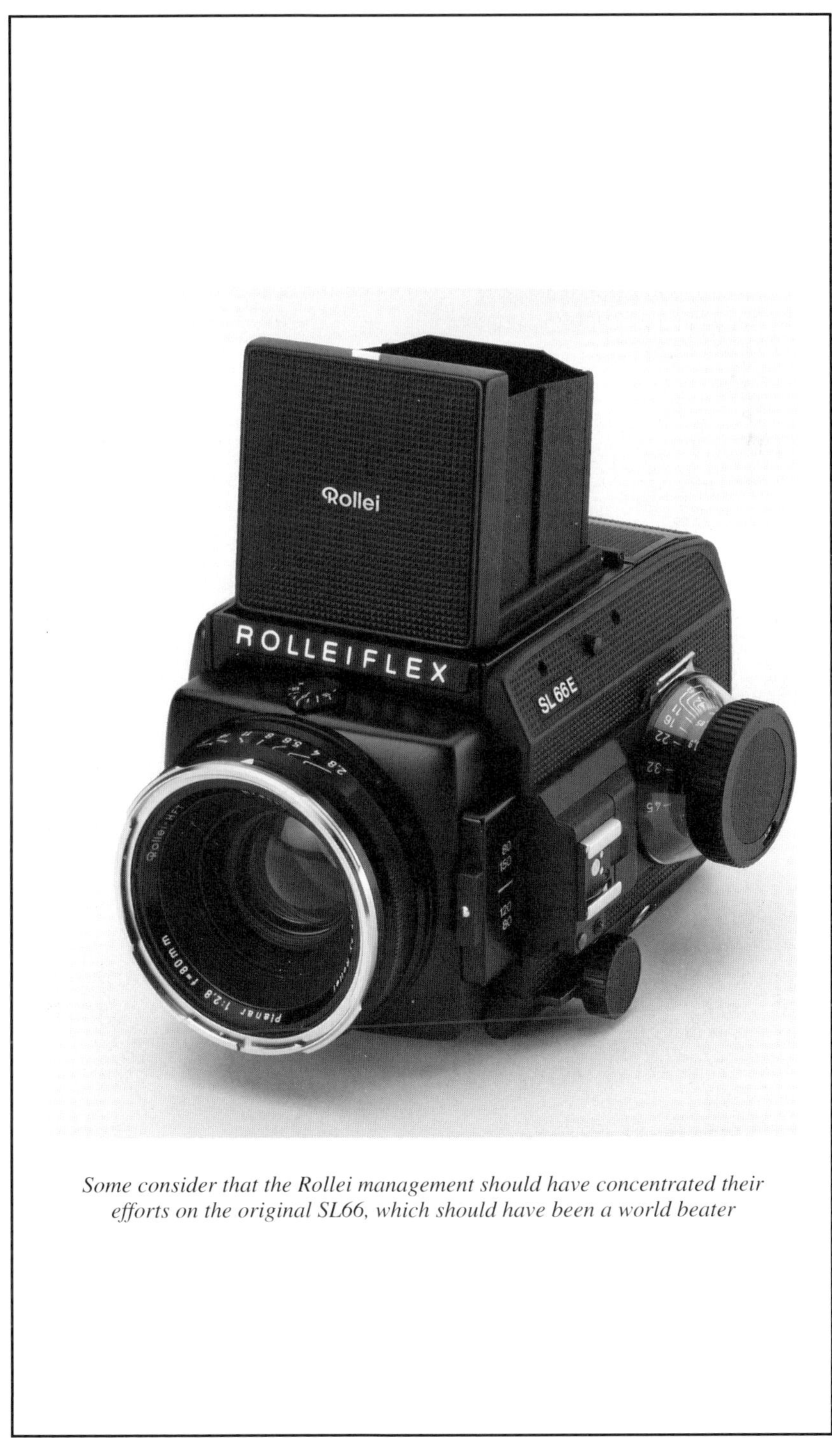

Some consider that the Rollei management should have concentrated their efforts on the original SL66, which should have been a world beater

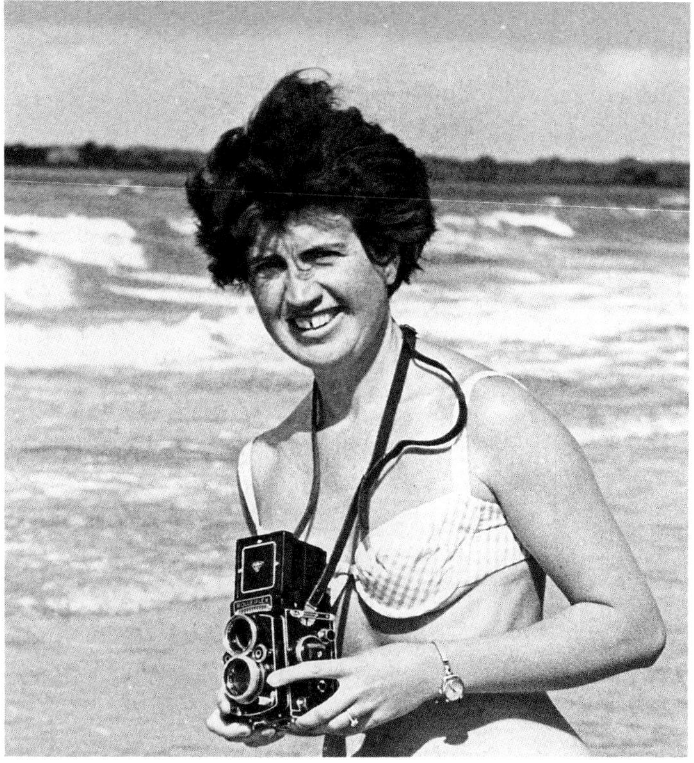

1959 pre-production 2.8F with Zeiss Planar lens, meter and 120/220 facility

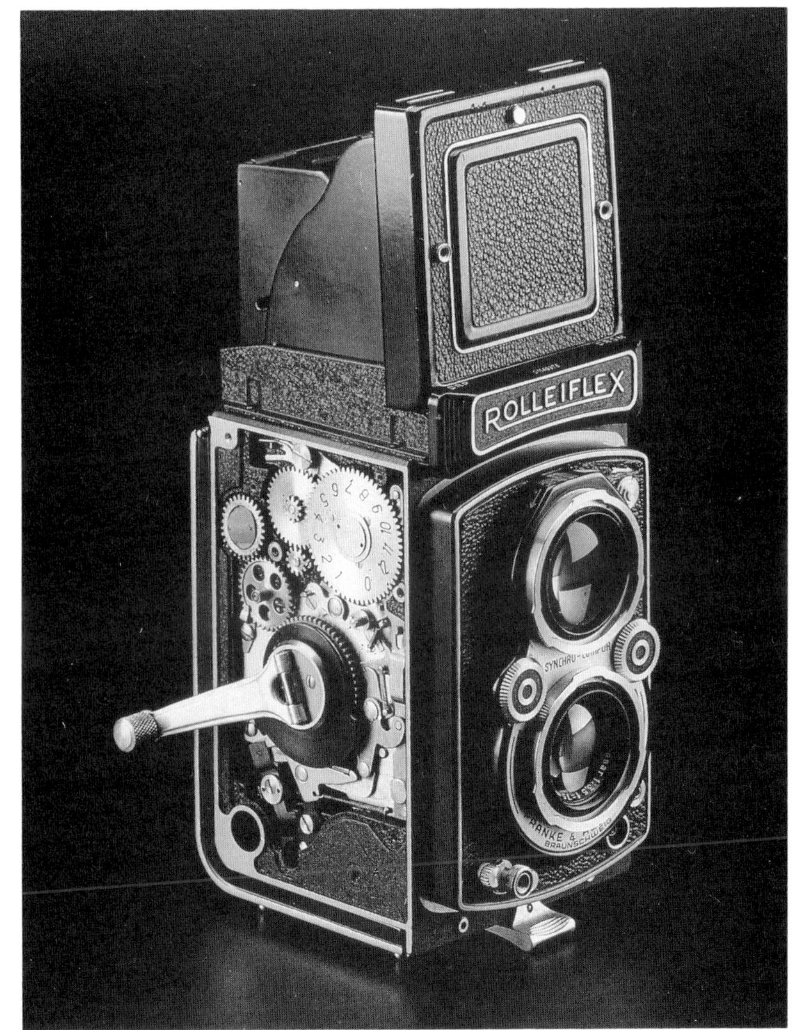

Rolleiflex MX (Type I) shown with side panel (lever wind) removed.
Photo: T. Sheehy.

and enabled Rollei to return from the ashes. It was not long before they regained their previous position providing the world's best medium format cameras.

I am sure both Franke and Heidecke would have been delighted with today's 2.8GX and in particular the Special Edition to honour their first 1929 roll-film T.L.R. Maybe the new camera does not have the same feel as the old F3.5 or F2.8, but today a flash shoe has to be provided and of course there is the excellent new metering system. Strange how Joe Public will criticise something they want, but will not accept their ideal product. Many still prefer the old T.L.R.s which operate without a battery even though the new 2.8GXs only requirement for a battery is for the meter. Sadly perhaps, changes inevitably take place and as during the war the firm of Rollei braced themselves for the changes that swept Europe, coming from Japan.

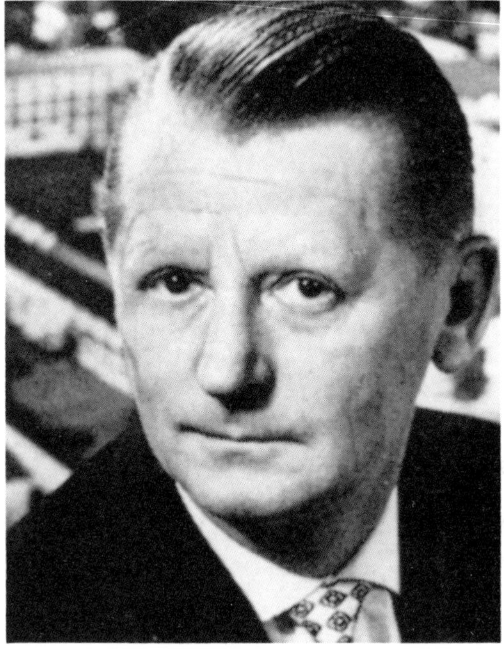

Horst Franke, son of Paul Franke, 1963.

CHAPTER 12

REINHOLD HEIDECKE - 1960

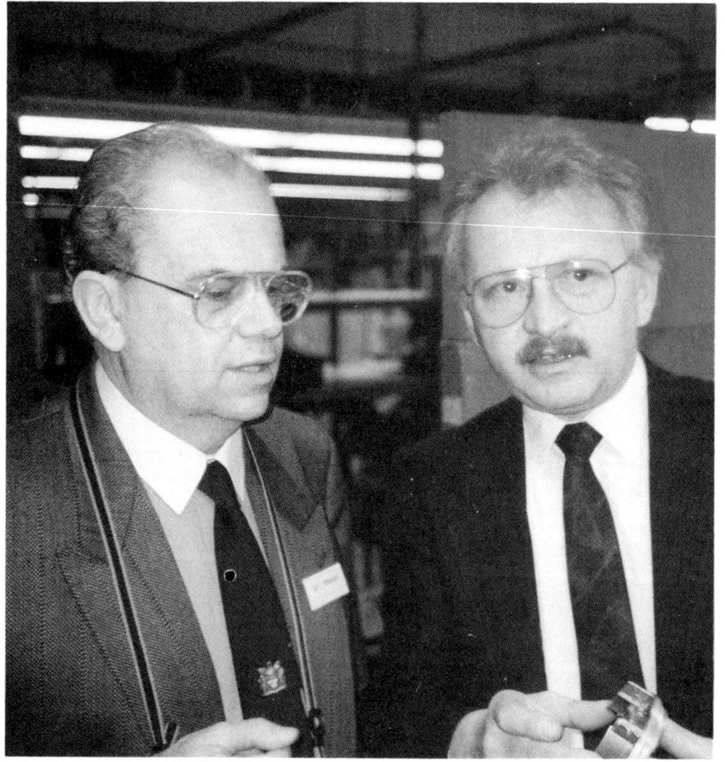

Peter Sheen discussing a point with Works Manager J. Wenzel, April 1991.

REINHOLD HEIDECKE - 1960

Reinhold Heidecke died on Friday 26th February 1960, in his eightieth year, almost ten years to the day after his partner Paul Franke died at only 62. Paul Franke was a jovial father figure who liked the good life and above all was the business brains of the partnership, coming from a middle-class family who were reasonably well off. Reinhold Heidecke came from an entirely different background. He had a quick temper in his early years, was rather shy and would shut himself away from the outside world in his drawing office. Feared by his employees, he was unpredictable and left his partner Paul Franke to sort out the turmoil caused by his frequent outbursts. Later on in life he mellowed, like most of us, and was finally accepted, at the age of 70, to receive his doctorate for having made a contribution to the world of science. Paul Franke's son Horst recommended that Heidecke should receive this recognition for his work, not only as an innovator whose ideas were taken up and used by designers a few years later, but for his life's work in starting a business with little capital, the eventual product of which became almost a household name synonymous with quality. No-one else in Braunschweig had achieved so much: a new product and a factory which had supported many families through good and bad times. Reinhold Heidecke was a respected engineer the world over, bad temper and all, and Horst felt it was about time the other self-esteemed members of the Braunschweig engineering society recognised his contribution to the design and manufacture of Rollei precision products.

Without doubt Reinhold's adolescent formative years had a bearing on his behaviour throughout his life. Today, with so many young couples living together and having no desire to become wedded, even when children appear, no-one today would have bothered too much about his lifestyle. There cannot be any doubt that Heidecke was determined in getting his own way and in that he succeeded. His children, like himself, cherished the day when they could leave home, and young Reinhold Ernst, although working for Rollei, was never taken into his father's confidence and never achieved any position, whereas Paul Franke's son Horst became Managing Director. Heidecke senior refused to give up control, even to his son, and he watched over the research and design department right up to his death.

Many have asked which was Dr. Heidecke's favourite camera. He would never answer correctly. All he would say was that he liked them all. However, his son did say that his father's favourite camera was the ill-fated studio camera. Dr. Heidecke was, not like his partner, a keen photographer, but at home he had an old Kodak No.41911 camera for 4 x 5 exposures on 123 film and also a folding No.4A that gave six exposures 4 1/4 x 6 1/2 on 126 film and several old Kodak 1 and 3 folding cameras. Young Heidecke remembers his father talking to his mother when he was around 26 years old about a studio camera 9 x 9cm and how it would become their best-seller. He went on to say that after the studio camera his father liked the first Rolleicord with the metal finish. That camera had made everyone look again. In the early 1930s many poorer people who could not afford a wireless would buy the case. Wireless sets in those days were very large. The cases could be used as a storage cupboard, some for storing sewing cottons and wools. Young Heidecke thought the Rolleicord art deco model would be bought as a cigarette box and put on the mantelpiece.

The studio camera must have been considered again by Heidecke in the 1950s. It is easy to forget that most photographs taken in the early twenties and thirties were never enlarged. Nothing has changed you may well say, but today's 35mm films are capable of giant enlargements, up to 20" and 30" or larger. Today's films and paper have remarkable definition which was not available in 1932. In those days very few amateurs had an enlarger and there were few photographic competitions or photographs appearing in magazines or newspapers as they required expensive blocks. Photographs were mainly taken to send to friends and relatives or stuck in the family album. Surely there must be a demand for large contact prints, he thought. In fact he did make a 6 x 9 prototype in 1954.

Over the past thirty years, 1960-90, Rollei alone have been able to offer a T.L.R. medium format camera: the Rollei Magic 1960/67 with built-in coupled light meter, automatic exposure, Tele Rollei 1959/75 and, as most Rollei collectors will tell you, the hardest camera to find, the Wide-angle Rollei 1961/67. The Weitwinkel Rolleiflex, with 55mm f4.5 Zeiss Distagon as the factory correct designation, has a curious story behind its origins. In 1958 the Yashica Japanese optical company copied the 1957 grey baby Rollei. So much so that they could hardly be told apart in the photographic shop window. Burleigh Brooks, Rollei importers in America, took Yashica to court and the Japanese 4 x 4 grey baby Rollei copy was dropped. The case was settled out of court, but during the preliminary proceedings the court heard discussion on how the 1956 Mamiya T.L.R."C" with an 85mm and 135mm interchangeable lens was affecting the sale of Rollei cameras. The following year Rollei, unable to redesign their basic camera to take interchangeable lenses, introduced the 135mm f4 Zeiss Sonnar.

Wedding and portrait photographers welcomed the new Tele Rollei and it sold very well. A questionnaire was distributed to wedding photo-graphers asking their opinions on the Tele Rollei. Several replied that the camera was very suitable within the studio or for fashion shots on location, but for weddings they found that too many amateurs were getting in front of their Tele and stealing their picture. Why not have a wide-angle Rollei, whereby the professionals could be in front of the wedding guests, who would not be able to get a group picture, thus creating more sales for their photos. Thus the wide-angle was launched as the professional wedding camera for groups and the standard 75mm for taking portraits. Professional photographers are slow to

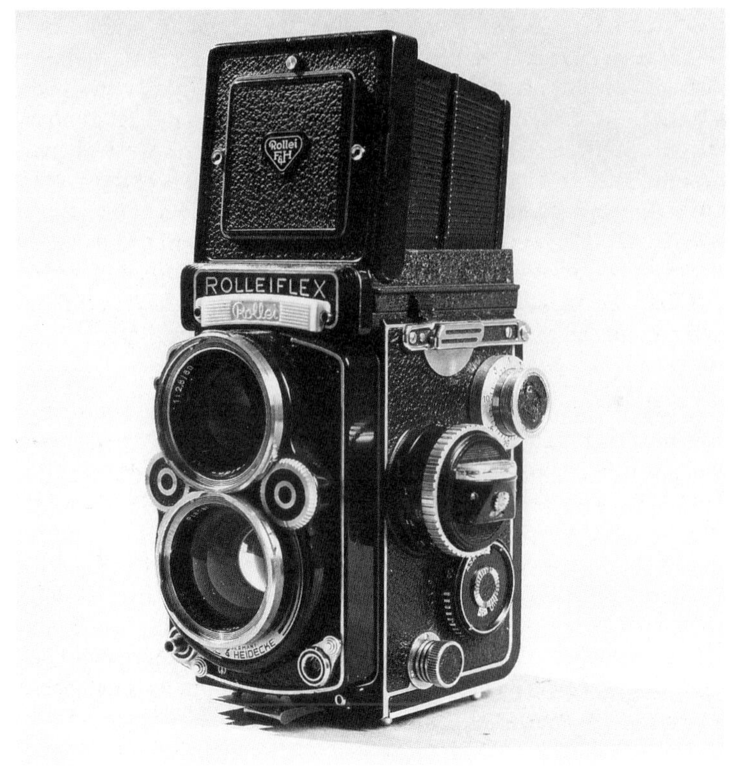

2.8F Rolleiflex with optical back and 35mm film facility from the collection of V. H. Seymour

change their ways, so sales of the wide-angle only met with moderate success. I have seen some remarkable landscape photographs taken with the wide-angle, using a bayonet IV red filter. Landscapes require a sturdy tripod, a sharp lens with excellent contrast to obtain an eye catching exhibition print. The Rollei wide-angle with no moving mirror Zeiss Distagon lens has many advantages over other cameras. Even so, only 3000 were constructed and sold, hence the rarity of this camera.

The F3.5 and F2.8 Rolleiflexes continued with modifications until the early 1980s and of course can still be seen in use today with Rolleicords and the older Rolleiflexes. The death knell of the T.L.R. has sounded many times, only to reappear a year or so later. With the growing popularity of Rollei cameras with collectors, we saw the golden Aurum in 1983 with f2.8 Planar lens. This camera has 23-carat gold plate on the metal exterior parts and the body and hood are covered with alligator leather. This most attractive camera came in a wooden presentation box and no-one ever thought that the camera might be used. Wedding photographers found the camera a great advertisement as a photographer who had a gold camera must be someone special. Several photographers quickly reprinted their visiting cards adding the word “society” in front of “professional photographer” and charged more for their assignment. So popular was the gold Aurum that eventually 1250 were constructed, including Herr Sass’ camera, without a number.

In 1986 the Platin edition appeared. This black crocodile camera with platinum-plated lens mount saw a production run of 400. Again this came with a black wooden presentation box and was priced at $9000 in the U.S.A. and £5000 in the U.K. In 1987 a Platin edition camera was stolen from a London shop. The thief, not realising that this was a special camera, decided to obtain some film and take the camera away on holiday. Liking the results, he took up photography and took many photos. In 1989 he was caught by the police after breaking into a house. On searching his home the police found the camera, which they thought was new as no scuff damage was evident, so good was the finish, The Jersey Photographic Museum bought the camera from the insurance company. The Platin edition is the best-finished of the 2.8F T.L.R.s but regrettably the price deters anyone from actually using one to take pictures unless they are not aware of its value.

The last of the 2.8F cameras, and by far the most collectable, is the Aurum Platin edition of 1989 with only 99 cameras constructed. Almost the entire production was sold in Japan. The camera is similar to the Platin edition but has a gold plate with camera number and close-up Proxars, all contained in a presentation box. The Jersey Photographic Museum camera is numbered 33/99. With no more available parts, the cost of hand-assembly has at last dealt the death knell of the “F” range of Rollei T.L.R.s that first appeared in 1959 and finally died in November 1989.

The ever growing Club Rollei may well have inspired Rollei in October 1987 to launch the new T.L.R. GX at Photokina in Cologne and the special edition 2.8X launched in Jersey in November 1989. This camera has the latest T.T.L. metering and dedicated flash to ensure accurate metering. Now with Planar HFT multicoated to eliminate flare, quiet shutter and overall operation the camera can be used on film sets, in churches and anywhere where a normal camera's noise would spoil the occasion. Dr. Reinhold Heidecke would have approved of this new twin lens reflex medium format camera. The 2.8GX special edition is certainly a camera for the collector, with only 1500 cameras constructed. The camera comes in a presentation box with gold nameplate, typical of the 1930s Rolleiflex typeface. The camera, finished in grey with nappa leather comes with close-up filter kit, a book on Rollei cameras, and at only the same price of the standard black 2.8GX.

Where does Rollei go now, you may well ask. True, they have a thriving market for the 6006/8, SL66SE and 3003 cameras as well as various specialist cameras seldom seen outside studios, laboratories and the aerospace industry. The twin lens reflex will stay in production so long as the market wants a reliable quality precision-engineered Rolleiflex 2.8GX – a camera designed for lasting value.

The 1990 Cologne Photokina saw the launch of a new range of binoculars, in 1991 the Auto-Focus compact Prego and a special edition of the baby 35 compact S for Sonnar lens. This camera, the 35 S Classic contains over 550 parts all assembled by hand. The small production run of 2500 cameras spread over three years shows that today's Rollei Fototechnic, as the firm is now known, still has the ability and skill to construct cameras by hand.

The T.L.R. edition 2.8GX line of 1500 cameras is now completed, the last batch was numbered 6,013,705. The standard black 2.8GX is still in production during 1992 with camera numbers in the 7,000,000-plus range. Today the only other manufacturers of T.L.R. cameras are Seagull in China, Mamiya in Japan and the Lubitel made in Russia. The Rollei T.L.R. is the only model available with T.T.L. metering.

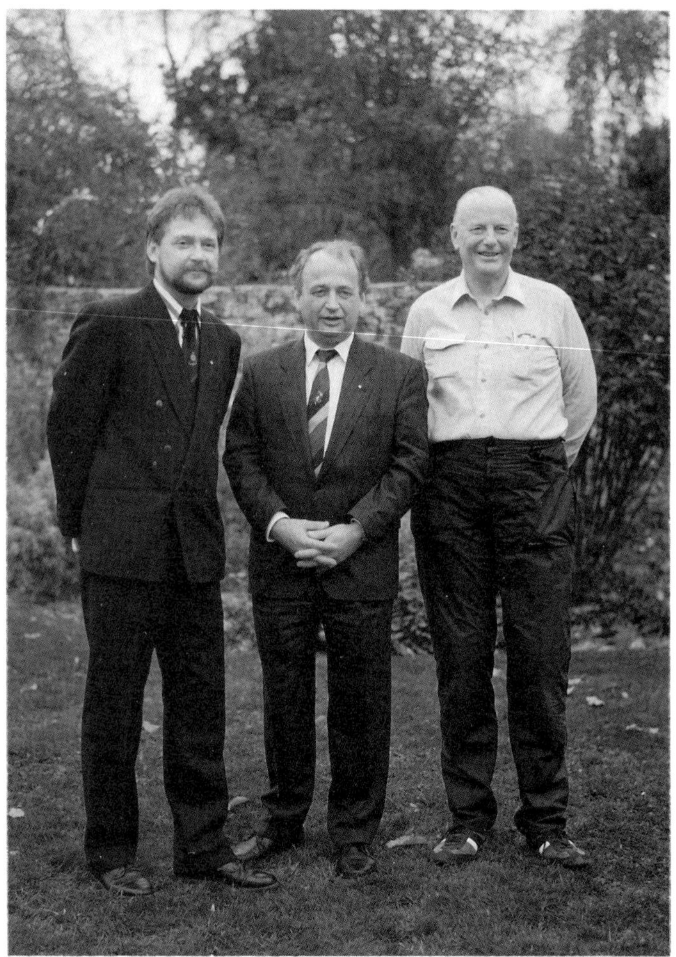

Dietmar Kanzer, Wolfgang Saß & Ian Parker
Jersey, November 1989

CHAPTER 13

THE FUTURE

Your future with Rollei
At photokina 1976 Rollei presents the progress of photography.
New pocket cameras. New SLR cameras. New flashguns. A new movie sound camera.
A new enlarger system.
And the successful products of the year 1976:
Rollei A 110, Rolleiflex SL 35 M, Rolleiflex SL 35 ME, Rolleiflex SLX, Rollei P 3800.
A dozen solid reasons to go to Cologne and to see Rollei.

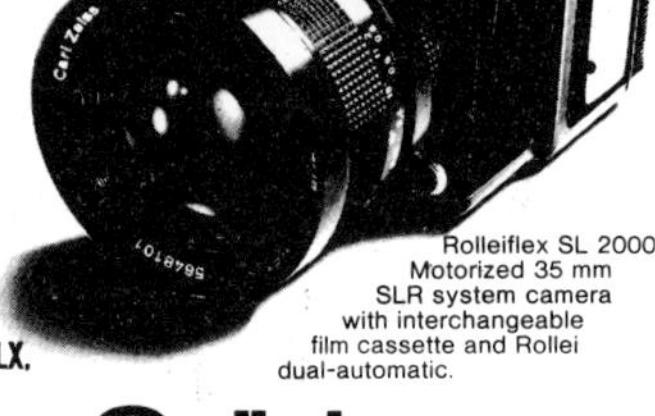
Rolleiflex
SL 2000
Carl Zeiss
Rolleiflex SL 2000.
Motorized 35 mm
SLR system camera
with interchangeable
film cassette and Rollei
dual-automatic.
Rollei
Progress in Photography.

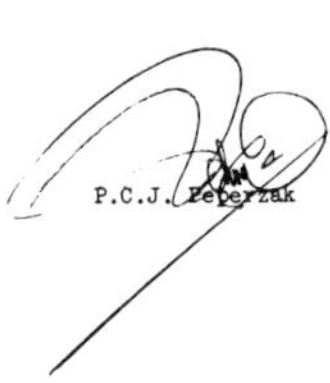
P.C.J. Peperzak

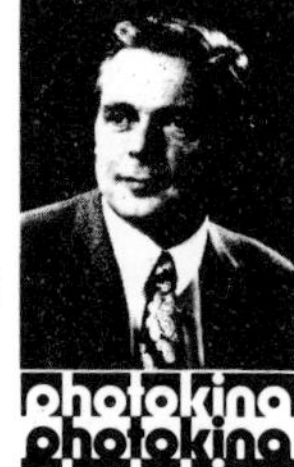
P. C. J. PEPERZAK
PRESIDENT OF THE
ROLLEI GROUP OF
COMPANIES

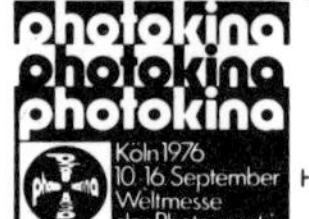
photokina
photokina
photokina
Köln 1976
10.-16. September
Weltmesse
der Photographie
Halle 1, Gang C, Stand 51.

THE FUTURE

Four years after Dr. Reinhold Heidecke died the family business seemed to fall apart. A new Managing Director, Dr.Ing Peesel, was appointed and on the surface Rollei was becoming a major photographic manufacturer with many new products. 1970 was a year of triumph when the Rollei Singapore factory was opened. This property is now occupied by Varta, the German battery manufacturer.)

In 1981 the company went into receivership, rescued by the British United Scientific Holdings P.L.C. of London who were well-known as the proprietors of Alvis cars, who built the British Army light armoured cars, and also of many electronic scientific manufacturing companies. Most of their turnover was derived from military orders but with the decline of defence expenditure they decided to sell Rollei Fototechnic to help reduce their large bank loans.

On 14th July 1987 Heinrich Manderman added Rollei to his Schneider-Kreuznach and B & W filter business. In 1991 Pentacon Praktica of Dresden were also added to the group.

Rollei Fototechnic is now managed by the very capable Wolfgang Saß and an excellent dedicated team of young and enthusiastic junior management which should ensure the future well-being of Rollei and you the user or collector can be assured that your investment will continue to be well worth that money, hard-earned no doubt, that you have spent in acquiring a little piece of history and a dependable instrument of the highest workmanship.

Dr. Reinhold Heidecke was able to witness the launch of the 3.5F and 2.5F T.L.R.s. Since then Rollei Fototechnic have successfully launched a range of cameras that neither the two founders way back in 1929 could have dreamt of. Even in 1960 I suspect that Dr. Heidecke would have guessed that some of the new cameras that he saw as prototypes in 1954/5 would be marketed. Secretly he wanted a studio camera to avenge the past, but this was not to be.

I am sure that one of Rollei's range of cameras in production today, 1992, will suit your requirements.

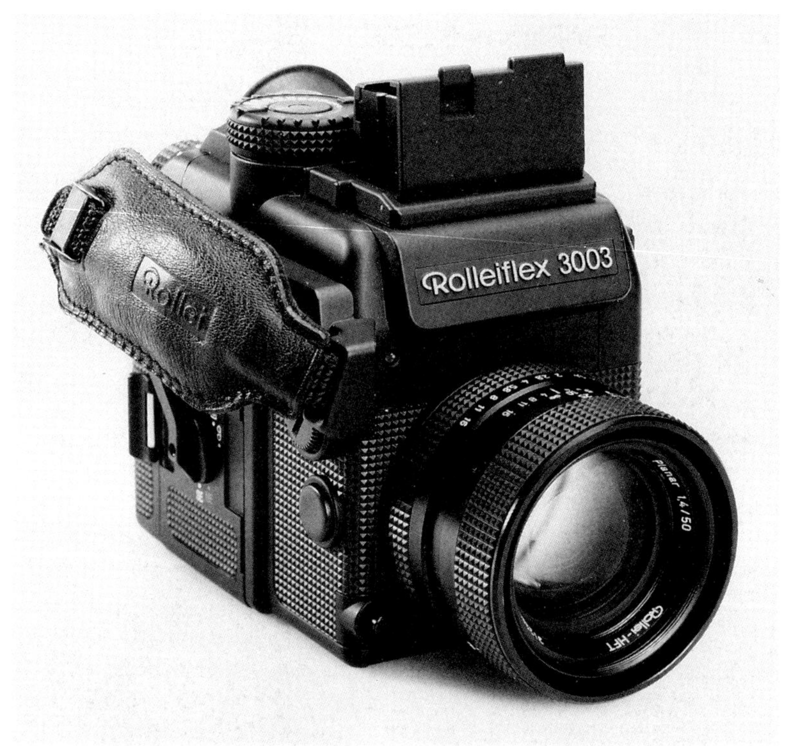

Rolleiflex 3003. The 35mm reflex system with the creative potential of medium format cameras.

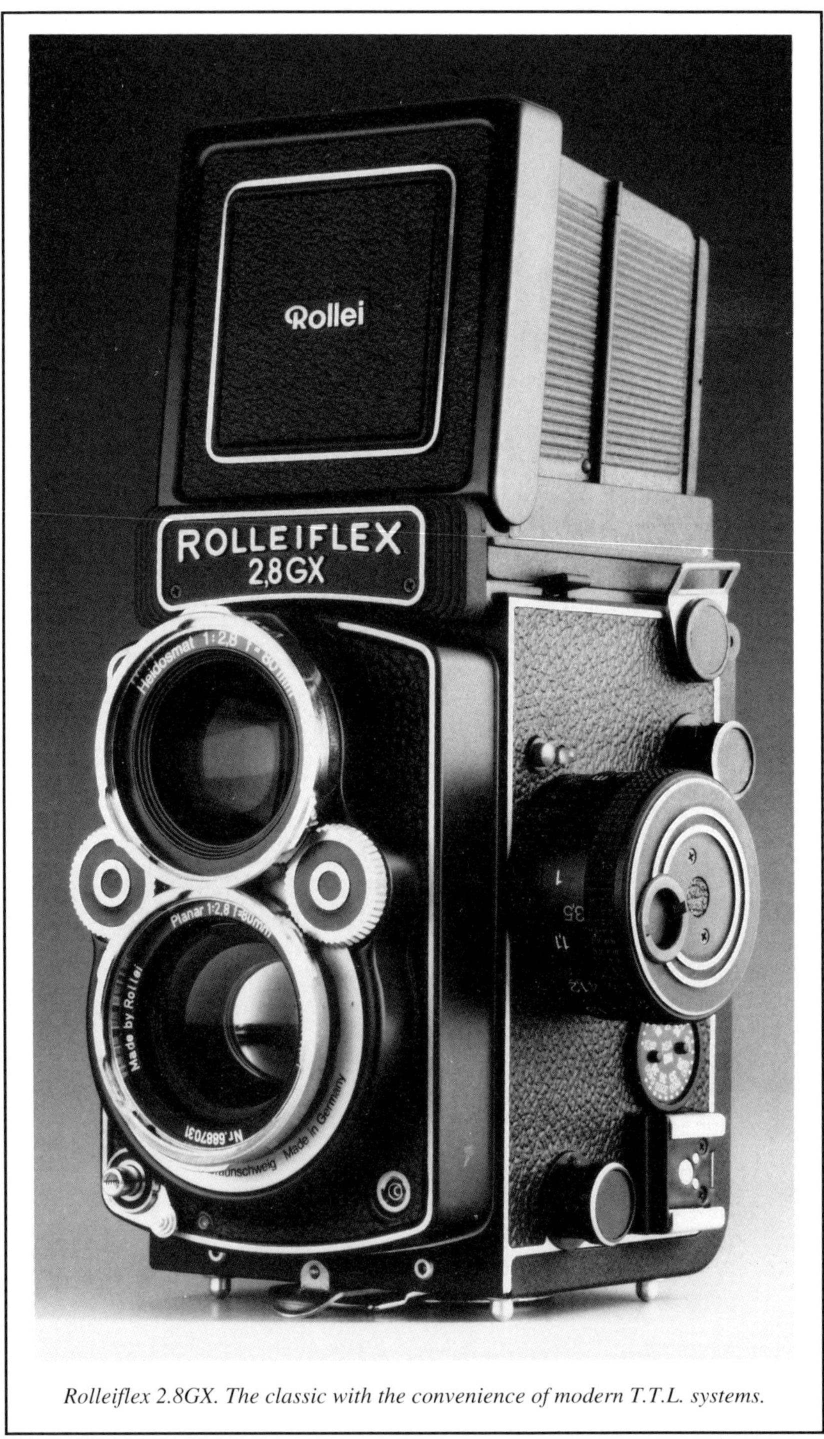

Rolleiflex 2.8GX. The classic with the convenience of modern T.T.L. systems.

HAVE YOU NOTICED A.V.'S ADVERTISING?

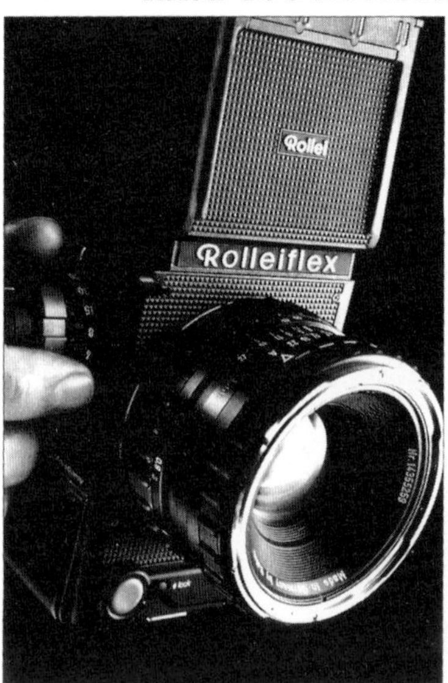

6008
Typical Rollei.

When speed and creativity are going to be a real challenge for the photographer the Rolleiflex 6008 is the right choice.

It is the most **complete** medium-format camera on the market, and can compete with the best 35mm cameras in features and ease of handling. The easy-to-operate exposure system, the ingenious quick-change film system and the modern high-performance lenses of Zeiss and Schneider-Kreuznach make it unique.

Anybody who aims for professional results cannot afford to pass up the chance of owning the Rolleiflex 6008.

Rolleiflex 6008 Professional – the sum of our experiences.

For a full colour brochure, and list of stockists, send the coupon to:
A.V. Distributors
21/22, St. Albans Place
London N1 0NX
Tel: 071-226 1508

Rollei
fototechnic

- ★ Aperture-priority, shutter speed-priority and programmed AE
- ★ Full manual override
- ★ Spot, multi-spot and multi-zone readings
- ★ Automatic bracketing sequences and TTL flash metering
- ★ Leaf shutter 30–1/800th sec, with 2 fps motordrive
- ★ Zeiss and Schneider lenses from 40mm–500mm

Please send me details about the Rolleiflex 6008

Name: ____________

Address: ____________

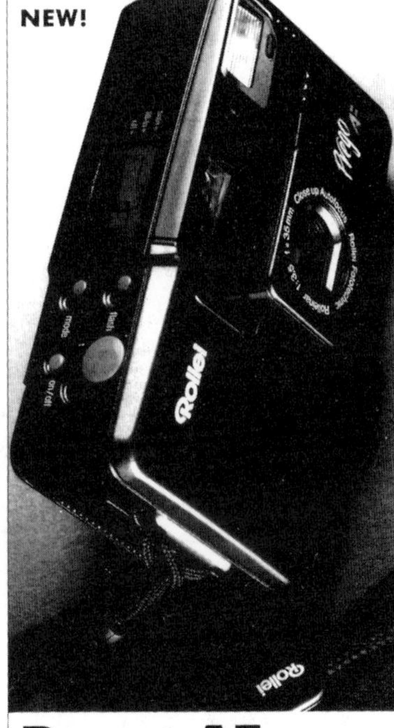

Prego AF.
Typical Rollei.

This new fully automatic super compact from Rollei, fitted with a Rolleinar 35mm f3.5 four element lens, is one of the most highly specified cameras of its type available today.
Send the coupon to the address below for a full colour brochure, and list of stockists.
A.V. Distributors
21/22, St. Albans Place
London N1 0NX
Tel: 071-226 1508

Rollei
fototechnic

- ★ 180-step autofocus motor
- ★ Programmed automatic exposure system
- ★ Built-in flash with auto operation
- ★ Data-back system
- ★ Self-timer and interval timer
- ★ DX-coding system
- ★ Auto-macro mode

Please send me details about the
Rollei Prego AF.

Name:

Address:

BC

CHAPTER 14

THE HISTORY OF ROLLEI FOTOTECHNIC

PhotoMagic.

Rollei's New Digital ScanBack

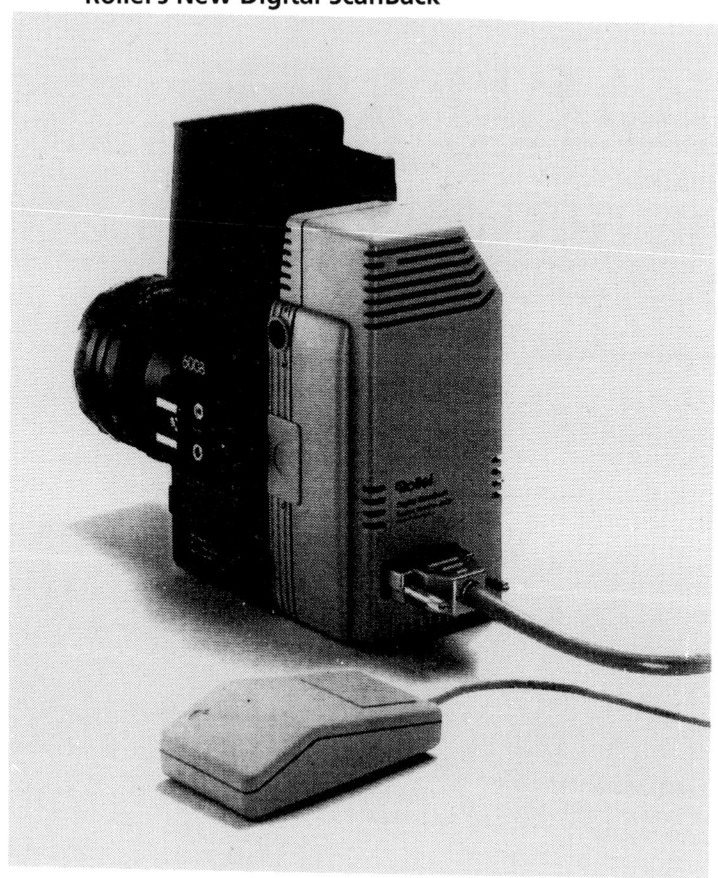

Rollei
fototechnic

THE HISTORY OF ROLLEI FOTOTECHNIC

1900

- Paul Franke joins Voigtländer, a recently formed company, aged 18. He starts work in the accounts office, and rises to the position of Office Manager in 1908 then to Sales Manager in 1911. Following W.W.II he pursued a career in the field of photography as a photo dealer in Berlin.

1906

- Reinhold Heidecke, aged 26, is very interested in opthalmology. He writes to Dr. David Robertson, the Principal of Glasgow University, concerning camera design and lenses.

1907

- Herr Heidecke joins Voigtländer as a junior in the design department.

1919

- Herr Heidecke, on meeting many war veterans who would like to have owned a truly portable camera, strongly constructed, small and easy to use, designs the Heidoscop, a reflex stereo plate camera. He writes to Paul Franke and they agree to set up business on a 50/50 basis. The agreement was still in existence on the death of Herr Franke on 18th March 1950.

1920

- The partnership of Franke & Heidecke starts life in rented rooms of a Braunschweig apartment house on Viewegstraße 31.
- A number of prototypes are made and tested with Goerz lenses – German lenses made in Berlin.

1921

- The first Stereo Heidoscop goes on sale, with two Carl Zeiss Jena Tessar 55mm,f4.5 taking lenses and Carl Zeiss Jena Sucher-Triplet f3.2 finder lens.
- Sales progress better than expected. This camera featured a bright view finder image and rounded corners on the casing. It accepted the smaller 45 x 107mm glass plates.
- By the end of the year the payroll numbers twelve.

1923

- The original Heidoscop is redesigned as the Rolleidoscop, a roll-film reflex stereo camera, taking 117 film.
- The Rollei name appears on the market for the first time.

1925

- The larger Heidoscop, size 60 x 113mm, goes on sale with Carl Zeiss Jena 75mm,f4.5 taking lens.
- Annual production exceeds 6000 cameras.

1926

- Previous problems fitting 117 film into cameras are solved.
- The Rolleidoscop goes on sale. Many devotees converted their Rolleidoscop to take 120 film, many of which are still in use today.

1927

- The first designs on the twin lens roll-film camera get under way.
- Stereo camera annual production reaches 12,090.

1928

- This is an historic year for photography, with the onslaught of the world's first roll-film twin lens reflex cameras. Ten prototype cameras are built, nine of these prototypes have a Tessar f4.5 taking lens and the tenth is fitted with a sample f3.8 Tessar. Both types use the Heidoscop f3.2 finder lens. Apart from the different taking lens, all cameras are identical. By Christmas the final design is agreed upon and patents are applied for. It is decided to market both types simultaneously.

1929

- On 17th January, France grants patent No. 604896 for the original Rollei camera, the Germans follow with No.526509 and world patents are applied for. Tools are made, parts are ordered and on 10th August production commences.
- By the end of the year the new T.L.R. is finally completed. The price of the f4.5 is £16.37, 198 Reichmarks, and £18.75, 225 Reichmarks, for the f3.8. The enormous difference between prices ensure the most popular camera is the less expensive f4.5. Orders throughout the world are far greater than either Franke or Heidecke could have expected.

1930

- With back orders for over 8000 T.L.R.s but only 22 employees, the original apartment house where they occupy two units is far too small. Sub-contractors, who could not always be relied upon to deliver when required, are abandoned. With frequent modifications and improvements being made to the cameras the sub-contractors could not adapt to the rapid changes.
- A factory is acquired in Salzdahlumer Straße, Braunschweig, and with the exception of the lens, shutter, mirror and screen, virtually all the manufacturing is done in-house. It was now possible, with a larger workforce, to build 20,000 cameras annually.
- Cameras are still very basic and it is not until after W.W.II that a large number of employees are required for assembly of the many complex moving parts.

- The final prototype of a new camera, the Baby Rolleiflex, is completed by Christmas.

1931
- The smaller 4 x 4 Baby Rolleiflex goes into production with an improved design, incorporating a lever film wind advance and positive film stop, taking 127 size film. This was the first camera able to take advantage of the in-house facilities at the new factory, the site of today's factory.

1932
- The 6 x 6 camera is re-designed, using 120 size film for 12 exposures, incorporating a lever wind as on the 1931 4 x 4 camera.
- Designs start on a new budget camera for the mass market.
- A giant camera using 122 film is designed for a Berlin studio. Fourteen cameras are built but sales do not materialize, as professional photographers prefer the larger plate cameras. The only known example of this camera was presented by Rollei to the Braunschweig Museum in 1981. Parts and some of the original film can be found in the Jersey Photographic Museum.

1933
- The Rolleicord with f4.5 Zeiss Triotar is launched with metal art deco panels, priced at 88 Reichmarks against the 198 of the f4.5 Tessar Rolleiflex. The first deliveries are not in time for Christmas.
- During January 600 cameras leave the factory, and at the end of the year over 20,000 cameras have been built.

1934
- The new Rolleicord with f3.8 Triotar and black leather covering is in circulation in time for Christmas.
- Annual camera production reaches 24,616, all types including stereo and Rolleiflex.

1935
- Total export camera sales worldwide reach 18,000.
- Total number of employees is now 496.
- Annual production exceeds 26,000.
- This is a year of consolidation, with all employees endeavouring to satisfy the large volume of orders. The design team spend two years improving manufacturing methods, tools and extensions to the factory.

1936
- The new Rolleicord production line is completed, and the redesigned camera, designated Rolleicord 1A, goes on sale in time for Ester.
- The design team start on a new Rolleiflex production line.

1937
- The Rolleiflex Automat is launched at the Paris World Fair and gains a Grand Prix.

- This camera, completely redesigned with automatic crank mechanism, allows the film to be positioned without the need for a window. The design is essentially the same as for the later 3.5F.
- Annual production reaches 36,800 – all designs of camera.

1938

- Annual turnover exceeds 7,277,000 Reichmarks.
- 27,000 Rolleiflexes, 22,000 Rolleicords, 700 Baby Rolleiflexes and 200 stereo cameras have been manufactured.
- The 300,000th Rolleiflex camera is sold.
- The factory now employs 725 staff.
- The Rolleicord II is redesigned with an f3.5 Zeiss Triotar finder lens and a double bayonet I mount on the taking lens.
- The Sports Rolleiflex is launched.

1939

- The finder lens on all Rolleicord and Rolleiflex cameras now has a double bayonet mount as on the taking lens, allowing a filter and hood to be used.
- With the outbreak of war Franke & Heidecke are involved in a defence contract.
- Camera production drops to just under 40,000.

1940

- During the war period no new cameras are designed, and most overseas markets are lost.
- The 400,000th camera is sold.
- The labour force drops to around 600 and defence work now occupies most of the factory.
- Production of the stereo camera comes to an end.

1944

- The factory is partially destroyed on 11th January 1944 and again on the 15th. Slight damage is caused on 13th August when 1275 tons of bombs are dropped by the R.A.F. on Braunschweig (see *Club Rollei,* issue 16, page 17). Production re-commences with 72 employees even though 65% of the factory has been destroyed.

1945

- Braunschweig is occupied by the British 21st Army Group.
- Camera manufacture re-commences, and the entire production is sold to the British Ministry of Defence.
- As things return to normal, the number of employees gradually increases, as old employees return from war. By Christmas employees total 178.

1946

- Rebuilding the factory workshops proves difficult with material in short supply. Those not living in war zones did not realise the problems of those who did. Who has priority for materials – shops, factories or houses? Everyone wants everything at once. Progress is slow, but little by little problems are overcome.

1948

- With rebuilding and equipping almost completed, once again new designs are the order of the day. Lessons are learnt from the war – the coating of lenses – synchronisation.
- Employees now number 600.

1949

- New prototype Rolleicord and Rolleiflex production lines are prepared.
- Old models are still selling and the total accumulated production of all Rollei cameras exceeds 1/2 million.
- Rolleicord III with Compur-Rapid shutter, 1 – 1/500th second (which is now standard in all cameras), is available with West German Schneider f3.5 Xenar coated lens.

1950

- Rolleicord III is launched in November with X synchronisation, coated Zeiss Triotar or Schneider Xenar 75mm,f3.5 taking lens, and f3.2 Heidosmat finder lens. Also with automatic film wind.
- A new Rolleiflex is launched in October with synchronisation, known as the Automat II. A choice of three lenses is available. The Tessar, supplied by the East German company Carl Zeiss Jena, or the West German Zeiss Opton Tessar or Schneider Xenar coated lenses.
- Sadly Paul Franke dies on 18th March aged 62. He lived to see the firm he began with his partner, each with 50% share in 1920, grow to become one of the most respected names in the photographic business worldwide.
- 30 years later Franke & Heidecke has surpassed its pre-war size, now employing almost 1000.
- Paul Franke is succeeded by his son, Horst Franke.

1951

- A new Automat model is launched with flash synchronisation.
- The Synchro-Compur MX shutter now replaces the Compur-Rapid on the Rolleiflex.
- Reinhold Heidecke receives a degree of honoary Dr. at the Institute of Technology, Braunschweig.
- The 2.8A Rolleiflex is launched in February. It sports a Tessar 80mm,f2.8 lens with a new bayonet III mount.

1952

- The 2.8B with f2.8 Carl Zeiss Jena Biometer lens is launched.
- A self-timer is now a standard fitting in all T.L.R.s.
- A new production line is installed for 2.8 cameras.
- 400 additional staff are recruited.

1953

- The 2.8C with West German Schneider Xenotar is launched in April together with a range of bayonet III filters, hoods, and close-up lenses.
- The Rolleicord IV is launched in August with Synchro-Compur MX shutter.
- All T.L.R.s now have double exposure facility, coated lenses, and bayonet mounts on both lenses.

1954

- Rolleiflex Silver Jubilee. A photographic contest is organised to help commemorate the occasion.
- Hans Hass designs the Rollei Marine underwater housing, now in Jersey Photographic Museum, in collaboration with Dr. Heidecke.
- The Rolleicord V is launched with a large focussing knob and West German f3.5 Xenar lens.
- Rolleiflex with MX-EVS is launched in April.
- The 2.8C Rolleiflex is now available with Zeiss Planar lens.

1955

- Usual cosmetic changes appear on the 3.5 Flex and Cord.
- Sales expand and labour force now numbers 1500.
- 2.8D Rolleiflex with f2.8 Planar or Xenotar and EVS system is launched.

1956

- The millionth Rolleiflex camera is produced.
- Employees now rise to 1600.
- 3.5E Rolleiflex is launched in October with f3.5 Xenotar or Planar lens, bayonet size II. This camera, along with the 2.8E, is available with built-in exposure meter.

1957

- The 4 x 4 Baby Rolleiflex is re-introduced after 16 years, with grey leather and dark grey trim. it is only available with Schneider Xenar 60mm,f3.5 taking lens and f2.8 Heidosmat finder lens, both with bayonet I double mounts.
- The 5A Rolleicord is launched in April with the focussing knob positioned on the left-hand side.
- Annual sales continue to rise.
- Employees now total over 2000.

1958

- Two new models are shown at Photokina, the photographic exhibition held in Cologne, Germany. The Rolleiflex 3.5F with coupled exposure meter, and the Rolleiflex T, which is able to take multiple picture sizes with the aid of an automatic switchable frame counter for 12 6 x 6cm exposures (21/2 x 21/2in.), or 16 4.6 x 6cm exposures (13/4 x 21/2).
- Women are employed for the first time in camera assembly.

1959

- Tele Rolleiflex is launched with Zeiss Sonnar 135mm,f4 taking lens, f4 Heidosmat finder lens, bayonet III mounts, and removable hood.
- 3.5E2 and 2.8E2 are introduced with a removable hood enabling viewing screens to be interchanged, as well as the addition of a pentaprism.
- Grey Baby Rolleiflex is discontinued, over 80,000 have been sold.

1960

- Reinhold Heidecke dies on 26th February in his 80th year. His favourite camera has been the 1937 Automat.
- The PII universal dual slide projector for 35mm and 6 x 6 is launched.
- Rollei Magic is launched, with built-in coupled light meter for automatic exposure.

1961

- Wide-angle Rolleiflex is launched in April with Zeiss Distagon 55mm,f4 lens, accepting new bayonet size IV mounts – perhaps Rollei's most valuable T.L.R. camera, excluding special editions.

1962

- Vb Rolleicord is launched with removable hood.
- Rollei Magic II is launched with Xenar f3.5 lens, bayonet II mount. Features include removable hood, switchable exposure and automatic or manual metering – the fully automatic camera.
- Company name is changed to Rollei-Werke Franke & Heidecke.

1963

- The 12 x 17mm Rollei is launched, the Rollei 16. Rollei's first ultra miniature. Features full exposure automation and Tessar f2.8 lens.
- 4 x 4 Baby Rolleiflex is re-launched, with black finish.

1964

- The company is completely re-organised with many management changes. Dr. H. Peesel becomes Managing Director.
- Workforce is reduced to 1624.
- The T.L.R. camera market continues to decline as many amateurs buy 35mm cameras and professionals switch to 6 x 6 S.L.R.s with interchangeable lenses.

1965

- Rolleiscop home slide projector is launched. Features push/lift slide change and fully adjustable condenser.
- Total re-organisation of domestic and foreign distributors is carried out by Dr. H. Peesel, Managing Director.
- Improved 16S ultra miniature is launched in Germany (available in black snake leather, red or green leather).

1966

- To combat falling sales, new models are shown at Photokina.
- The new SL66, Rolleiflex S.L.R. is available with interchangeable lenses, bellows, tilting lens-board, and features lens retro-mounting for macro work. If available only six years earlier it would have been a winner.
- A worldwide sensation is launched, the 35 Rollei, the smallest full frame viewfinder camera, size 24 x 36. With Tessar f3.5 lens.
- The 2.8F T.L.R. becomes available for use with 120 or 220 film.

1967

- New products include computer flash guns E60 and E66.
- The Rollei Magic II, the wide-angle T.L.R., and the Tele-Rollei are discontinued to help reduce production costs.
- Labour force is reduced to 1478.

1968

- Rollei pension scheme for employees gets under way.
- The high cost of tooling and marketing and the slow return on capital result in the Norddeutsche Landesbank becoming a shareholder.
- SL26 is launched using 126 format, supplied with standard Tessar 40mm,f2.8 lens, with bayonet I mount. Additional 28mm,f3.2 pro-Tessar and 80mm,f4 pro-Tessar were available. Voted the best 126 camera ever made by several photographic magazines.
- A new range of Strobonar flash and studio units are launched, the E50, E55 and E20.

1969

- 35mm compact 35B is launched with 40mm,f3.5 Triotar and meter.
- 35C is launched, a budget camera also with f3.5 Triotar lens but without meter.
- New range of flash units include the E17, E17C, E22, E22C, and C27C.
- 4 Super-Eight cameras are launched, adding to the ever-expanding range of Rollei products; the SL81, SL82, SL83 and SL84.

1970

- The Tele-Rollei is re-launched with factory-fitted meter and provision for 220 film. Note that the Rolleiflex T with 220 feature was never available. There is some confusion between the 12/16 feature which some thought allowed 220 film to be used. Lack of space in the T precluded a 220 film mechanism to be fitted.

- Rolleiflex SL35 is launched, a 35mm S.L.R. camera, available with 50mm,f1.8 Schneider Planar or Xenon lens, filter size 49mm.
- P35 AF, autofocus 35 slide projector is launched.
- A new factory is built at Uelzen (about 50 miles, 80km, from main factory) on Lüneburg Heath.
- In an attempt to reduce high German labour costs, and to try and stay on a par with Japanese and Far East manufacturers, Rollei decide to manufacture cameras in Singapore. A new company is formed, Rollei Singapore (PTE) Ltd., and pilot production starts on two rented floors in Alexandra Road.

1971

- Rollei becomes Singapore's largest investor. Employing 600 Singaporean staff and 3 German staff. Production was officially started.
- The production of the P35, P35A, and P37A projectors is transferred to Rollei Singapore.
- The E15B flash unit is produced at the Rollei Singapore plant.
- A special 35 gold edition is launched in Germany.
- The Hessische Landesbank takes over part of the shareholding.
- With new products being launched, the Rollei workforce in Braunschweig is increased to 2177 employees.
- New sales subsidiaries are formed – Rollei of America Inc., Rollei Canada Ltd., Rollei (U.K.) Ltd., and Rollei Austria GmbH.

1972

- With a workforce of 800 Singaporeans and 50 Germans, Rollei Optical in Singapore commences production on high quality lenses, pentaprisms, finder optics and shutters.
- Rollei's main factory is now situated in Chai Chee Road, Singapore.
- Workforce now numbers 1800 Singaporean and 70 German.
- Assembly starts on Rollei 35, 35B, A26, and a Rolleiflex S.L.R., the SL35 camera.
- Rollei acquire Rollei France S.A. and Optische Werke Voigtländer.
- New flash units E34C, E24C, E24 and E36 RE are launched.
- New projectors P37 and P37 AF are launched.

1973

- 100 journalists worldwide are invited to an international press conference held by Rollei in Singapore.
- The SLX is launched, the world's first microprocessor-controlled roll-film S.L.R. Features include automatic exposure, motordrive, 120/220 capability, all built-in. Some 17 years later it is still the only medium format, excluding newer Rollei cameras, that has all these functions. The original

prototype can be seen at the Jersey Photographic Museum. Rolleiflex was once again on top.

- The VF 102 (Voigtländer) flash gun is launched.
- The Rollei S is launched, a small 35mm compact with f2.8 Zeiss Sonnar lens, made by Rollei under licence. Still a most sought-after camera, able to produce negatives that can be greatly enlarged.
- New flash units are launched – the 121 BC, 128 BC, 140 RES, and 140 REB.
- New slide projectors P66 A and P66 AF, both for the medium format 6 x 6 are launched.

1974

- Voigtländer Vertriebsgesellschaft (VVG) is formed as a marketing subsidiary.
- An entirely new pocket camera taking 110 cartridge film for 12 or 24 exposures is launched, the A110 camera.
- A 35mm compact rangefinder camera, the XF35 with f2.3 Rollei Sonnar lens is launched.
- New projector P35 OA and a range of Voigtländer flash units, VC21 B, VC315, VC38 S, and V38 RES are launched.
- The SLX now heralded as the most advanced medium format camera takes Photokina by storm. Also on show is the compact 35 S camera in a special gold edition.
- Rollei employees in Braunschweig number 1648; in Uelzen, Lüneburg Heath, West Germany 316; and in Singapore 5696 – a total of over 8500 when you take into account subsidiaries!

1975

- Dr. Peesel resigns and is succeeded as Managing Director by Peter C.J. Peperzak.
- New products include the VF 135 camera and V21 B flash unit.
- New projectors launched are the VP 135A, VP 135AF, V 35A and the V 35AF.
- Design staff commence work on a new 35mm camera with interchangeable backs.
- SL35 E prototypes are made with a shutter speed of 1/2000th second.
- Production of the Rolleicord declines.

1976

- A new subsidiary is formed, Rollei Nederland B.V.
- SL35 M, SL35 ME, and VSL 2 S.L.R. cameras are launched.
- E110 and Voigtländer Vitoret 110 cameras are launched.
- A host of new products are available. P3800 Projectors, V200 BC, V200 B, 100XL, and 100 XLC flash units, and the Rolleimat enlarger.

- Rolleiflex SL2000 prototype is shown for the first time at Photokina. This camera can be seen in the Jersey Photographic Museum.
- Peter C.J. Peperzak becomes President of the Rollei group.

1977
- New subsidiary is formed, Rollei Japan.
- XL8 and XL12 movie cameras, made in Japan, are launched.
- P36OA and AF slide projectors are launched.
- Mr. H. Wehling becomes Managing Director.
- Production of the T.L.R. is declining, it is only available through special order.
- Employees now number 1217 in Braunschweig, 112 in Uelzen and 4649 in Singapore.

1978
- Not a very good year for T.L.R. sales, which are almost nil.
- Compact Rollei 35 LED economy model appears on the market.
- P355 A and AF slide projectors are launched.
- Sales are rapidly declining due to the heavy advertising and promotion of cameras. A sad fact that whole-page advertising pays off.
- Rollei re-organisation results in the sale of the new Uelzen works and a loss of 112 jobs. At nearby Braunschweig, employees are reduced to just under 700, a total of 500 lose their jobs.

1979
- Company is renamed Rollei-Werke Franke & Heidecke GmbH & Co. KG.
- The Singapore factory, which is fighting for survival, has to seek outside commissions.
- Design work on the SL2000 is halted through lack of funds.
- Problems occur with the electronics in the new Voigtländer S.L.R. which could not operate above 1/1000 second.
- Rollei make a frantic effort to recoup previous year's losses and launch the Japanese made Rolleimat F with f2.8 Rolleinon lens and built-in flash. A very reliable small plastic camera.
- Further new products include the 35 LED compact camera.
- SL35 E, S.L.R. Rolleiflex is launched with metal focal plane and shutter to 1/1000th second. A very nice camera, used today by many satisfied photographers. For the instruction book reprint see *Club Rollei*, issue 14, June 1989.
- Voigtländer VSL 3-E S.L.R. (same as Rollei SL35 E) is launched.
- The Beta 1 to Beta 4 flash range is launched.
- The faithful T.L.R. is no longer in production. Orders are taken from old stock.

1980

- Rollei 35 TE, 35 SE, and the Rolleimatic are now produced in Singapore.
- Rollei moves production of the P3800 dissolve projector and the P66 S from Germany to Singapore.
- A Japanese Rolleimat AF camera is launched.

1981

- On 26th June at Braunschweig District Court, an application for composition proceedings shocks the world.
- A bankruptcy petition is filed for by Rollei-Werke Franke & Heidecke GmbH & Co. KG., on 6th November. This included Singapore and all self-contained sales subsidiaries.
- Rollei employees fight to keep the company alive. The SL2000 F goes on sale in Germany, the Rolleimat AFM with motorised advance is launched, and the Rolleimatic with an unusual lens cover goes on sale. Most of the stock is sold at knock-down prices, and anything else the liquidators can lay their hands on. Meanwhile the banks, among others, were trying to devise a way to rescue Rollei.

1982

- With many foregoing Christmas a deal is reached on 1st January, and from 2nd January 1982 a new Rollei Fototechnic GmbH is founded.
- Rollei is saved by an English company – United Scientific Holdings P.L.C. of London, who become the majority shareholder.
- Production resumes on professional-orientated cameras and equipment, and commissioned work outside the Rollei photographic trade is accepted.
- SLX and SL66 production is resumed. The cost of developing the SLX cost Rollei dearly. The concept using linear motors had never been used on a shutter within a lens before.
- P3801, P801S, and P66S projectors are launched.
- The SL2000 F is redesigned, and with all the faults rectified it finally goes on sale worldwide.
- The SL2000 and SL35 SE utilise new technology, possibly beyond the reach of a firm the size of Rollei.

1983

- Eager to get Rollei back on the road to profits to fund research and design, parts for the 2.8F are made into a special edition of 1000 Gold Aurum 2.8F cameras. This camera is today considered to be one of the most attractive special editions ever made.
- Projector production of the P66 S and the manufacture of the 50mm,f1.4 Planar are relocated from Singapore back to Braunschweig.
- With enthusiasm for the future a new SL66, the E, with built-in exposure meter, and the 6006, successor of the SLX, with interchangeable backs, are launched.

1984

- Photokina year comes round again and new products are required.
- Rolleiflex 3003 is launched together with the new Rolleivision 35 Twin, infrared dissolve projectors.
- A new extended range of accessories for the SL66 E and 6006 is introduced.
- 7 x 42 binoculars are launched, picking up many major awards along the way, and also military contracts.
- An industrial camera division is set up for holographic testing.
- Remaining 2.8F parts, combined with a new HFT Zeiss Planar lens, are made into a limited edition, the Platin. Only 500 are made.

1985

- Sub-contract work from space agencies in America, Germany, France and United Kingdom is received with great enthusiasm.
- Rolleiflex 3000 P, derived from the 3003, is supplied to the police for surveillance purposes.
- A new professional product for the amateur who does not require interchangeable backs is launched, the 6 x 6 Rolleiflex 6002, with 3 budget-priced Rolleigon lenses, 50mm,f4; 80mm,f2.8; and 150mm,f4.

1986

- Scientific Instrument division appears for the first time, and Rollei's own product developments appear at the German Geodetics September exhibition, featuring the Rolleimetric MR and Rolleimetric RS.
- Formation of Club Rollei, whose headquarters are in Jersey, and a magazine of the same name is published five times a year.
- New products are shown at Photokina. A budget S.L.R. Rolleiflex, the 3001 – a simpler version of the 3003. Rolleivision 66AV projector evolved from the P66. The Rolleiflex SL66 SE top-of-the-range camera, mechanically controlled roll-film S.L.R. features full-area and spot exposure metering.
- Rolleiflex SL66 X with T.T.L. flash automation, exposure control, supersedes the SL66 which is now discontinued.
- The Rolleivision 66 supersedes the P66 projector.
- A limited edition of 444 Rollei 35 Platinum cameras is launched to commemorate the success of this camera 20 years earlier. So successful was the secrecy of manufacture that many people did not know of their existence until three years after the launch. The Jersey Photographic Museum now has one of these cameras, thanks to Wolfgang Sass, the man in charge of Rollei. Incidentally most of the special platinum Rollei 35 editions were sold to Japan.

1987

- United Scientific Holdings of London sell their shareholding in July to Heinrich Manderman, West German agent for Praktica cameras. Mr. Manderman also owns Jos. Schneider Optische Werke Kreuznach GmbH & Co. K.G.

- Once again Rollei have a name change, this time to Rollei Fototechnic GmbH & Co. K.G.
- Managing Directors are now Heinrich Manderman and Dr. Joachim Herzke. The General Manager is Wolfgang Sass who has been with Rollei for 13 years and previously managed Rollei Singapore.
- A new T.L.R., the 2.8GX, is shown at the Club Rollei annual meeting in Jersey during November, and goes on sale in West Germany in time for Christmas.

1988

- Supplies of the new 2.8GX slowly arrive into the U.K. during January.
- Collaboration with Jos. Schneider results in two high resolution and quality AV-Xenotar lenses being devised for the successful Rolleivision 35 twin dissolve projector.
- New products are launched at Photokina in October, and at Club Rollei November meeting in Jersey. Included is the new top professional medium format, electronic roll-film S.L.R. camera, the 6008. Features include three metering methods including spot metering, as on the SL66 SE, four exposure control modes, various exposure correction provisions, L.E.D. panel of exposure data in the finder, faster sequences of up to 2 f.p.s., removable hand grip, and an integral feature, part of the three sequence bracketing mode. A first for any medium format camera. Not many 35mm cameras have this feature. The Nikon F4 and Minolta 9000 professional cameras have to have, at a great additional cost, bolted-on backs to provide a bracketing sequence. See *Club Rollei,* issue 11, December 1988.
- A new range of professional quality lenses for the 6008 is available. Schneider 60mm,f3.5 Curtagon HFT PQ, which many buy as a standard lens, 80mm,f2.8 Xenotar HFT PQ, and 150mm,f3.5 Tele-Xenar HFT PQ. The new lenses, each with larger linear motors, are able to function at 1/500th second day after day, year after year, in busy modern studios.
- A special 3003 is launched, finished in grey lizard skin, also shown at Photokina.

1989

- New versions of the Rolleivision 35 twin digital and 35 twin digital P dissolve projectors are launched – now with programmable memory chips, microprocessors and controlled functions.
- Production of the 6008 can hardly keep pace with the vast amount of orders, which results in a backlog of orders, enough for five months' production.
- Binoculars and projectors now have their own dedicated production lines.
- Rollei employees now number 505.
- The big surprise for the annual Club Rollei meeting in November is the world launch of the special edition 2.8GX T.L.R., to celebrate 60 years of the T.L.R. Unfortunately due to a postal delay the camera never arrived until after the meeting, but the author who had seen the prototype camera in

production, along with Wolfgang Sass and Dietmar Kanzer from Rollei Braunschweig, were able to assure those present the camera did exist! The special 2.8GX edition, of only 500, is sold in a special kit in the English-speaking world. It includes a presentation box, 2.8GX camera with original Rolleiflex name in gold, finished in grey nappa leather, Rollei guide book and close-up filter kit.

- A further very special Platin Gold Aurum 2.8F T.L.R. is made for the Japanese market with an order for 44 units. Being hand-made proves far more costly than envisaged. News of a production cost of £1750 for this camera accounted for the rise in auction prices of mint late 1970 2.8F cameras, selling for £860.

1990

- Photokina year. New products include the new Schneider and Rolleinar lenses for the 3003, 35mm S.L.R. and the new fast 80mm,f2 Xenotar HFT PQ, and 180mm,f2.8 Tele-Xenar HFT PQ for the 6008. Plus a range of new accessories for the 2.8GX and 6008.
- The cost of tooling new products has become so costly that 1990 will be a year when the research and design departments will be exploring new ways and means to improve reliability within their products, and at the same time in improving production and purchasing costs, all to ensure Rollei products are sold as competitively as possible.
- 1990 is the year when all medium format manufacturers will be looking at their obsolete designs, many will start to redesign and produce new models. They will no doubt discover many problems, just as Rollei did with the SLX. On paper ideas may look great but the actual product is sometimes not what is expected.

1991

- Launch of compact AF Prego, probably the world's best compact AF camera.
- Breakthrough with New Digital Scanbak for the Rollei 6008, shown with great success at Frankfurt photo show, resulting in over 55 confirmed orders.
- Launch of the new Schneider PQ lens for the Rollei 6000 series of cameras.
- Growing back orders on lens, prisms and 6008 cameras causing problems in increasing production of this popular system.
- Compact 35 Classic with Rollei f2.8 Sonnar lens. Entire production for two years sold. It is planned to increase output of this remarkable handconstructed camera.

1992

- Rollei cameras will still be in use by many photographers in 100 years' time. They say small is beautiful. There is a market for well-made, reliable products – let's hope Rollei keeps it that way. To exploit the brand name in worthless mass-produced disposable products would be a mistake. Please support the Rollei tradition.

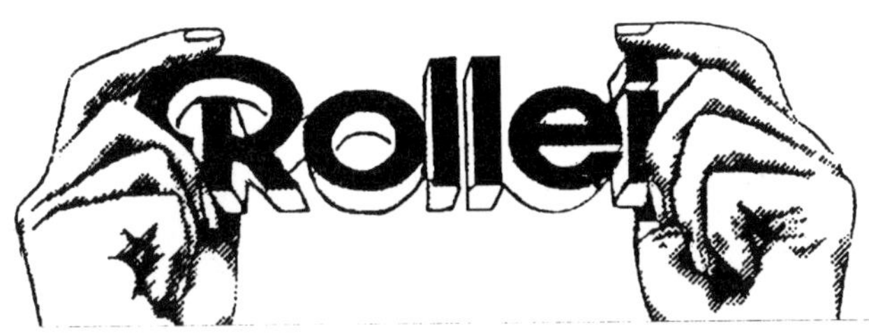

CLUB ROLLEI - ***A Camera Club with a difference!***

Club Rollei is situated in the Hotel de France Jersey, the largest hotel in the Channel Islands.

Club Rollei's magazine is published five times a year.

Twentysix back issues are available for £35 or separately at £2.50 each.

The joining fee is £17.50 that includes a years subscription which is £14 per annum to be payed annually after the first year.

MEMBERSHIP APPLICATION

To: CLUB ROLLEI,
Hotel de France, St. Saviour's Road,
St. Helier, Jersey,
Channel Islands, JE4 8WZ, U.K.

Name ....

(Business Name) ....

Address ....

....

Telephone Number Day.............................. Night ....

Occupation / Business ....

Rolleiflex Equipment Owned ....

....

I/We enclosed a cheque/credit card No.

-----------------------------------/ EXP;----------------

Signed .... Date ....

CREDITS

Photographs and Illustrations

Jersey Photographic Museum:
12, 14, 19, 21, 36, 39, 53, 54, 55, 56, 57, 58, 93, 120, 121, 144.

The author and his family:
26, 31 bottom, 32, 46, 49, 50, 54, 62, 63, 64, 77, 78, 81, 82, 116, 119, 152, 156.

Rollei Fototechnic:
10, 22, 28, 31 top, 34, 40, 69, 72, 74, 75, 97, 98, 112, 114, 134, 147, 148, 149, 151, 154, 169, 170, 172, 190.

Terry Sheehy:
viii, 84, 94, 124, 133, 140, 153.

Carl Zeiss, Oberkochen:
24, 153.

W.T. Harrison A.R.P.S.:
101

Daily Express:
117

Dennis Parker A.R.P.S.:
138

John G. Banks L.R.P.S.:
128, 130.

V.H. Seymour:
159

A.V. Distributors (London):
167, 168.